Multinational Warfare

MULTINATIONAL WARFARE

AN ENORMOUS EXERTION

Brig. (Retd.) P.V. Mann

PRASHANT PUBLISHING HOUSE

DELHI-110094

Published by :

Prashant Publishing House

C-34, 28 Foota Road, Gali-3,

West Karwal Nagar, Delhi-110094

Phone : 011-22963970, Mob. : 9810396373

Multinational Warfare

An Enormous Exertion

First Pubished

ISBN 978-93-80565-17-0

PRINTED IN INDIA

Published by Mr. R.K. Jha M/s Prashant Publishing House and Published at H.S. Offset House Press, Delhi.

Preface

From the beginning of recorded history, war has played a major role in shaping the course of events. Though geography changes, nations come and go, vanquished turn into conquerors, and victors become victims, one of the constant elements of warfare is its degrading effects on the environment. Concurrent with war's deleterious effects on the environment, man has from time to time attempted to harness the overwhelming powers inherent in the environment and unleash them on his enemies. This was graphically demonstrated as recently as the 1991 Gulf War. The environmental destruction that occurred in that short war appalled the world and set new levels in man's willingness to destroy his surroundings while waging hostilities. Many observers expected similar environmental warfare during the 2003 Gulf War, and there is clear evidence that there were plans to do so that were never executed.

It has become commonplace in the last decade to say that "the importance of protecting the environment has become increasingly obvious." The events of the Persian Gulf Wars have only served to accelerate that trend. While there are more than 900 treaties that have provisions dealing with environmental protection, none attempts to create an integrated approach to environmental warfare regulation. The following is a brief analysis of the most significant international law documents that directly or indirectly provide protections for the environment during war. This analysis will be divided into two areas: protection of the environment from passive wartime effects (when the environment is the victim of hostilities), and prevention of and limitations on active environmental warfare (when the environment is the weapon in hostilities).

The book is a comprehensive and authentic living record of the whole gamut of Warfare.

—*Editor*

Preface

Contents

1

Introduction

INFORMATION WARFARE

Information warfare is the use and management of information in pursuit of a competitive advantage over an opponent. Information warfare may involve collection of tactical information, assurance(s) that one's own information is valid, spreading of propaganda or disinformation to demoralize the enemy and the public, undermining the quality of opposing force information and denial of information-collection opportunities to opposing forces. Information warfare is closely linked to psychological warfare.

Overview

Information warfare can take many forms:

- Television and radio transmission(s) can be jammed.
- Television and radio transmission(s) can be hijacked for a disinformation campaign.
- Logistics networks can be disabled.
- Enemy communications networks can be disabled or spoofed.
- Stock exchange transactions can be sabotaged, either with electronic intervention, leaking sensitive information or placing disinformation.

The US Air Force has had Information Warfare Squadrons since the 1980s. In fact, the official mission of the US Air Force is now: "To provide sovereign options for the defence of the United States and its global interests. To fly and fight in Air,

Space, and Cyberspace", with the latter referring to its Information Warfare role. As the Air Force often risks aircraft and aircrews to attack strategic enemy communications targets, remotely disabling such targets using software and other means can provide a safer alternative. In addition, disabling such networks electronically (instead of explosively) also allows them to be quickly re-enabled after the enemy territory is occupied. Similarly, counter information warfare units are employed to deny such capability to the enemy. The first application of these techniques were used against Iraqi communications networks in the first Gulf War.

Also during the 1991 Gulf War, Dutch hackers stole information about U.S. troop movements from U.S. Defence Department computers and tried to sell it to the Iraqis, who thought it was a hoax and turned it down. In January 1999, U.S. Air Intelligence computers were hit by a co-ordinated attack, part of which appeared to come from Israeli and French hacking.

Information Operations

Information Operations (Info Ops) is an evolving discipline within the military. It has emerged from earlier concepts such as "Command & Control Warfare" and "Information Warfare"-mainly US-dominated, originating in the 1990s and considering lessons learned from the Gulf War(s), phenomena like the so-called "CNN Effect" and enormous advances in Information Technology. Today, Germany leads a multinational effort on developing Info Ops as an integrating function/joint mission area within the military, called the "Multinational Information Operations Experiment" (MNIOE). The current 20 MNIOE partners define Info Ops as: "The advice to and co-ordination of military activities affecting information and information systems – including system behaviour and capabilities – in order to create desired effects". This definition-and its related context-differs from extant national views (e.g. those of the USA or the UK) and provides an advanced approach to multinational and interagency information activities in support of crisis management and effects-based operations.

Designing and implementing guidance for Coalition actions to affect information and information systems (information activities) is a challenge; it applies to the whole scope of civil-military efforts from pre-crisis situations to post-conflict reconstruction, and spans all levels of involvement.

Non-military

Organized teams of non-military, even non-governmental information fighters become an increasingly common phenomenon. They can advance different political agendas, be involved in astroturfing or participate in election campaigns.

ELECTRONIC WARFARE

Electronic warfare (EW) is now considered a branch of information operations, which includes technical measures such as computer security and attacking hostile computers, but also "soft" disciplines such as psychological warfare and deception. Current usage really refers to the entire electromagnetic and acoustic spectra, not just the traditional radio and radar frequencies. It includes passive infrared light heat-seeking guidance and thermal viewing. It includes directed energy from lasers. Indeed, the basic principles are extended against weapons using acoustic energy, principally involving submarines and torpedoes.

Even though current designers of critical civilian systems need to consider the threat, it is hardly a new discipline. In the Russo-Japanese War of 1905, a Russian captain became aware of a Japanese ship transmitting the Russian position, but was denied permission to jam the signal; the decisive Japanese victory at the Battle of Tsushima Strait might have been prevented had the Russian admiral given permission for EW. Perhaps this can better be described as the first command misunderstanding of the potential value of EW.

EW is often discussed in terms of means and attacks. Effects are produced by the means; the effects may be either permanent ("lethal") or transient ("nonlethal"). The techniques are the means of causing the effects; one distinction, not always clear-cut, is whether they use physical or energy-based methods: a lethal attack can destroy a radar with the blast and fragmentation of a anti-radiation missile, or by an electromagnetic pulse or other high-intensity energy source that burns out, rather than "dazzles", components in the radar.

Nonlethal attacks on the same radar could confuse it with physical but passive decoys (e.g., chaff or with active false signals (e.g., deceptive jammers) that do not damage the equipment.

Given the constant challenge-response-counterchallenge nature of EW, some research has suggested that the complexity of electronic warfare systems make it extremely difficult to use standardized acceptance procedures.

Since the starting conditions in which an EW system will have to operate are unpredictable, models using chaos theory may need to be used in planning and evaluation. Rather than observe, attack, and protect, the traditional three categories, what is the purpose of electronic warfare? A model from the U.S. Air Force splits it into three tenets:

- Control: dominate the spectrum, so that friendly forces can gain information on the adversary or attack his systems, and, simultaneously, protect themselves from enemy information-gathering or attack.
- Exploit: use the spectrum to your advantage: detecting the enemy, denying him use of the spectrum, disrupting his C3I-ISR and destroying his resources
- Enhance: use EW as a force multiplier. EW, as part of suppression of enemy air defence, ensures all of one's attack hit their targets, rather than having to send spares because some might be shot down

Electronic warfare has offensive and defensive aspects that work in a "movecountermove" fashion. Often, these aspects are used simultaneously and synergistically to support the mission. In the same way that air superiority allows friendly forces the freedom from attack, freedom to manoeuvre, and freedom to attack, the proper coordinated use of EW allows friendly forces to use the EM spectrum.

As examples, the offensive denial of a command and control (C2) network by jamming disrupts the adversary's ability to marshal forces that would otherwise engage a friendly strike force. The proper use of EP allows friendly radar and communications to continue operating in the presence of enemy jamming.

Exploitation

Of the five fake landing plans under Plan BODYGUARD deception operations preceding the WWII invasion of Europe, the one the Allies most wanted the Germans to believe FORTITUDE SOUTH, to believe that the main attack would come further north, at the Pais de Calais, the shortest distance across the English Channel. The actual attack at the Battle of Normandy was farther south than the FORTITUDE SOUTH area.

It was to the Allies' advantage to have the shortest ocean crossing to their targets. If they were to land at the FORTITUDE SOUTH area, it would be reasonable to have the invasion force preparing in Kent. They created the fictitious First United States Army Group (FUSAG) under the flamboyant and feared GEN George Patton, and had the U.S. 3103rd Signal Battalion and the British 3118th Signal Service Group created a great deal of radio traffic, coming from locations in Kent. Meanwhile, an absolute minimum of radio traffic came from the real camps in Devon and Dorset in southern England. The dummy radio traffic, the sightings of Patton, and other deceptive information exploited the beliefs of Adolf Hitler, who, for some time after the Normandy landings, insisted they were a fake and held back reserves to use against the "real" invasion.

Other information operations complement EW. For example, the overall deception plan may use many means to convince the enemy of something untrue, which you want him to believe. One of those means is electromagnetic deception, or the deliberate radiation, reradiation, alteration, suppression, absorption, denial, enhancement, or reflection of EM energy in a manner intended to convey misleading information to an enemy or to enemy EM-dependent weapons, thereby degrading or neutralizing the enemy's combat capability." In the FUSAG case, the form of electromagnetic deception was simulative EM deception, or actions to simulate friendly, notional, or actual capabilities to mislead hostile forces. The radio silence at the camps of the real invasion force was manipulative EM deception, or actions to eliminate revealing, or convey misleading, EM telltale indicators could have given German intelligence the knowledge of another large force.

Enhancement

To enhance is to use EW as a force multiplier. Careful integration of EW into air and space operations will detect, deny, disrupt, deceive, or destroy enemy forces in varying degrees to enhance overall mission effectiveness.

Through proper control and exploitation of the EM spectrum, EW functions as a force multiplier and improves the likelihood of mission success. If the enemy used identification-friend-or-foe techniques to recognize his own forces,*imitative EM deception'* would send the proper "don't kill me" EM signal into enemy systems that imitates enemy emissions.

Techniques of EW

A common distinction breaks EW into three sets of techniques:

- Learning about an opponent's electronic capabilities, resources and their deployment. At the national/strategic level, this is usually called electronic intelligence, and electronic support (ES) at the tactical level.
- Interfering with the opponent's systems, called either electronic attack (EA) or, traditionally, electronic countermeasures (ECM).
- Minimizing the effects of enemy counteractions on one's own electronics, called electronic counter-countermeasures (ECCM) or electronic protection EP. The latter is a newer and less frequently recognized term.

ES, EA, and EP are preferred terms because, as newer terms, the "E" can be thought of as "electromagnetic" rather than "electronic". This newer thinking helps remember that directed energy and passive sensing are included in the modes. In Soviet doctrine, EW was called Radio-electronic Combat (REC) [Radioelektronaya Bor'Ba]. They divided it into:

- radio intelligence/intercept, specifically rejecting the U.S. distinction between ELINT and ES
- radio countermeasures (jamming)
- physical suppression/attack
- radio concealment and deception

In each of these sets, purely electronic or computer software/network attacks are called soft kill, while physical destruction of enemy electronic resources is hard kill; there will be countermeasures against both hard and soft kill. Some of the hard kill concerns are general military ones; a tank driving through the building will kill it whether it is the communications centre or the cookhouse. Even with the softer methods, it often is hard to draw the line among the three branches. For example, if an aircraft detects that it is being "painted" by the terminal guidance radar of a surface-to-air missile, the detection being in the electronic support area, the aircraft computer may immediately and automatically respond with jamming (i.e., electronic attack) and launching decoys (i.e., electronic protection). Not to take those immediate steps may mean the airplane is seconds away from becoming a fireball.

Nuances of these distinctions include that EP should not be confused with self-protection. When an aircraft is threatened by heat-seeking air-to-air missiles (AAM), which use the infrared light part of the spectrum, it can release flares for self-protection. The flares are hotter than the engines on which the missile normally homes; they act as decoys. While flares are self-protection, they are not EP, but rather *EA against the missiles*. Equipping one's own heat-seeking AAMs with software and electronics to ignore decoy flares is electronic protection *of the missile*. The flare rejection technique is EP for the missile. It ensures friendly use of the infrared part EMS to track the intended target despite the adversary self-protection/defensive EA actions (i.e., the flare) to prevent or reduce friendly use of the EMS. While defensive EA actions and EP both protect personnel, facilities, capabilities, and equipment, EP protects from the effects of EA (friendly and/or adversary), while defensive EA is primarily used to protect against lethal attacks by denying adversary use of the EMS to guide and/or trigger weapons.

ELECTRONIC SUPPORT

In this article, the focus of ES is on tactical warning, of electronic threats against oneself or friendly forces, such that immediate action is necessary. Consider how a radar works: it sends out energy, some of which reflects from the target and is received. It follows, therefore, that if a target is at the very edge of the radar transmitter's range, there may be just enough energy in the beam so that it can be detected, but not enough energy to reflect back a signal that the hostile receiver will recognize.

Radar warning

Against traditional radars, a radar warning receiver can usually detect an enemy radar farther away than the radar can detect the target carrying the warning receiver. With newer low probability of intercept radar, the rules may change; some radars cannot be detected by conventional electronic support receivers.

Directed energy ES

A laser warning receiver (e.g., AN/AAR-47) designed to detect and analyse a laser signal is, in EW terms, ES. Laser warning presents technical problems different than traditional radio or radar warning: the signal of interest will have have a much smaller beam to intercept. Especially during the day, the signal will coexist with broadband background interference, such as sunlight, or fire or flares at night. New detector and discriminator technologies are needed. There will be different requirements for detection of laser rangefinders versus laser designators and laser-beam-riding missiles.

ELECTRONIC ATTACK

According to the U.S. joint doctrine, "EA involves the use of EM energy, directed energy, or antiradiation weapons to attack personnel, facilities, or equipment with the intent of degrading, neutralizing, or destroying enemy combat capability and is considered a form of fires." The term "fires" has come full circle, to include soft kill as well as hard kill. This definition includes the very hard kill of the AGM-88 HARM anti-radiation missile (ARM), which is a "fast gun" that hits radar very quickly, as opposed to the mixed soft-hard kill of the British BaE Systems ALARM. ALARM will strike a radar if one is active, but, otherwise, it dangles on a parachute over the battlefield, daring a radar to show itself. Either approach denies the enemy the use of radar. Long after bomber aircraft gave up their aerial gunners, they still needed electronic warfare specialists. When much strategic bombing became the job of fighter-bombers, they needed electronic warfare aircraft, such as the Panavia Tornado ECR, EF-111 and EA-6B Prowler as escorts, with the EF-18 Growler and EW unmanned aerial vehicles (UAV) coming on line, as well as major EW enhancements to multirole aircraft such as the F-22 Raptor.

Directed energy example

A laser or other light source (e.g., xenon arc) designed to blind or disrupt optical sensors is, in EW terms, EA. Directional infrared countermeasures (DIRCM), such as the AN/AAQ-24, do, however, attempt to blind the guidance seeker of the missile attacking the platform — aircraft or tank — while its function is electronic attack, its goal is self defence. Typically, infrared countermeasures interfere with the final, terminal attack part of a missile trajectory. Directed energy countermeasures, such as the Russian Shtóra-1 EOCMDAS (electro-optical countermeasures defensive aids suite) has modes that try to foil the terminal attack (i.e., the final dive into the target) as well as to interfere with midcourse guidance. Blinding 'must not' be directed at people, but only at equipment. A widely ratified international agreement forbids the use of weapons whose "sole combat function or as one of their combat functions, is to cause permanent blindness to unenhanced vision." The protocol does not apply to blinding as a collateral effect of other laser-based systems, such as weather instrumentation, rangefinders, etc., but it is a widely accepted principle that unless the device is a true laser weapon intended to kill, it is unwise to give even an incidental blinding capability. After all, the beam could accidentally hit onto friendly forces or civilians.

Offensive EA

While an enemy who knew ALARM was in use would be very cautious about bringing up his radars, a deceptive operation in the Gulf War, Poobah's Party (Poobah was the call sign of the EW commander, BG Larry Henry) encouraged the Iraqi air defence to turn on radars. After the defenders were frustrated after the first "invisible" wave from F-117 Nighthawk stealth bombers and hard-to-detect BGM-109 Tomahawk cruise missiles, they finally sensed large numbers of aircraft, and turned on their fire control radars. What they first saw were flocks of drones that showed up brightly on radar. What they saw next were a massive number of anti-radiation missiles from almost every airplane that could carry an AGM-88 HARM. For many people, jamming brings up an image of high-power, broad-spectrum noise. In the real world, it can be much more complex, if for no other reason that if the frequency(ies) of the threat are known, flooding that frequency will be a more efficient use of the available power. More sophisticated jamming, however, requires more intelligence in the jammer.

In a simplified example of more intelligent jamming, the protection system receives the pulse, sent by the radar transmitter, and repeats it at a higher power level than the real reflection, on the chance that the receiver will assume the weaker but real return is a secondary reflection, and believe the stronger echo, remembering the weak signal and screening it out. Then, on successive pulses, the deceptive jammer would transmit the signal slightly before or slightly after the real return, to give the receiver the impression the target is closer or farther away than its real range.

Self-protection as defensive EA

The AN/ALE-47 Countermeasures Dispenser System [CMDS], is a "smart" electronic warfare expendables dispenser that can integrate with defensive avionics such as radar warning receivers, radar reflector (i.e., chaff) dispensers, radar jammers, as well as helping the pilot with situational awareness of the threat. Such a dispenser may still get additional control from an electronics countermeasures suite controller such as the Danish-developed AN/ALQ-213.

Meaconing

Meaconing is a specific form of deceptive jamming directed at navigational systems. It will receiving radio beacon, or navigational radar, signals and rebroadcasting them, on the same frequency to confuse navigation. The meaconing stations cause inaccurate bearings to be obtained by aircraft or ground stations. Meaconing also includes deception directed at active navigational aids, which, in normal operation, transmit a response signal on a different frequency than used to trigger the aid. In such cases, meaconing sends out a stronger faked response to confuse other receivers. Even before the Battle of

Britain, in March 1940, British scientific intelligence, under R.V. Jones, became aware of the Luftwaffe setting up navigational aids to direct their bombers over Britain. These were not used significantly during that Battle.

After the Battle, however, a new bombing campaign began, until the Allies invaded the continent and captured the German airfields. During this campaign, there was a constant back-and-forth between the German navigational systems and the British electronic warfare specialists in meaconing those systems. The British also were aware that the Germans were building their own radar-equipped integrated air defence system, and Jones added the task of electronic attack against the German air defenses.

ELECTRONIC PROTECTION

A good deal of electronic protection (EP) needs to be carried out well in advance of the threat. It focuses on the ensuring friendly use of the [electronagnetic spectrum], such as frequency agility and spread spectrum in a radio, or variable pulse repetition frequency in a radar." These measures keep the enemy from finding the friendly signals to interfere with them. Procedures to shut down nonessential emanations (EMCON) must be preplanned and the appropriate commands distributed and understood. Operational testers of a new Canadian Forces Situational Awareness System, expressed concern that the EMCON imposed at higher level may prevent lower-level commanders from keeping tactical awareness, unless there are local relaxations for tactical EMCON.

A 2006 comment from the head of the Iranian military electronics sector indicates both the perception of the standards of NATO EP, but that other countries do not intend to have large "kill me" signs on their own equipment. "If our main enemy wants to carry out electronic warfare and jamming operations, our standards are at the NATO level," Ebrahim Mahmoudzadeh, said Iran's radars, passive and active electronic protection "can combat anything that wants to harm us".

Spectrum management

Frequency management is the discipline of assigning radio frequencies to functions, units, regions, etc. It includes wartime reserve modes (WARM), an example of which would be a radar frequency never used in training, perhaps with new antennas or transmitters installed just before a combat mission. An obvious use for such modes would be the terminal guidance radar signal for a semi-active radar homing missile, the function of the AN/SPG-62 on AEGIS battle management system equipped ships. Even the existence of WARMs for a particular system will be classified, with the modes themselves even more so.

Passive protection

A filter for equipment, or goggle designed to filter out the harmful wavelength of laser light is, in EW terms, EP. Sunglasses are a trivial form of natural protection against bright light. To protect the crew while its jammers are operating in high power, the cockpit of the EA-6B Prowler is lined with a thin, transparent, but conductive layer of gold.

Organization

Once a military organization commits to EW, there will immediately be conflicts, among one's own side, even before direct confrontation with the enemy. The strategic intelligence organizations may want to get national-level information, which puts them against the operational-level organization who want to understand the specific threat confronting them. Once conflict begins, there will still be conflicts, between the ELINT/ES people who want to learn more about enemy capabilities, and the combat operations/EA/EP commanders who want to shut down the enemy systems. There will be concern that EA may affect friendly electromagnetic systems, and the activities will need to be deconflicted. If the organization is multinational, there will be complex challenges of allowing allies access to sensitive intelligence and EW capabilities. Even when a willingness to share is there, there will be interoperability problems, even among the services of one's own country, then against close allies (e.g., AU/CA/UK/US and NATO), and then *ad hoc* coalition partners, such as the U.S. and Syria, usually adversaries, allied in the Gulf War.

Intelligence preparation for EW

One of the first conflicts will be between the national/strategic level intelligence collectors and the combat operators.

Intelligence will be the foundation for EW planning, starting at the strategic scientific and technical intelligence (STINFO) level of understanding the adversary's basic capability.

Electronic probing

Before any operations begin, the strategic ELINT groups will want to do their own information collection, and may ask the combat operations to probe the enemy to trigger his use of signals. "Electronic probing is the intentional radiation into the devices or systems of potential enemies for the purpose of learning the functions and operational capabilities of the devices or systems. Obviously, probing, also called "ferret missions", puts crews, and, if not yet in a war, the peace, at risk.

Electronic warning

As conflict grows nearer, electronic warning centres alert friendly forces of impending threats. Detailed ELINT guides the preparation of reprogramming and WARM plans. Eventually, ELINT will blur into ES for specific missions. Russia, as mentioned previously, does not differentiate between the two. On July 24, 1965, an RB-66 electronic warfare aircraft, specifically flying in a warning mode, broadcast the call "Bluebells ringing, bluebells ringing" to a strike mission over North Vietnam.

That call was a warning that a fire control radar, for the S-75 Dvina (Western designation: SA-2 GUIDELINE) surface-to-air missile was active. While the U.S. was aware of the presence of SAMs, a civilian Defence Department official John McNaughton, Assistant Secretary of Defence for International Security Affairs, had ruled that the North Vietnamese would not actually use them.

McNaughton's theory was not borne out by reality; the RB-66 broadcast another warning five minutes later, and an F-4C fighter was knocked down by a SAM. While there had been sufficient EW concern to provide warning, the strike force was not prepared to counter the SA-2 threat. Warning alone was not enough. A specific counter-SAM capability was not ordered until August 13, 1965, and then built from off-the-shelf electronics. Soon, one of the classic EW dilemmas was seen: jammers interfered with ES receivers.

PLANNING OPERATIONAL EW

Factors influencing EW planning include available assets; desired effects (exploitation, deception, disruption, or destruction); placement limitations (altitude, range, time, or loads); frequency deconfliction; anticipated EW missions from other Services; and authentication requirements.

It is very easy for jammers to interfere with one's own systems, and, especially in multinational organizations, the planners must emphasize:

- Jammer system design includes directional antennas.
- Capabilities exist to lockout frequencies.
- Friendly forces state realistic restricted frequency requirements.
- A command and control process exists which is responsive to real-time frequency changes.

GLOBAL ENVIRONMENT AND CHALLENGES

Future Strategic Environment in an Era of Persistent Conflict

Framing the Future strategic environment in an era of persistent conflict is an immense challenge. Unlike during the Cold War era, the United States no longer has an overarching paradigm through which it can view the world. Nonstate actors and irregular warfare dominate America's attention as it continues to fight insurgencies while coping with terrorist threats like Al-Qaeda. Traditional threats persist in places like the Korean peninsula, while the rise of China presents the prospect of a future strategic competitor. Increasingly global forces in economics, the environment, and health have greater impact on citizens worldwide. The U.S. is not sure how to structure, fund, and oversee its national security apparatus to meet these future challenges. No overarching paradigm suffices, and the United States faces the prospect of racing from one crisis to the next.

Several institutions have conducted studies to help policymakers plan for national challenges beyond the next 20 years. Among the most recent are Mapping the Global Future by the National Intelligence Council; Joint Operating Environment by United States Joint Forces Command; Forging a World of Liberty under Law by the Princeton Project on National Security; The New Global Puzzle by the European Union Institute for Security Studies; and Global Strategic Trends Programme by the British Ministry of Defence Development, Concepts, and Doctrine Centre.

These studies suggest the trends that will characterize and shape the future strategic environment: globalization, demographics, and the rise of emerging powers, the environment and competition for resources, non-state actors and challenge to governance, and advances in technology. These trends will present complex, multidimensional challenges that may require careful use of the military along with other instruments of national power. To respond to this future strategic environment, the United States will most likely be involved in three types of missions: expeditionary warfare to manage violence and peace, defence of the command of the commons, and homeland defence. The land forces will spearhead expeditionary missions to "contested zones" to protect American interests abroad. Sea, air, and space forces will counter threats to the American command of the commons-air, sea, space, and cyberspace-where the American military currently has dominance. The military will also support the interagency effort in homeland defence as technological advances weaken traditional natural barriers to attack on U.S. soil.

FUTURE TRENDS OF THE NEXT 20 YEARS

Globalization will force future trends that present both optimistic and pessimistic likelihoods. The good-In Mapping the Global Future, the National Intelligence Council calls globalization the overarching "mega-trend" that will shape all other trends of the future. Globalization is an amorphous concept, but here it is meant in its broadest definition-the increasingly rapid exchange of capital, goods, and services, as well as information, technology, ideas, people, and culture. Markets for goods, finance, services, and labor will continue to become more internationalized and interdependent, bringing immense benefits to the world as a whole. Globalization will continue to be the engine for greater economic growth. The world will be richer with many lifted out of poverty. It is unclear, however, whether a richer world where America has less relative economic power will be better for the United States in terms of its global influence.

Studies before the recent economic shock had expected the global economy to be 80 percent larger in 2020 than in 2000, with average per capita income 50 percent higher. According to the European Union Institute for Security Studies, the world economy will grow at a sustained annual rate of 3.5 percent between 2006 and 2020. The United States, European Union, and Japan will likely continue to lead in many high-value markets, with the United States continuing to be the main driving force as the world's leading economic power. Emerging economies will continue to do well, with the Chinese and Indian gross domestic product tripling by 2025. The percentage of the world's population living in extreme poverty will likely continue to decline.

The bad-The benefits of globalization will not be global. The harsh realities of competitive capitalism will produce definite winners and losers, and result in increased social and economic stratification both internationally and within countries. Internationally, these losers will concentrate in certain areas of the "arc of instability," a "swath of territory running from the Caribbean Basin through most of Africa, the Middle East, and Central and Southeast Asia." Here, the gap between countries who are benefiting economically, technologically, and socially and the countries that are left behind will continue to widen. And although absolute poverty will decline worldwide, this will not be the case for these regions. In sub-Saharan Africa, for example, the number of people living in absolute poverty-on less than one dollar a day-has increased from 160 million in 1981 to 303 million today. Poverty and aggravated income inequality will remain a monumental challenge in the next 20 years.

The Defence Development, Concepts, and Doctrine Centre notes, "Absolute poverty and the comparative disadvantage will fuel perceptions of injustice." The disparities will be evident to all because of globalized telecommunications. Populations of "have-not" countries that perceive themselves to be losing ground may continue to be breeding grounds for extremist and criminal ideologies that lead to violence within and outside those countries.

Greater economic interdependence will lead to greater political interdependence. Although such a scenario diminishes the prospects of major industrialized war between two nations, it also means that what happens in one part of the globe will affect other parts of the globalized world. Economic shocks will reverberate throughout the globe. A drastic downturn in the U.S. economy, for example, has caused a global economic recession, perhaps requiring global or regional political solutions.

And the ugly-The new era of globalization also means that the United States cannot depend on geography to shield it from the many problems of the developing world. This was clear on 9/11 when the hate espoused by the extremist ideology of radical Islam manifested itself in attacks on U.S. soil. The dangers of interdependence are manifest in other areas as well. Effects of climate change, disease, and pandemics originating from remote parts of the world will affect the United States. Infectious disease is already the number one killer of human beings. AIDS is a scourge in most of the world and poses an extreme societal threat in portions of sub-Saharan Africa. Even more frightening is the threat of a global avian influenza pandemic. The ever increasing connectivity of nations resulting from globalization means that a virus originating in a remote part of an undeveloped country can spread throughout the world at a frightening pace, as evidenced by the recent "swine flu" panic. A pandemic would also cause economic hardship, even if the disease were physically kept out of the United States.

DEMOGRAPHIC TRENDS

Experts expect the world's population to increase by 23.4 percent from 2005 to 2025. The population growth in the developed world, however, will remain relatively stable. The United States will have 364 million citizens by 2030, while the population of the European Union will grow from 458 million to 470 million in 2025 before declining. Japan and Russia will experience a decrease in population, with Japan's population falling from 128 million to 124.8 million and Russia's population falling from 143.2 million to 129.2 million within the next 20 years. Developed countries will also experience significant population aging. In the European Union, the ratio of employment age citizens (15-65) to the retired (over 65) will shift from about 4 to 1 in 2000 to 2 to 1 by 2050. Japan will approach 2 to 1 by 2025, and the median age in Japan will increase from 42.9 to 50 years. This trend will fortunately not have as severe an impact on the United States due to higher fertility rates and greater immigration. Europe and Japan could face societal upheaval as they try to assimilate large numbers of migrant workers from the developing world. These factors will soon challenge the social welfare structure of these countries, their productivity, and discretionary spending for defence and foreign assistance.

Developing countries

Ninety percent of global population growth by 2030 will occur in developing and poorer countries. Population growth in these areas will be 43 to 48.4 percent in sub-Saharan Africa, 38 percent in the Middle East/North Africa region, 24 percent in Latin America, and 21 percent in Asia. Nine out of ten people will be living in the developing world in the next 20 years.

In contrast to the developed world, a significant portion of the population growth will be the "youth" of the region with a "youth bulge" occurring in Latin American, Middle East, and Sub-Saharan Africa. About 59 percent of the population of sub-Saharan Africa will be under 24 years by 2025. In the Middle East, the working-age population will expand by 50 percent and in North Africa area by 40 percent, challenging governments to provide employment for a young and undereducated populace with little employment opportunities and setting up the potential for violent conflict. As a recent Economist article notes, these young men without "either jobs or prospects" will trade "urban for rural poverty, head for the slums, bringing their anger, and machetes, with them." In the last two decades, 80 percent of all civil conflicts took place in countries where 60 percent or more of the population was under 30 years of age.

Migration

Significant portions of the global population will be on the move, mostly to the cities. By 2030, 61 percent of the global population will live in cities as compared to 47 percent in 2000. And while the urbanization ratio will be greater in developed countries compared to developing countries (81.7 percent versus

57 percent), the developing countries will struggle to control the transition to urban societies. Shantytowns will likely proliferate in "mega-cities" struggling with crime and disease. Migration to wealthier countries will also continue as workers search for better economic opportunities. The Defence Development, Concepts, and Doctrine Centre reports that the number of people living outside their country of origin will increase from 175 million in 2020 to 230 million by 2050. Environmental degradation, natural disasters, or armed conflicts will also forcibly uproot populations. How both the developing and developed countries absorb the influx of migrants may determine the level of conflict associated with these movements.

Identity

How segments of the global population identify themselves may drastically change in the next 20 years. Individual loyalty to the state and state institutions will become increasingly conditional. Identity will increasingly be based on religious convictions and ethnic affiliations. Religious identity may become a greater factor in how people identify themselves. Although Europe will remain mostly secular, religion will have greater influence in areas as diverse as China, Africa, Latin American, and the United States. In some areas of the developing world, Islam will continue to increase as the overarching identity for large numbers of people. In other regions, ethnicity and tribal loyalties will continue to be the dominant form of identification.

EMERGING POWERS

The rise of powerful global players will reshape how we mentally map the globe in an increasingly multipolar world. *Mapping the Global Future* likens the emergence of China and India to the rise of a united Germany in the 19th century and the rise of the United States in the 20th. The global centre of gravity will shift steadily toward the Pacific.

China

China will become a powerful actor in the global system. The rise of China has been called "one of the seminal events of the early 21st century." China's economic and diplomatic influence will continue to expand globally. Its gross national product is expected to surpass all economic powers except the United States within 20 years. China's demand for energy to fuel this growth will make it a global presence as it ventures out to secure sources of energy. In East Asia, China is likely to wield its growing influence to shape the region's "political-institutional contours" to build a regional community that excludes the United States. All this will likely be accompanied by a continued Chinese build-up of its military to reinforce its growing world power status. Whether China continues to pursue a peaceful rise will have a profound impact on the course of international affairs in the next 30 years. The rise and fall of great powers has been one of the most important dynamics in the international system, a dynamic that is often accompanied by instability and conflict. Defence Development, Concepts, and Doctrine Centre believes China will approach international affairs with a fair amount of pragmatism, but face daunting challenges as it develops. It may exert its growing hard and soft power to either protect its growth or ensure internal stability. When China does establish itself as a global power, it may be less restrained in its conduct of foreign affairs.

Other powers

Other nations may also play a greater role in the international arena. Among those mentioned in the studies are India, Russia, Indonesia, South Africa, and Brazil. Depending on its ability to achieve greater political cohesion, a more united European Union could also play a greater role, especially as a model of global and regional governance. Another possibility would be the rise of a rival alliance. The rise of these powers may mean a decline of the relative power of the United States. Though the United States would continue to play the major role in international affairs, its overwhelming dominance may decline. In the next 20 years, a more multipolar world may develop with political, economic, and military power diffused throughout the globe and America's ability to influence dialogue in key global issues relatively diminished.

ENVIRONMENT AND COMPETITION FOR RESOURCES

Scientific consensus increasingly points to human activity as a main contributing factor in global warming. Although climate science is complex and the estimates of probable damages differ, the possibilities of catastrophic effects caused by global warming are real. Major consequences are likely because of "melting ice-caps, thermal expansion of the oceans, and changes to ocean currents and flows." Possible consequences on land include increased desertification, reduced land for habitation and agriculture, spread of diseases, and an increase of extreme weather events. The worst-hit regions will likely face political, economic, and social instability. These regions will be an arc of instability affecting the non-integrated areas of the globe and particularly worsening the already marginal living standards in many Asian, African, and Middle Eastern nations. The likelihood of more failed states collapsing will increase as weak governments are unable to cope with decreases in food and water and increases in disease and violent uprisings.

Competition for resources

Exacerbating the environmental concerns is the ever-increasing competition for resources. As countries grow richer and modernize, the demand for resources will greatly increase in the next 20 years. According to the International Energy Agency, demand for energy will likely grow by more than 50 percent by 2035, with fossil fuels projected to meet 80 percent of this increase. The world economy will remain heavily dependent on oil through 2025 at a minimum. Similarly, global consumption of natural gas will increase by 87 percent. The United States has so far shown little inclination to seriously address its addiction to oil. Growing Asian powers' consumption of oil will also skyrocket; China will have to increase consumption by 150 percent and India by 100 percent by 2020 to maintain current growth. Such explosive consumption will exacerbate global warming in the absence of a global framework to tackle the problem.

Because of global growth, competition for these resources will intensify as the United States and other major economies vie to secure access to energy supplies. The competition will bid up energy prices, making it even more difficult for developing nations to afford minimal energy for their populations. As Isaiah Wilson notes, resource security has persistently been the primary objective of advanced-nation security and military strategies. Quests for this security will continue to draw nations into military and economic engagement in the "arc of instability." The United States will continue its involvement in the Middle East for years to come. China will continue to build bilateral agreements with various nations in Africa to secure its oil supply.

The degradation of the environment and increased economic growth of nations will cause competition not only for traditional energy sources, but also for necessities like food and water. Major portions of the population will live in areas of "water stress," and the amount of arable land may diminish. The consumption of *blue water* (river, lake, and renewable groundwater) will continue to increase, depriving even more people of access to clean drinking water. Concurrently, environmental degradation, intensification of agriculture, and a quickened pace of urbanization will all contribute to the reduced fertility of and access to arable land. Increased reliance on biofuels for growing energy needs will reduce food supply crop yields. Competition for other food sources, including fish, will increase. Even now, African fishermen bemoan the disappearance of their livelihoods while Europeans bemoan the increasing prices for fish in restaurants.

NONSTATE ACTORS AND CHALLENGES TO GOVERNANCE

Scholars view the rise of nonstate actors as a fundamental challenge to the Treaty of Westphalia-based international system. The United States, as the leader and architect of the Westphalian system, has been and will continue to be the primary focus of this challenge. Nonstate actors that do not see themselves bound by national borders are likely to continue to grow in strength and lethality. Small, empowered groups will be increasingly able to do greater things while states' near monopoly on information and destructive power continues to diminish. Various factors have aided their cause. The National Intelligence Council sees a "perfect storm" in certain regions of the underdeveloped world as weak governments, lagging economies, religious extremism, and the unemployed youth fuel extremist movements. Al-Qaeda remains a formidable near-term threat. Recent testimony by American intelligence officials reported that Al-Qaeda is continuing to gain strength from its sanctuary in Pakistan and is "improving its ability to recruit, train, and position operatives capable of carrying out attacks inside the United States." Even if the West neutralized Al-Qaeda, the National Intelligence Council believes that the factors that gave rise to Al-Qaeda will not abate in the next 15 years and predicts that by 2020, "similarly inspired but more diffuse extremist groups" will supersede it.

Challenges to governance

Nonstate actors such as Al-Qaeda will play a major role in spreading extreme and violent ideologies. Fueled by the perceived injustices in a globalized world and by frustration with the oppressiveness of regional authoritarian regimes, major segments of the population in the arc of instability may rally to radical Islam and attack the institutions of traditional government through violent means. These forces may also cross national boundaries to form a transnational governing body dedicated to terrorism and jihad. The National Intelligence Council, for example, sees a possible scenario in which political Islam provides a context to form a Sunni Caliphate and draws on Islamic popular support to challenge traditional regimes. The Princeton Project on National Security presents another scenario where a radical arc of Shi'ite governments rules areas from Iran to Palestine, sponsors terrorism in the West, and tries to destabilize the Middle East. Governments in the arc of instability will face daunting challenges to stability. They will have to deal with the adverse effects of globalization, climate change, unemployment, and a new form of identity politics. To succeed, they will need to fight internal corruption and reform their inefficient, authoritative governments. They will need to do this as a radical ideology fiercely attacks their legitimacy and any connections to the Western world.

International crime will also challenge governance. Criminal activities will continue to increase in sophistication and lethality as enhanced communication technologies and weapons continue to proliferate. Such activities will be increasingly intertwined with civil conflict and terrorism as criminal groups leverage the benefits of increased globalization and their alliances with states and nonstate actors, to include terrorists. Nonstate actors may also provide opportunities for increased cooperation to meet these future challenges. International, regional, and nongovernmental organizations will continue to grow in capacity. Although governance over international trade and crime has increased due to expanded transnational government networks, new collaborative institutions and mechanisms will be required to cope with increasingly complex global and regional problems. These networks must continue to grow in strength to solve global problems.

Technology

Advances in technology elicit great hope as well as great fear, because major technological breakthroughs have an impact on every aspect of our lives. We can expect further progress in information technology and nanotechnology, innovations in biotechnology, and increased investments in research and development. Faster computers combined with elements of nanotechnology and biotechnology may improve our ability to deal with daunting challenges such as human health, environmental issues, and malnutrition.

On the other hand, technology's availability and ease of transfer allow broader access to previously unavailable weapons. The ease of use of commercial technology has also exacerbated the problem of proliferation. This is most dangerous in terms of weapons of mass destruction. The Princeton Project on National Security asserts that the "world is on the cusp of a new era of nuclear danger." North Korea does possess nuclear weapons. Despite the findings of the recent United States National Intelligence Estimate, it seems likely that Iran is still determined to acquire the ability to build nuclear weapons. If the international community cannot rein in these countries, other countries in the Middle East and East Asia will likely also attempt to join the nuclear club.

Countries will also continue to pursue chemical and biological weapons, as well as delivery capabilities for these weapons. Chemical and biological weapons can be integrated into legitimate commercial infrastructures to conceal a country's capabilities. At the same time, more countries will be able to acquire ballistic and cruise missiles, as well as unmanned aerial vehicles. By 2020, the National Intelligence Council believes that both North Korea and Iran will have intercontinental ballistic missile (ICBM) capabilities, and several countries will develop space-launch vehicles. A preview of such capabilities came on 5 February 2008 when Iran launched a Kavoshgar-1 rocket into space using technology similar to that needed for long-range ballistic missiles.

Concurrently, many in the United States fear the waning of American domination in research and development of new, emerging technology. The number of American Ph.D. engineering students is decreasing while the number of foreign students returning to their countries from U.S. universities is on the rise. At the same time, the *Economist* notes that the domestic trends in American politics and immigration policy are keeping the world's best and brightest talents from "darkening America's doors."

Technology and terrorists

The potential nexus of terrorist groups and nuclear weapons is perhaps the most frightening scenario for national security experts. The increasing ease with which terrorists can acquire weapons to deliver a nuclear attack on the United States presents a nightmare scenario. Graham Allison notes that there are more than 200 addresses around the world from which terrorists can acquire nuclear weapons or fissile material. Russia, Pakistan, and North Korea are among the likely sources. If terrorists cannot acquire a nuclear bomb, the technology and tools are now available for them to build their own. The difficult part is acquiring the fissile material needed for a homemade bomb. There is evidence that Al-Qaeda attempted to acquire a nuclear weapon for an attack on the United States. The prospect of Iran gaining nuclear capabilities is also of great concern because of the capabilities of its proxy force, Hezbollah.

OPERATING ENVIRONMENT AND THREAT EVALUATION

This chapter explores the ramifications of these trends for each type of mission set by explaining the operating environments and the nature of the threat. There are obvious limitations to such framing. First, missions will likely be joint and interagency ventures with success not achieved purely through the application of military force. Second, labelling these challenges as "threats" inherently implies an adversarial relationship, which may not always be the case. The emergence of great powers, for example, may not necessarily lead to adverse conditions in international affairs. Third, some challenges do not fit neatly into these categories, so we may not always identify an emerging threat. The emerging radical Islamic community in Europe might be an example.

However, categorization does highlight the vastly different types of missions our military forces may perform during the next 20 years. With tighter budgets for discretionary spending, the U.S. must prioritize missions and use military forces efficiently and effectively. Examining and analyzing mission sets allows each service to plan accordingly and adapt to myriad possibilities the future strategic environment may hold.

So, what do these trends mean for our military forces? American expeditionary forces may need to enter what Posen labels "contested zones." These zones correspond to areas the Pentagon has called the global "arc of insecurity." Any mission in these zones will be both dangerous and difficult because political, physical, and technological realities negate many American military advantages. Although this will have to be a joint venture, land forces will likely spearhead such missions. The air, sea, and space forces, on the other hand, will lead the effort in countering threats to the "command of the commons." With the rise of emerging powers and advances in technology, countries will venture into the commons where the U.S. military has traditionally maintained dominance. Finally, all forces will continue to support the Department of Homeland Security and other federal agencies in defending the homeland against nontraditional actors. For each mission type, the U.S. military will face increasingly capable threats seeking to take advantage of any vulnerabilities.

EXPEDITIONARY WARFARE TO CONTESTED ZONES

Although both the Navy and Air Force have begun structuring their forces for expeditionary warfare, the land force will likely spearhead the missions into the "contested zones" in the arc of insecurity. These areas, running from the Caribbean Basin through most of Africa, the Middle East, and

Central and Southeast Asia, will disproportionately involve the losers from globalization. In fact, these zones are where the many trends of the next 20 years will converge. Increased poverty or at least relative poverty, large numbers of unemployed youth, environmental degradation, competition for resources, emergence of deadly nonstate actors, failed states, and proliferation of devastating technology will be the most evident and severe here.

The American expeditionary force may be drawn into these areas for a variety of reasons. First, these areas will continue to be breeding grounds and safe-havens for extremist ideologies and criminal elements. Second, increased global demand and competition for energy sources could require military intervention in these contested zones. Third, tribal wars or genocides may oblige the United States to join multilateral forces in stabilizing failed states or regions. Fourth, humanitarian interventions may increase if natural or man-made disasters cause mass suffering or death. In these zones, the American forces will be involved in both the management of violence and management of peace, forcing it to "fight" wars in a different fashion.

Political, physical, and technological facts will make the missions in these areas particularly difficult. Local actors have stronger interests in a war's outcome than the United States, and our adversaries will have a plentiful supply of males of fighting age. They will also have the "home-court advantage." They have studied the way the U.S. military fights, and the weapons required for close combat are inexpensive and plentiful. In addition, conflicts that involve more than battles between traditional armies will also require nontraditional expertise in areas like cultural awareness, working with and training allied nations, interagency operations, and diplomacy. Major General Robert Scales goes as far as to say that the next World War will be the social scientists' war, describing the wars to follow as "psycho-cultural wars" requiring officers with knowledge based on the discipline of social sciences. These factors negate the traditional advantages of the American way of war built on technology and organization.

What will the operating environment look like for U.S. expeditionary forces in the contested zones? A survey of the literature suggests that U.S. forces will have to operate in an environment characterized by the following factors:

- Highly urban environment/megacities. Approximately 60 percent of the world's population will live in cities by 2030. Some of these cities will grow into megacities containing huge shantytowns. They may have high crime rates, ineffective or corrupt police forces, and high levels of instability. Some megacities may collapse into chaos.
- Extreme environments. These regions may become increasingly inhospitable due to human activities and climate change. There may be less access to basic resources needed for survival, like food and water. These conditions could often obligate U.S. forces to provide such resources to populations in countries in which they operate.
- Communicable disease. Countries may also have high levels of communicable disease, such as HIV/AIDS, malaria, hepatitis, and tuberculosis.
- Endemic hostility. There may be underlying hostility among the populace caused by transnational or intercommunal conflicts or virulent anti-American ideologies, such as militant Islam.
- Collapse of functioning state. U.S. forces may have to operate in regions where the government has failed and local warlords use extreme violence to control populations.
- Nonmilitary partners. U.S. forces will have to understand how to work with other government agencies and elements of society to combat adversaries. The management of peace will undoubtedly be an interagency affair as the integrated instruments of national power become increasingly crucial for success. The presence of media and internet coverage will also complicate missions. The military will need heightened awareness of legal implications and the rules of engagement.
- Cheaper and deadlier weapons. Adversaries will continue to benefit from wide availability of weapons, and they will continue to modify what is cheaply available to cause maximum damage on U.S. forces.

- Weapons of mass destruction. Advances in and the proliferation of technology may make the use of nuclear, chemical, and biological weapons on U.S. forces a real possibility.
- Greater collaboration with developing country militaries. Demographic declines and fiscal pressures will result in reduced military capabilities among developed-country allies. Future coalitions will increasingly rely on less well-trained and poorly equipped developing country forces that may not share the U.S. professional military ethic.
- Media on the battlefield. The media will likely cover the actions of the expeditionary force on the ground and communicate them in real time to a global audience.
- Humanitarian disasters. Increasingly devastating natural disasters caused by climate change could require more military humanitarian assistance.

Threats will come from multiple sources:

- Terrorists. Terrorists will continue to target U.S. interests abroad, seeking soft targets to send messages and inspire similar groups to action.
- Paramilitary forces. These forces will be intermingled with the local population and ally themselves with terrorist groups. The United States will face rebel groups, gangs, insurgents, and private military companies.
- Tribal forces. Armed tribal forces may be a big challenge because they have the potential to switch from being adversaries to allies depending on American strategy and tactics and on shifting local political calculations.
- Criminal elements. Weak governance will allow both transnational and local criminal elements to thrive. Drug cartels will continue to be an international presence and the most notorious criminal networks.

MAINTAINING THE COMMAND OF THE COMMONS

Posen describes the "commons" as those areas that no state owns but that provide access to much of the globe. It is analogous to the command of the seas, although Posen also includes command of the air and space. The Joint operating environment includes the command of cyberspace as well. According to Posen, "command of the commons" means that the United States gets vastly more military use out of the commons than other states, that the United States can generally deny its use to others, and that others would lose access to the commons if they attempt to deny its use to the United States. The command of the commons has been "the key military enabler" of America's global position and has allowed the United States to better exploit other sources of power.

The United States sea, air, and space forces will lead in responding to these challenges to the command of commons. Though the command of the commons will most likely remain uncontested in the near-and medium-term, the rise of emerging powers could lead to competition over time. Posen notes that the sources of U.S. command include American economic resources and military exploitation of information technology. As American economic power begins to decline relatively, and as advanced technology becomes more diffused, other nations may exploit these factors to become viable contenders. Already, nations have launched missiles into space, started investing in blue water navies, and increased their cyber warfare capabilities.

The following are critical considerations for the operating environment:

- Increased interest in space. Emerging powers will continue to expand their space programs. Advances in technologies will enable more nations to launch rockets and satellites. The United States will be increasingly concerned about capability of nations to convert this technology into intercontinental ballistic missiles as well as weapons threatening to U.S. space capabilities.
- Nuclear proliferation. As more countries acquire nuclear weapons, American ability or proclivity to intervene in various areas of the commons (or contested areas) may decline due to the threat of nuclear retaliation.
- Missile technology proliferation. Missile technology proliferation may deny certain areas of the commons to the United States. Examples include sea-lanes in the Straits of Hormuz, the Suez Canal, and the Strait of Malacca.

- Connectivity vulnerabilities. Increased automation and reliance on information technology leave the United States more vulnerable to cyber-attacks as adversaries use techniques such as worms, viruses, Trojan horses, botnets, or electromagnetic pulse.
- The rise of great powers will feature nations with increased conventional military capabilities like that of the United States. They will possess "information-enabled network" forces as well as naval forces with air and undersea capabilities. Nations may be able to challenge command of their regional sea-lanes, as well as U.S. dominance in space and cyberspace. Also, nonstate actors may be able to exploit technology to conduct cyber warfare.

MILITARY SUPPORT TO HOMELAND DEFENCE

With globalization and advances in technology shrinking the world, the homeland of the United States will be more vulnerable. 9/11 was a watershed moment in America as national policymakers began reexamining existing defenses and the balance between security and liberty. Many fear that terrorist and other criminal elements will continue to exploit the openness of American civil society to attack our financial, energy, or governmental infrastructure. The increasing availability of nuclear weapons may result in an attack that dwarfs the physical and psychological damages of 2001.

Despite the lack of terrorist attacks in the United States since 2001, it is still unclear if security measures implemented so far have made America safer. Many doubt the effectiveness of our changes and criticize the behemoth Department of Homeland Security and the restructuring that occurred with the creation of this agency. The Federal Emergency Management Agency's performance during Hurricane Katrina heightened these concerns. Some scholars also doubt the wisdom of the creation of the Office of National Intelligence and the preservation of the Federal Bureau of Investigations as the lead law enforcement agency on domestic intelligence. Still others call for reform of Congressional committee jurisdictions and oversight capabilities. How the U.S. military will best support this interagency effort is still unclear. The military has been viewed simultaneously as the last and greatest safety net for devastating events as well as a possible threat to civil liberties when operating within the U.S. borders. The demand for higher levels of security in the homeland leads to tension with many of the political and cultural traditions of America. Increased domestic surveillance conflicts with cherished civil liberties. Similarly, increased border protection affects immigration and even openness to foreign business travelers, both of which can have negative economic and cultural impacts. The vigorous, often partisan, debates in Washington on wiretapping, torture, and immigration will likely continue well into the future. Following are the areas of major concern:

- Weapons of mass destruction-Proliferation of nuclear, biological, and chemical technology and material will leave the United States increasingly vulnerable to attacks with weapons of mass destruction.
- Natural disasters-Hurricane Katrina may have been a sign of things to come, with the nation looking more to the military as the most effective institution for dealing with devastating natural disasters.
- Economic shocks-Terrorist elements may target key financial nodes in the United States such as the New York Stock Exchange to attack the global financial system.
- Energy crisis-Shortages of supplies relative to increasing demand may leave the United States susceptible to energy shocks.
- Refugee flows-Economic and environmental factors may increase both legal and illegal migration from Latin America and elsewhere.
- Cyber-attacks-Increased automation of our financial systems, physical infrastructure, and government operations renders the homeland more vulnerable to attacks on our information systems by both state and nonstate actors.

There are multiple probable sources of threat. Al-Qaeda and other terrorist groups remain the biggest threat to U.S. homeland. Other Islamic terrorist groups may emerge not directly linked to Al-Qaeda, but inspired by similar extremist ideology. Elements of our society may become disposed to extremist Islamic ideology and independently plan attacks. Transnational criminals, including drug cartels, will continue to have a presence in the U.S. Although state attacks on U.S. homeland will be rare, hostile states may use proxy forces to attack vulnerable sites using difficult-to-trace methods, such as cyber attack. States could also potentially use economic measures, such as energy embargos or financial measures as holders of U.S. debt, to damage the U.S. economy.

FACING THE CHALLENGES

The challenges of the next 20 years are immense and diverse. Some are immediate and others are long term or systemic. In this context, the U.S. military must be sufficiently flexible and multi-talented to play the various roles the nation may ask of it. Operations in the contested zones will be extremely complex and multidimensional, and perhaps more frequent; the military will have to redefine the concept of war and the nature and utility of military forces. Great-power politics will continue and may manifest itself in a challenge to American command of the commons. America may have to reexamine its hegemonic status and the role of U.S. forces in maintaining the international system. Threats to the U.S. homeland will continue and increase. The military will need to function effectively in the interagency process to aid in the defence of our homeland. Yet, our military must do this in an era of likely declining military funding. Forward-thinking analysis of likely trends on these various military missions will prove essential to preparing for the challenges ahead.

2

Warfare in the 21st Century

SPECIAL WARFARE'S NAZI PROVENANCE

Since the end of World War II, the United States has acted through proxies either to defeat leftist insurgencies or to subvert "hostile" governments, e.g. those states viewed by Washington and the multinational corporations they serve as ideological competitors. Historically, U.S. unconventional warfare (UW) doctrine was derived from Nazi experiences in countering "partisan warfare" across Europe during World War II. As analyst and scholar Michael McClintock detailed in his essential study on the topic.

American special warfare doctrine would draw considerably on *Wehrmacht* and SS methods of terrorizing civilian populations and, perhaps more importantly, of co-opting local factions to combat partisan resistance. The Department of the Army's *A Study of Special and Subversive Operations* (November 1947) was an early assessment of the lessons learned from World War II in the context of Cold War imperatives.But the United States did more than translate captured *Wehrmacht* and SS documents: they recruited many Waffen SS veterans, often with an assist from high Vatican officials. Tens of thousands of war criminals were spirited out of Europe along "ratlines" into U.S. hands for clandestine war against the new enemy: the Soviet Union and the international left.

Pathological killers such as SS veteran Klaus Barbie, the Butcher of Lyons, was instrumental when the CIA and the Argentine death-squad generals launched their 1980 "cocaine coup" in Bolivia. Barbie, along with operatives linked to the

CIA, Sun Myung Moon's Unification Church and preexisting Nazi networks, "reorganized" Bolivia's intelligence services to reflect the Southern Cone's "changing realities."

Even when the "competition" was peaceful and confined to the political-economic spheres, once the U.S. intervened, violence, civil war and chaos followed. This scenario was played out in Chile during the 1970s, Afghanistan, Angola, Mozambique, Nicaragua and El Salvador throughout the 1980s, in Yugoslavia and the Balkans generally during the 1990s, today in Bolivia and Venezuela and on a planetary scale under the rubric of the "global war on terrorism" (GWOT). The lesson for those who buck the global hegemon? U.S. political subversion and state terror will wreck havoc and halt independent development in its tracks.

And when the global Godfather's military forces directly intervene? Although the U.S. was defeated in Southeast Asia, target countries such as Vietnam, Laos and Cambodia were destroyed by the United States in the process. Devastated economically and socially, decades later these nations have yet to fully recover from the depredations wrought by their American "liberators." However, the U.S. military did learn certain unique skills, not least of which was the application of selective violence against the communist National Liberation Front's civilian infrastructure.

The Phoenix Program, meticulously analyzed in researcher Douglas Valentine's definitive account, was launched in 1967 by the CIA and U.S. Special Forces as a means to win "hearts and minds." But from its inception, Phoenix operators worked in tandem with drug-linked South Vietnamese and Laotian "allies" and morphed into an assassination and torture program that killed thousands. Long after the U.S. withdrew from Southeast Asia, lessons learned through Phoenix and related programs such as Condor and Gladio, were "refined" during the 1970s-1980s in Afghanistan, Italy, Turkey and Central America, and now constitute the bedrock on which the Pentagon's unconventional warfare doctrine operates today. Throughout the Cold War, U.S. power in proxy states was exercised through repressive police, intelligence agencies and by far-right civilian allies. Such forces, trained and funded by the U.S., combined a neofascist political outlook with organized criminal activities generally, though certainly not limited to, the international narcotics trade.

NATO's infamous "stay-behind" Operation Gladio networks in Italy and Turkey for example, worked directly with international narcotics syndicates and pro-fascist political parties such as the Italian Avanguardia Nazionale (National Vanguard) founded by the terrorist drug trafficker Stefano delle Chiaie and the Turkish Milliyetçi Hareket Partisi (National Action Party, MHP) and the drug-linked terror gang, the Grey Wolves, founded by Alparslan Türke°, a German sympathizer during World War II. With links to those nations' intelligence services, the CIA and the Pentagon, these organizations waged a relentless war against the left through terrorist bombings, murders and assassinations in a bid to destabilize their governments and spark a full-fledged military takeover. Along with the CIA, the United States Special Operations Command (USSOCOM) have been instrumental in organizing and waging unconventional warfare with the express purpose of maintaining the economic-political status quo in target countries.

As long-time readers of *Antifascist Calling* are aware, among the more critical issues explored here are those relating to the intersection of corporate and military power and how those interactions play out on the contemporary political plane to subvert democracy and movements for social justice.

IDEOLOGICALLY COHERENT

The authors of FM 3-05.130, far from being militarist troglodytes are knowledgeable and erudite, presenting a broad and ideologically coherent narrative that is both informative and historically intriguing in its transparency and methodological purpose. In other words, unlike their political masters, they don't pull any punches. Right up front they inform the reader that UW establishes a "litmus test" which is warfare conducted "by, with or through surrogates" and that their preferred assets are irregular forces:

Irregulars, or irregular forces, are individuals or groups of individuals who are not members of a regular armed force, police, or other internal security force. They are usually nonstate-sponsored and unconstrained by sovereign nation legalities and boundaries. These forces may include, but are not limited to, specific paramilitary forces, contractors, individuals, businesses, foreign political organizations, resistance or insurgent organizations, expatriates, transnational terrorism adversaries, disillusioned transnational terrorism members, black marketers, and other social or political "undesirables." While "conventional warfare" is viewed as a conflict between states, Irregular Warfare (IW) and UW according to FM 3-05.130 is "about people not platforms." Irregular and unconventional warfare "does not depend on military prowess alone."

It also relies on the understanding of such social dynamics as tribal politics, social networks, religious influences, and cultural mores. Although IW is a violent struggle, not all participating irregulars or irregular forces are necessarily armed. People, more so than weaponry, platforms, and advanced technology, will be the key to success in IW. Successful IW relies on building relationships and partnerships at the local level. It takes patient, persistent, and culturally savvy people within the joint force to execute IW.

Indeed, FM 3-05.130 explicitly states that its "strategic purpose [is] to gain or maintain control or influence over the population and to support that population through political, psychological, and economic methods." While both IW and UW seek to influence "relevant populations," UW in contrast to IW, "is always conducted by, with, or through irregular forces." In other words, local surrogates drawn from relevant far-right and/or organized crime-linked assets are the means of eliciting "influence" over "relevant populations."

In Bosnia and Kosovo during the 1990s, "irregular forces" deployed during U.S./NATO destabilization operations in the former Yugoslavia included elements of the Afghan-Arab database of disposable intelligence assets, e.g. al-Qaeda, which have been linked to the CIA, Britain's MI6, Germany's Bundesnachrichtendienst (BND) and Pakistan's Inter Services Intelligence agency (ISI), as well as long-established drug, arms and human trafficking networks aligned with the Albanian and Turkish Mafias. Indeed, "irregular forces" such as the Kosovo Liberation Army (KLA) demonstrated *all* of these relationships in spades.

According to FM 3-05.130, the constituent elements of contemporary IW theory include: Insurgency; COIN (counterinsurgency); UW; Terrorism; CT (counterterrorism); FID (foreign internal defence); Stability, security, transition, and reconstruction (SSTR) operations; Strategic communication (SC); PSYOP; Civil-military operations (CMO); Information operations (IO); Intelligence and counterintelligence (CI) activities; Transnational criminal activities, including narco-trafficking, illicit arms dealing, and illegal financial transactions that support or sustain IW; and Law enforcement activities focused on countering irregular adversaries. Its but a short step as far as it goes, from citing the elements of UW to deploying the most dubious players as strategic assets in planetary-wide U.S. destabilization operations.

The Media's Role

Explicitly stated is the media's role in advancing the goals of United States national power. As recent exposés in *The New York Times* and elsewhere have documented, "message force multipliers" such as retired Pentagon officials and former high-ranking officers, often linked to corporate defence firms that rely heavily on Pentagon largesse, have leveraged their expertise and conducted illegal domestic psychological operations (PSYOPS) and information warfare, with the complicity and full knowledge of the giant media firms.

It is important for the official agencies of government, including the armed forces, to recognize the fundamental role of the media as a conduit of information. The USG uses SC to provide top-down guidance for using the informational instrument of national power through coordinated information, themes, messages, and products synchronized with the other instruments of national power. The armed forces support SC themes and messages through IO, public affairs (PA), and defence support to public diplomacy (DSPD). The armed forces must assure media access consistent with classification requirements, operations security, legal restrictions, and individual privacy. The armed forces must also provide timely and accurate information to the public. Success in military operations depends on acquiring and integrating essential information and denying it to the adversary. The armed forces are responsible for conducting IO, protecting what should not be disclosed, and aggressively attacking adversary information systems. IO may involve complex legal and policy issues that require approval, review, and coordination at the national level.

Indeed, as the authors aver, since UW consists of operations conducted "by, with or through irregular forces," engagement with the "human terrain" is "fundamentally a conflict of ideas"! In a nutshell, the "human terrain" explicitly includes the American public who are also the targets of Pentagon propagandistic "information operations." This is stated explicitly:

By contrast, USG-controlled specific instruments of informational power, while narrower in scope, can achieve specific and measurable results useful to prosecuting UW. ARSOF [Army Special Operations Forces] can work with DOS [Department of State] counterparts to identify and engage select TAs [target audiences] that are able to influence behaviour within a UWOA [unconventional warfare operating area]. Such TAs may be inside the UWOA itself or outside but able to influence the UWOA. The USG can then subject these TAs, directly or indirectly, to a DOS public diplomacy (PD) campaign coordinated to support the UW effort. Similarly, since UW may be a long-duration or politically sensitive effort, ARSOF and its DOS partner, the Bureau of Public Affairs, can craft a PA campaign intended tc keep the U.S. domestic audience informed of the truth in a manner supportive of USG goals and the effective prosecution of UW.

ECONOMIC SUBVERSION

For the authors of FM 3-05.130, "properly integrated manipulation of economic power can and should be a component of UW." Never mind that such "manipulation" can and did result in the deaths of hundreds of thousands of human beings in Iraq prior to the 2003 U.S. invasion and occupation as well as in a score of other nations that have defied the U.S. The cases of Chile and Nicaragua are instructive in this regard, where the disgraced president, Richard Nixon, vowed to "make the economy scream," prior to the 1973 coup, or the crippling sanctions and economic embargo imposed on Nicaragua's Sandinista government. Various sanctions regimes unambiguously "can build and sustain international coalitions waging or supporting U.S. UW campaigns." A similar methodology is being applied today against Iran as "punishment" for its legal development of civilian nuclear power.

Like all other instruments of U.S. national power, the use and effects of economic "weapons" are interrelated and they must be coordinated carefully. Once again, ARSOF must work carefully with the DOS and intelligence community (IC) to determine which elements of the human terrain in the UWOA are most susceptible to economic engagement and what second- and third-order effects are likely from such engagement. The United States Agency for International Development's (USAID's) placement abroad and its mission to engage human groups provide one channel for leveraging economic incentives. The DOC's can similarly leverage its routine influence with U.S. corporations active abroad. Moreover, the IO effects of economic promises kept (or ignored) can prove critical to the legitimacy of U.S. UW efforts. UW practitioners must plan for these effects.

Indeed, ARSOF plans for waging UW take an integrated approach and assert that they "can and should exploit the active and analytical capabilities existing in the financial instruments of U.S. power." The application of financial warfare however, including the "persuasive influence" of state and nonstate "actors" regarding the availability and terms "of loans, grants, or other financial assistance" is predicated on towing the U.S. line. The authors aver that "such application of financial power must be part of a circumspect, integrated, and consistent UW plan." In other words, threats, bribery and economic subversion generally can work wonders in getting the attention of recalcitrant states not "on board" with the U.S.

Narcotrafficking Networks and the "Global War on Terror"

For decades, investigative journalists, researchers and analysts have noted the symbiotic relationship amongst international narcotrafficking syndicates, neofascist political groups, U.S. intelligence agencies and U.S. Special Forces in the war against leftist adversaries. Dozens of books and hundreds of articles by journalists and writers such as Alfred W. McCoy, Peter Dale Scott, Henrik Krüger, Robert Parry,

Gary Webb, Jonathan Marshall, Douglas Valentine, Daniel Hopsicker, Bill Conroy as well as exposés by former DEA investigators such as Michael Levine and Celerino Castillo III, have documented the long and bloody history of U.S. complicity in the global drugs trade.

While the United States has pumped billions of dollars into so-called drug eradication programs in target countries such as Colombia, Peru, Bolivia, Afghanistan and Mexico through ill-conceived projects such as Plan Colombia and the Mérida Initiative, also know as Plan Mexico, recent reports, most notably by *The Narco News Bulletin*, have documented the close interrelationships amongst narcotraffickers, rightist extremists, political elites and U.S. intelligence agencies. Indeed, investigative journalist Bill Conroy recently documented how a U.S. trained and equipped special operations group within the Mexican army (the Zetas) "is now assisting the Mexican military in its narco-trafficking operations along the border."

None of this however, phases the authors of *Unconventional Warfare*. And why should it. As they themselves describe the doctrine, unconventional warfare is "conducted by, with, or through surrogates; and such surrogates must be irregular forces," the next logical step in the equation is the utilization of transnational criminal networks to advance U.S. national power. The section, "Law Enforcement Instrument of United States National Power and Unconventional Warfare," states this explicitly: no tinfoil hat needed here!

Actors engaged in supporting elements in the UWOA may rely on criminal activities, such as smuggling, narcotics, or human trafficking. Political and military adversaries in the UWOA will exhibit the same sensitivity to official exposure and engagement because criminal entities routinely seek to avoid law enforcement. Sometimes, political and military adversaries are simultaneously criminal adversaries, which ARSOF UW planners must consider a threat. At other times, the methods and networks of real or perceived criminal entities can be useful as supporting elements of a U.S.-sponsored UW effort. In either case, ARSOF understand the importance of coordinating military intelligence preparation of the battlefield (IPB) for specific UW campaigns with the routine intelligence activities conducted by U.S. law enforcement agencies.

During subversive operations by U.S. ARSOF soldiers in target areas, indigenous networks, many of whom are linked to far-right and narcotrafficking groups (Nicaragua, Bosnia, Kosovo), including "former" allies such as al-Qaeda, are referred to as "The Underground" and "The Auxiliary" in FM 3-05.130. Details however, are few and far between and the authors state unambiguously: There is more SF participation in developing and advising underground [and auxiliary] elements than is widely understood or acknowledged. Most such participation is classified and inappropriate for inclusion in this manual.

Preparing the ground for U.S. attacks and/or subversive operations by proxy forces aligned with American goals are a key component of UW theory. Whether a population is "on-board" with U.S. geostrategic goals or the tactical modalities employed in such campaigns is irrelevant to the new cold warriors of the GWOT. When "persuasion" fails the muscle moves in to get the attention on the "natives." Organization of the larger indigenous population from which the irregular forces are drawn–the mass base–must likewise be conducted primarily by the irregular organization itself under indirect guidance of SF. The primary value of the mass base to UW operations is less a matter of formal organization than of marshaling population groups to act in specific ways that support the overall UW campaign. The mass base, or general population and society at large, is recognized as an operational rather than a structural effort for ARSOF in UW. Elements of the mass base are divided into three distinct groups in relation to the cause or movement–pro, anti/con, and those who are uncommitted, undecided, or ambivalent. ARSOF, the underground, and the auxiliary then conduct irregular activities to influence or leverage these groups. These groups may be witting or unwitting of the UW nature of the operations or activities in which they are utilized.

In Colombia for example, U.S. "counterdrug" assistance to the corrupt Uribe government flowed directly to the narcotrafficking far-right death squad, the Autodefensas Unidas de Colombia, or AUC. Though designated a Foreign Terrorist Organization by the U.S. State Department, the Uribe government's military high command, directly advised by the Pentagon, funneled weapons and intelligence that was used by the narcofascists to murder union organizers, often after payment by U.S. multinational corporations such as Chiquita Brands International, of anyone the group identified as a "guerrilla." In ARSOF parlance, AUC "influence"–dragging unsuspecting citizens off a bus and beheading them in front of their children, for example–is what is meant when corporate- or drug-linked death squads "conduct irregular activities" to "leverage these groups." But the international community has another term to describe these activities: *state terrorism*. In 2004, as part of broad U.S. efforts to unseat Venezuela's socialist President Hugo Chávez, Venezuelan authorities arrested some 100 AUC fighters who were planning to attack specially-selected targets in Caracas. According to published reports, several high-ranking American and Colombian military officers were implicated in the operation.

The parapolitical scandal which continues to rock Bogotá, revealed high-level involvement by Colombia's political and military elite with the narcofascist AUC. But the scandal also revealed the involvement of the U.S. 7th Special Forces Group and the 1st Psychological Operations Battalion in directly training and advising Colombian military units responsible for the worst human rights abuses. Numerous reports have emerged that detail these linkages, including the 2007 disclosure by the National Security Archive that Colombian Army commander General Mario Montoya "engaged in a joint operation with a Medellín-based paramilitary group. 'Operation Orion' was part of a larger military offensive in the city during 2002-03 to attack urban guerrilla networks. The sweep resulted in at least 14 deaths and dozens of disappearances. The classified intelligence report confirmed 'information provided by a proven source,' according to comments from the U.S. defence attaché included in the document."

This is but the tip of the proverbial iceberg, however. In Afghanistan, the world's number one producer and processor of opium and its finished "product" heroin, bound for European and U.S. markets, drug trafficking according to the United Nations Office on Drugs and Crime (UNDOC) in their *2008 World Drug Report*, is "out of control." According to UNDOC, drug money is used as "a lubricant for corruption, and a source of terrorist financing: in turn, corrupt officials and terrorists make drug production and trafficking easier." Indeed, since the 2001 U.S. invasion and occupation, opium production has skyrocketed some 1,000% and accounts for a large percentage of the country's gross domestic product. Tellingly, some of the staunchest U.S. allies in the area are directly tied to international narcotics organizations. According to UNDOC, the global increase in opium production "was almost entirely due to the 17% expansion of cultivation in Afghanistan, which is now 193,000 ha [hectares]" reaching 8,700 metric tons in 2007, accounting for a staggering 92% of global opium production! Despite these horrendous statistics, the authors of FM 3-05.130 can asset that "the methods and networks of real or perceived criminal entities can be useful"! Indeed they can, as a seemingly limitless source of black funds earmarked for U.S. planetary subversion in the interest of expanding American corporate power.

According to a June 2008 report by *The Times*, after last year's bumper crop sent the price of opium spiraling downwards, the Taliban and U.S.-connected drug lords linked to Hamid Karzai's government, are stockpiling vast quantities of opium in order to induce a rise in world prices. And *Time Magazine* reported in October that the value of hoarded opium may be as much as $3.2 billion. Celebrated by the Pentagon and the U.S. media as a "splendid victory," the 2001 invasion and occupation of Afghanistan quickly spiraled out of control and the country now faces a resurgent Taliban, a new base of operations for al-Qaeda in the tribal areas of Pakistan and evidence of Pakistani ISI involvement in aiding the fundamentalist insurgents and the global drugs trade. But for American unconventional warriors, a full accounting of war crimes that ARSOF supervised and their Northern Alliance "allies" carried out have yet to be answered.

As Peter Dale Scott noted in 2002, It's a bitter irony: The largely successful U.S. campaign against the Taliban and al Qaeda in Afghanistan is resulting in an increase of funds for terrorists around the globe.

It is true, as President Bush has insisted, that global terrorism is financed by the flow of illicit drugs. Yet by installing and rewarding a coalition of drug-financed warlords in Kabul, the United States has itself helped restore the flow of Afghan heroin to terrorist groups, from the Balkans and Chechnya to Tajikistan, Pakistan and Kashmir. Indeed, among the staunchest U.S. allies in the region, characters such as Hazrat Ali and Gul Agha, "have been 'bought off' with millions in deals brokered by U.S. and British intelligence." But while America was happy to endorse a drug-linked status quo that relied on its so-called "warlord strategy" to "stabilize" Afghanistan, part of the blowback from these dubious alliances included allowing bin Laden to escape into Pakistan in 2001 after the "battle" of Tora Bora.

But for Pentagon proponents of unconventional warfare, the "price is always right" when it comes to strategic and tactical alliances with narcotraffickers and international terrorists. After all, since "UW must be conducted by, with, or through surrogates; and such surrogates must be irregular forces," everything is permitted.

3

Global Space Warfare and Technology

SPACE WARFARE

Space warfare is combat that takes place in outer space, i.e. outside the atmosphere. Space warfare therefore includes *ground-to-space warfare*, such as attacking satellites from the Earth, as well as *space-to-space warfare*, such as satellites attacking satellites. It does not include the use of satellites for espionage, surveillance, or military communications, however useful those activities might be. It does not technically include *space-to-ground warfare*, where orbital objects attack ground, sea or air targets directly, but the public and media frequently use the term to include any conflict which includes space as a theatre of operations, regardless of the intended target. For example, a rapid delivery system in which troops are deployed from orbit might be described as "space warfare," even though the military uses the term as described above.

A film was produced by the U.S. Military in the early 1960s called *Space and National Security* which depicted space warfare. From 1985 to 2002 there was a United States Space Command, which in 2002 merged with the United States Strategic Command. There is a Russian Space Force, which was established on August 10, 1992, and which became an independent section of the Russian military on June 1, 2001. Only a few incidents of space warfare have occurred in world history, and all were training missions, as opposed to actions against real opposing forces. In the mid-1980s a USAF pilot in an F-15 successfully shot down the P78-1, a communications satellite in a 345 mile (555 km) orbit.

In 2007 the People's Republic of China used a missile system to destroy one of its obsolete satellites, and in 2008 the United States similarly destroyed its malfunctioning satellite USA 193. To date, there have been no human casualties resulting from conflict in space, nor has any ground target been successfully neutralized from orbit. International treaties governing space limit or regulate conflicts in space and limit the installation of weapon systems, especially nuclear weapons.

History

Early efforts to conduct space warfare were directed at space-to-space warfare, as ground-to-space systems were considered to be too slow and too isolated by Earth's atmosphere and gravity to be effective. The history of active space warfare development goes back to the 1960s when the Soviet Union began the Almaz project, a project designed to give them the ability to do on-orbit inspections of satellites and destroy them if needed. Similar planning in the United States took the form of the Blue Gemini project, which consisted of modified Gemini capsules that would be able to deploy weapons and perform surveillance. One early test of electronic space warfare took place in 1963 when the United States exploded a ground-launched nuclear weapon in space to test the effects of an electromagnetic pulse. The result was a deactivation of many then-orbiting satellites, both American and Soviet. The deleterious and unfocused effects of the EMP test led to the banning of nuclear weapons in space in the Outer Space Treaty of 1968.

1970s–1980s

Through the 1970s, the Soviet Union continued their project and test-fired a cannon to test space station defence. This was considered too dangerous to do with a crew on board, however, so the test was conducted after the crew had returned to Earth. Space warfare strongly influenced the final design of the United States Space Shuttle. The distinctive delta wing shape was needed if the shuttle were to launch a military payload towards the Soviet Union and perform an immediate de-orbit after one rotation to avoid being shot down.

Both the Soviets and the United States developed anti-satellite weaponry designed to shoot down satellites. While early efforts paralleled other space-to-space warfare concepts, the United States was able in the 1980s to develop ground-to-space laser anti-satellite weapons. None of these systems are known to be active today; however, a less powerful civilian version of the ground-to-space laser system is commonly used in the astronomical technique of adaptive optics.

2000s

China successfully tested a ballistic missile-launched anti-satellite weapon on January 11, 2007. This resulted in harsh criticism from the United States of America, Britain, and Japan.

Space warfare system

A space system has three segments, each of which, in principle, offers opportunities for attack to an enemy. The system comprises: (i) the satellite, perhaps the constellation of satellites in orbit; (ii) the up and down links to and from the orbiting vehicle, commands from the ground stations and information flow from the satellite; (iii) and the ground station that controls the behaviour of the satellite and distributes its information to the users."

THEORETICAL SPACE WEAPONRY

Ballistic warfare

In the late 1970s and through the 1980s the Soviet Union and the United States theorized, designed and in some cases even tested an astonishing variety of bizarre and exotic weaponry designed for warfare in outer space. Space warfare was seen primarily as an extension of nuclear warfare, and so many theoretical systems were based around the destruction or defence of ground and sea-based missiles. Space-based missiles were not a target due to the Outer Space Treaty, which banned the use, testing or storage of nuclear weapons outside the Earth's atmosphere.

Systems proposed ranged from measures as simple as ground and space-based anti-missiles to railguns, space based lasers, orbital mines and other such futuristic weaponry. Deployment of these systems was seriously considered in the mid-1980s under the banner of the Strategic Defence Initiative (popularly known as Star Wars). If the Cold War had continued, then many of these systems could have seen deployment: the United States got as far as developing working railguns, and a laser that could destroy missiles at range, though the power requirements of both were phenomenal, and the ranges and firing cycles utterly impractical.

Electronic warfare

With the end of the Cold War and continued development of satellite and electronics technology, attention was focused on space as a supporting theatre for conventional warfare. Currently, military operations in space primarily concern either the vast tactical advantages of satellite-based surveillance, communications, and positioning systems or mechanisms used to deprive an opponent of said tactical advantages.

Accordingly, most space-borne proposals which would traditionally be considered "weapons" (a communications or reconnaissance satellite may be useful in warfare but isn't generally classified as a weapon) are designed to jam, sabotage, and outright destroy enemy satellites, and conversely to protect friendly satellites against such attacks. To this end, the US (and presumably other countries) is researching groups of small, highly mobile satellites called "microsats" (about the size of a refrigerator) and "picosats" (approximately 1 cubic foot (H"27 litres) in volume) nimble enough to manoeuvre around and interact with other orbiting objects to repair, sabotage, hijack, or simply collide with them.

Kinetic bombardment

Another theorized use involves the extension of conventional weaponry into orbit for deployment against ground targets. Though international treaties bar the deployment of nuclear missiles outside the atmosphere, other categories of weapons are largely unregulated. Traditional ground-based weapons are generally not useful in orbital environments, and few if any would survive re-entry even if they were, but as early as the 1950s, the United States has toyed with kinetic bombardment, i.e. orbiting magazines of non-explosive projectiles to be dropped onto hardened targets from low-earth orbit. Kinetic weapons have always been widespread in conventional warfare—bullets, arrows, swords, clubs, etc.—but the energy a projectile would gain while falling from orbit would make such a weapon rival all but the most powerful explosives. A direct hit would presumably destroy all but the most hardened targets without the need for nuclear weapons.

Such a system would involve a 'spotter' satellite, which would identify targets from orbit with high-power sensors, and a nearby 'magazine' satellite to de-orbit a long, needle-like tungsten dart onto it with a small rocket motor or just dropping a very big rock from orbit (such as an asteroid). This would be more useful against a larger but less hardened target (such as a city). Though a common device in science fiction, there is no publicly-available evidence that any such systems have actually been deployed by any nation.

Directed-Energy Weapons

Weapon systems that fall under this category include lasers, linear particle accelerators or particle-beam based weaponry, microwaves and plasma-based weaponry. Particle beams involve the acceleration of charged or neutral particles in a stream towards a target at extremely high velocities, the impact of which creates a reaction causing immense damage. Most of these weapons are theoretical or impractical to implement currently, aside from lasers which are starting to be used in terrestrial warfare. That said, directed-energy weapons are more practical and more effective in a vacuum (i.e. space) than in the Earth's atmosphere, as in the atmosphere the particles of air interfere with and disperse the directed energy. Obviously, that problem would not occur in space.

Practical considerations

Space warfare is likely to be conducted at far greater distances and speeds than terrestrial combat. The vast distances involved pose difficult challenges for targeting and tracking, as even light requires a few seconds to traverse ranges measured in hundreds of thousands of kilometres. For example, if attempting to fire upon a target at the distance of the Moon from the Earth, the image one sees reflects the position of the target slightly more than a second earlier. A projectile from a railgun recently tested by the US Navy would take over eighteen hours to cross that distance (making the simplifying and optimistic assumption that it will travel in a straight line at a constant velocity of 5.8 km/s along its entire trajectory). Even a laser will need approximately 1.28 seconds, meaning a laser-based weapon system would need to lead a target's apparent position by 1.28×2 = 2.56 seconds.

Three factors conspire to make engaging targets in space very difficult. First, the vast distances involved mean that an error of even a fraction of a degree in the firing solution could result in a miss by thousands of kilometres. Second, space travel involves tremendous speeds by terrestrial standards—a geostationary satellite moves at a speed of 3.07 km/s whereas objects in low earth orbit can move at up to 8 km/s. Third, though distances are large, targets remain relatively small. The International Space Station, currently the largest artificial object in Earth orbit, measures slightly over 100m at its largest span. Other satellites can be orders of magnitude smaller, e.g. Quickbird measures a mere 3.04m. External ballistics for stationary terrestrial targets is enormously complicated—some of the earliest analog computers were used to calculate firing solutions for naval artillery, as the problems were already beyond manual solutions in any reasonable time—and the issues in targeting objects in space make a difficult problem even harder. Additionally, though not a problem for orbital kinetic weapons, any directed energy weapon would require large amounts of electricity. So far the most practical batteries are lithium batteries, and the most practical method of generating electricity in space is through photovoltaic modules, which are currently only 5-18% efficient, and fuel cells, which have limited fuel. Current technology might not be practical for powering effective lasers, particle beams, and railguns in space.

Regardless of one's reasons for going to war, at present those reasons are not likely to suggest major targets located in space. Most of the main theories which attempt to explain human proclivity for warfare—psychological, sociological, demographic, economic, political, or otherwise—would not indicate space as a likely location of conflict until a significant population is engaged in large-scale activity there. Until then, space warfare is likely to take a supporting role to conventional, terrestrial warfare. Aside from applications such as communications, reconnaissance, GPS, and the like, which would be difficult or impossible without satellites, there do not appear to be any major advantages to basing weapons systems in space. The main reason is simply cost. Space warfare that involves humans being deployed in space to fight each other is not currently practical because of the difficulty and cost of sustaining human life in space, especially over long periods of time.

Additionally, there are few things that could be accomplished by space warfare that any nation wealthy enough to finance them cannot accomplish far more cheaply through conventional means. Raising any significant mass beyond Earth's gravity will always require a large amount of energy, and the cost increases with mass. For example, though kinetic bombardment potentially offers the ability to strike any target anywhere in the world within minutes, both the United States and Russia, possibly the only nations with the resources and facilities necessary to implement such a system, have sufficiently long-range supersonic bombers that the same target could already be deployed in a matter of hours at a mere fraction of the cost.

POSSIBLE WARFARE OVER SPACE

Most of the world's communications systems rely heavily on the presence of satellites in orbit around Earth. Protecting these assets might seriously motivate nations dependent upon them to consider deploying more space-based weaponry, especially in conflicts involving advanced countries with access to space. Even without the further militarization of space, a future conflict conducted largely on the ground through conventional means might well be sparked by actions conducted entirely in space. Alternatively, the very threat of space warfare may be enough to put considerable pressure on the political system of a nation, such as the pressure which caused the formation of the Outer Space Treaty.

Relatedly, though no infrastructure or economic interests exist at the moment to warrant the occupation of terrain on other terrestrial bodies within the Solar system, or to occupy orbital trajectories in outer space, some futurists have predicted that should such infrastructure be deployed, space-faring nations may go to war for control of extra-planetary resources. Such a conflict could easily involve warfare both within and outside the Earth's atmosphere. One suggested point of conflict is the helium-3 resources in the south polar region of the Moon. Russia has already stated its intention of developing this resource, and the Chinese lunar mission is scheduled to land in that area in 2024. However, the high abundance of this isotope would make war quite unlikely.

Space warfare in fiction

Space warfare is a topic often touched upon in science fiction, with a wide range of realism and plausibility, from stories based on anticipated future technology and tactics, to fantasy or historically based scenarios that happen to take place in a science-fiction background. Some portray a space-borne military will be similar to an Air Force, whereas others depict a more naval analog. Still others suggest forces more like marines: highly mobile forces engaged in interplanetary and interstellar warfare but with most of the actual conflict occurring in terrestrial environments.

Both kinetic energy and directed energy weapons are often portrayed, along with various military space vessels. The Lensman series by E. E. Smith is an early example, which also inspired the term Space Opera due to the grandiose scales of the stories. The Ender's Game series by Orson Scott Card is a notable example in that it makes conjecture as to what sort of tactics and training would be required for war in outer space. Other science fiction authors have also delved into the tactics of space combat, such as David Weber in his Honorverse series as well as Larry Niven and Jerry Pournelle in their Mote in God's Eye series. A more recent example would be Alastair Reynolds' Revelation Space universe, which explores combat at relativistic speeds. Robert A. Heinlein's Starship Troopers is perhaps one of the best-known and earliest explorations of the "space marine" idea. Space-based vehicular combat is portrayed in many movies and video games, most notably Star Wars, the Halo Series, Descent, Macross and Star Trek. Games such as the Homeworld series provide interesting concepts for space warfare, such as the use of plasma-based projectors that receive their energy from a ships propulsion system, and automated unmanned space combat vehicles. Other series, such as Gundam, prominently feature vehicular combat in and among many near future concepts, such as O'Neill cylinders.

The distinct fictional settings in which space warfare occurs are far too numerous to list, but popular examples include Star Trek (in all of its various incarnations), Warhammer 40,000, Star Wars, Babylon 5, Buck Rogers, Flash Gordon, Battlestar Galactica, Mass Effect, Stargate, the Halo Series and many comic book franchises. Video games have frequently touched the subject, with the Wing Commander franchise serving as a prototypical example. Note that very few games attempt to simulate an environment with realistic distances and speeds, though Independence War and Frontier: Elite II both do, as does the board game Attack Vector: Tactical.

MILITARY SPACE TECHNOLOGY

One has to look to beyond forefront military space technologies in order to begin to map the future of space warfare. This is partly due to the fact that in recent years, research and development partnerships related to sensitive military space systems and dual-use commercial systems have grown broader and more inclusive. This trend has resulted in greater access for the United States to talented minds from all over the world and low-cost scientific contributions from university-based researchers and small commercial operations. It has also resulted in a greater probability for technologies developed in the U.S. to leak outside its borders. The realignment of the global economy stands to further shift the international balance of space power in the years to come. For nations that possess the relative wealth, infrastructure, and knowledge to develop space warfare technologies, their ability to become a leading military space power requires only the will to do so. The "brain drain" that hampered the space programs of many nations in decades past is weighing less on them today. The stagnancy of foreign economies that resulted in a flood of scientific minds to the U.S. is slowly ebbing, as many are now returning home to profitable jobs in booming defence and space industries.

This situation is compounded by increased competition in the launch services industry, which has resulted in reduced costs to place assets into orbit, as well as a decrease in the size and weight of satellites and space systems—developments that are conducive to space warfare. Consequently, access to space is no longer limited to nations with massive military budgets. In this rapidly changing environment, the greatest influence on the development of space warfare may rest on our ever-growing dependency upon satellites—for both military and commercial purposes—and their inherent vulnerabilities. Furthermore, as we venture forward into a globalized security environment fueled by advances in technologies such as directed energy (DE) systems, artificial intelligence (AI), and nanomanufacturing, both the warfighter and the diplomat will be presented with new tools to respond to security crises.

Military space technologies currently in development are the precursor to a world where threats can be neutralized at the speed of light and conflicts may escalate at a rate too fast to curtail. Accordingly, adjustments will soon have to be made across the entire spectrum of diplomatic and military affairs. If we fail to draft international treaties now that are in line with the pace of advancements in military space technology, a global technology free-for-all could result. This could contribute to a climate in which a spacefaring nation such as the U.S. would be bound to engage in a constant race against itself in order to maintain an effective defensive capability. The purpose of the following military space technology forecast and analysis is to provide new insights and specific recommendations that might protect peaceful cooperation in outer space. This forecast assumes that there are no binding constraints from international treaties. It depicts the current and future state of science related to military space systems, specifically systems that could lead to scenarios that could be precursors to or causes of warfare in space.

In the years leading up to 2020, tensions among military space powers have been mounting. This has been due, in part, to broad-spectrum advances that have materialized internationally in the "Five Ds" of counter-space operations: Deception, Disruption, Denial, Degradation, and Destruction. Even as nations flaunt their military space abilities as a means of intimidating and deterring space rivals, instances of space systems failures, though still uncommon, are slowly rising due to space-warfare systems testing and the increasing amount of space debris. Space systems failures in this new era are triggering accusations of systems disruption and sabotage between nations. The means to achieve an offensive and defensive military space capability in this heady space environment can be found in various force-multiplying arenas of technology, which we will now discuss.

2020

We enter 2020 to find that the disparities that existed in decades past regarding global space warfare capabilities have been fundamentally and irreversibly altered. Many leading nations are now operating on a near-level playing field. Complementary technologies are driving one another's progress; for example, as robotics concepts top out and undergo a momentary pause, they are soon catapulted ahead by explosive growth in the field of supercomputing. The arrival and subsequent establishment of strong artificial intelligence is approaching. Key strategists of military space warfare systems are chasing full-spectrum, real-time, and seamless situational awareness of sea, ground, air, and space. The world's brightest minds are reaching new heights as human intelligence is fused with intelligent agents and neural networks. These are the systems that will deliver humanity to the next echelon as nations become increasingly reliant on AI systems and their ability to process a now humanly unmanageable stream of information–a torrent to which our military is now inextricably connected.

The five theaters of combat: Cyber, Space, Air, Land, and Sea, now resemble a unified battlesphere. The international space community is being led by drivers such as the still plummeting cost of computational power, the continued free exchange of knowledge, and the refinement of nanomaterials applications, which are resulting in stronger, lighter, faster and more responsive space systems. Featured most prominently in this transition process is the influence of the smaller commercial space systems companies and non-military R&D providers, such as universities. The roles of large military and governmental-based, space-systems providers have been challenged effectively by the private space industry. This challenge was inspired in part by successes in the fields of launch services, satellite development, and niche emerging systems. During this era, the commercial launch industry in the United States is now spending as much as four times the total annual budget of NASA, with wide spread commercial space travel seeming more plausible than ever.

The threat spectrum for potential space-attack scenarios is no longer a distant hypothesis, nor does it seem an abstract possibility because the technology is unknown–in 2020 various advanced space-warfare technologies are openly displayed and touted as offensive attack systems. For many nations there is an ominous and increased probability of sustaining a space asset attack; running in parallel with such concerns are increasing fears of worst-case scenarios related to the accidental launch of nuclear forces. This is also due to measurable increases in space debris and the confusion that could arise should space systems be attacked or time-out for extended periods without explanation. As more countries than ever are now realizing their mounting reliance on space, and as tensions run higher, the range of possible deterrents and responses to a space systems attack are increasingly severe and include the possible use of nuclear weapons. Full-scale attacks on space systems can now deliver catastrophic effects upon economies, societal functions, and military operations that would take decades to recover from–even limited acts of space warfare could result in rapid conflict breakout and light-speed escalation scenarios. Intolerable demands have now been placed upon the government and military officials of the leading space powers, as the remaining human factors across the entire spectrum of military space operations must come to terms with the prospect that their continued presence might only serve as an impediment to the realized potential of computational efficiency.

Artificial Intelligence & Cyber Warfare

In light of the convergence process that is now taking place between AI and cyber warfare systems and their corresponding areas of responsibility relating to military space systems and space warfare technologies internationally, their sections have been merged to reflect this evolution.

Human-machine interactions and interfaces are radically changing many aspects of the military space command and control structure. In many cases, specific combat operations are now being conducted by human and artificial operators working together in a virtual environment, which delivers a real-time view of the target area with semi-autonomous and autonomous attack options just a blink or a voice-command away. In 2020, AI-driven systems are now supplying consolidated information and refined military options to high-level decision makers, who are now unable to decipher and analyse vast data flows alone. The role of the war planner is now found to be most critical during the process of selecting war fighting strategies generated and provided by AI systems.

The entire sphere of global military operations in 2020 has the potential to be fully interconnected for those with the means and the desire to do so, as successful military operations are decided by this complex network of systems. Vast protection measures have been taken to guard these systems, including actions to greatly reduce the number of network access points into military and national security systems and to centralize individual architectures in an attempt to prevent unauthorized access and lessen the probability of cyber attacks. This will prove to be a critical decision for many advanced military powers. As governmental network access points are reduced and their decentralized layout is eventually integrated, the potential for security breaches is greatly decreased. However, should a cyber denial of service or brute force attack prove successful, a full or near-full spectrum catastrophic failure could result. Scenarios such as these must be considered before the complete consolidation of information architectures is achieved. Decentralized systems lead to an increased potential for vulnerabilities; however they defuse the effects of successful attacks, thus minimizing the potential for significantly debilitating operational effects.

Threats posed to computer networks that support critical military satellite systems are in 2020 becoming increasingly complex and are occurring more frequently. Specifically, attacks targeting ground stations and command centres threaten military connectivity and the seamlessness of the Command, Control, Communications, Computer, Intelligence, Surveillance, and Reconnaissance systems (C4ISR). Such attacks have the potential to effectively induce a systems blackout. A military's ability to adequately secure C4ISR systems and protect ground segments ensures success not only in space, but in all dimensions of warfare. Advances in cryptology, quantum cryptology, and related technologies such as ciphers and crypto-keys for performing encryption and decryption of these data streams are vital to space-systems security. Specifically, the preservation of secure crosslink/uplink/downlink data transmissions will require constant enhancement efforts due to the availability of advanced computer processing capabilities and the adaptive nature of highly skilled adversaries. As with all military space-supporting computer systems, threat sources are not limited to code breakers and hackers trying to exploit weaknesses from outside government facilities in faraway lands, but from within the host government as well. In an environment where trust is everything, a weakness in the human element of security could jump all other protection measures. Additionally, if an attack were to succeed against the C4ISR supporting space systems, a self-healing capability or Self-Regenerative Systems (SRS) solution must be executed immediately in order to repair and secure the effected network. Such abilities to survive a debilitating space systems attack will be made possible by advances in AI.

Nanotechnology

In 2020 it is nearly impossible to find nanotechnology detractors as universal applications are benefiting countless industries in this multidisciplinary field. Up to this point, nanotechnology discoveries that improved space warfare capabilities had appeared mostly in the form of materials improvements, which enhanced solar power generation, survivability, and structural integrity. Now, micro-electro-mechanical systems (MEMS) and micro-opto-electro-mechanical systems (MOEMS) are beginning to lead to further improvements in sensors, such as Attitude Determination and Control (ADCS) and other components, such as actuators.

Meaningful research into the materials sciences has now been underway for nearly twenty-five years and novel applications are currently appearing and addressing key challenges. Specifically, developments made in the areas of carbon nanotubes (CNT) are resulting in materials capable of thermal and electrical conduction. Additionally, CNT in the proper configurations have led to the creation of materials with unprecedented ballistic protection and heat-shielding and load-bearing strength, including the ability to defuse and insulate against the effects of high-energy lasers. For example, 3D aerogels and xerogels are in 2020 capable of withstanding load-bearing pressures as extreme as 75,000psi. One can imagine numerous applications for such materials, especially when we factor in advances in oxide options. Nanocomposite materials such as those utilizing silica or polystyrene even demonstrate an ability to shield against the effects of high-power microwaves (HPM) and radio frequency (RF). This field of science is also delivering applications that provide the ability to blend an asset's thermal, visual, and radar appearance into its background. Through this research, advanced photovoltaics and power generation methods are evolving as well.

More elaborate, yet feasible, concepts are being pursued such as a Faraday Cage built on a nanoscale level, which would require doped and multi-walled carbon nanotubes (MWCNT). This concept uses carbon nanotubes to develop an enclosure for satellite subsystems and smaller satellite classes such as picosats and nanosats and would provide insulation against various DE threats. Such an enclosure could deter the effects of an electromagnetic pulse (EMP), electrostatic discharges and various other directed energy threats.

Also, self-healing materials are being researched by universities, industry, and militaries to develop self-repairing technologies to address damages such as those that could be sustained in space as a result of space debris or destructive space-asset attacks. Such impacts could lead to a satellite failure, and so a technology like this reaching the development stage would prove invaluable. These materials would use composite structures that contain nanoscale spheres, which encapsulate an unhardened polymer resin. When a satellite is hit, the resin would spread and then fill the cracks to prevent further damage. Such systems could also provide shielding.

Flexible nanoelectronic devices that are as thin as paper and mounted to a thin flexible substrate such a as a plastic would provide a flexible, conductive, and multiuse material, which could then be integrated into countless space systems.

A very attractive manifestation of this application would be in the form of a substrate on which electronic circuits could be printed on demand. Such a nanomaterial would also be durable and could be rolled up and stored. Flexible substrates and the use of various conductors could lead to thin-film solar cells for space applications or thin-film semiconductors. The next level: Molecular nanotechnology (MNT) promises to revolutionize countless products by engineering mechanical and electronic systems, including advanced materials, at the molecular scale. Such a capacity for discovery will touch upon every aspect of military technology in the realm of space warfare.

SATELLITES, ATTACK SATELLITES & ASSET DEFENCE SYSTEMS

In 2020 military satellites and, to a lesser degree, commercial satellites that perform functions critical to civilians, governments and militaries are now increasingly capable of performing active and passive defence, offensive interdiction and rendezvous operations, and covert and overt attacks, while simultaneously carrying out their primary missions. As a result of this trend towards a technology convergence, satellites, attack satellites, and asset defence systems will be included in the same section. Advanced autonomous satellites systems, may include the following subsystems: laser communications systems, high-powered electronic propulsion systems, advanced pattern recognition software, earth-space energy transfer, and/ or advanced photovoltaics. These discoveries, which originated in the fields of AI, nanotechnology, and DE are continually improving many other areas of satellite survivability and overall performance.

These advanced systems are in many cases complemented by elaborate suites of countermeasures including: aerosols, decoys, lasers, chemical munitions, high-and low-energy lasers, power-sapping methods, adhesives, adhesive materials, corrosives, destructive enzymes, charged projectiles, kinetic objects, kinetic collisions, cryogenically frozen micro-meteors, compact DE systems, jamming devices, electronic warfare (EW), high-powered microwave (HPM), RF, EMP, and electromagnetic interference (EMI), and various other methods to duplicate natural phenomenon. Countermeasure options also include thermal effects, foils, lures, methods to compromise sensors, crosslink/uplink/downlink transmission sabotage or interference, and, lastly, defence by an accompanying host/surrogate satellite or an independent escort/defence satellite. Such countermeasures could be employed to defend against attack or, in an offensive capacity, impose the 5Ds upon a rival satellite.

The satellites of leading nations may now be incorporating autonomous crash avoidance, self-monitored diagnostics utilizing low-cost sensors and plug-sense-and-play software, threat identification and reporting abilities, and even self-directed repair services. Satellites are now also incorporating advanced nanomaterials, which depending upon their configuration, can partly or fully insulate against many forms of DE attacks, EMP, charged particle beam (CPB), neutral particle beam (NPB), HPM, and RF, assuming that a significant blast wave does not take effect–though the effect of such pressure is being reduced during this period as well.

In the era of space warfare, nations with lumbering space systems that can be reached with ballistic missile capabilities are faced with two choices: Replace or defend. A prime example of such a vulnerability (both in 2009, and undoubtedly in 2020) would be a system like the European Union's four Helios observational satellites, which each weigh in at 4 metric tons and are located in low earth orbit (LEO). In contrast, deployed formation-flying microsatellite constellations are beginning to evolve into pico satellite and nanosatellite swarms, providing an enhanced means to defuse the effects of space warfare against satellite systems. Such satellite configurations would also further upgrade the overall integrity of a global, seamless, real-time, and integrated data stream, which is the ultimate pursuit of the military war planner. Such systems would be equipped with versatile features such as electrical propulsion systems, multiple-agent-based autonomy, and laser communications systems–all technologies delivered via the fields of directed energy, artificial intelligence, and nanotechnology.

Directed Energy Weapons (DEW)

Various ground-based DEW platforms, which can deliver effects utilizing CPB, NPB, HPM, RF, and high-energy laser

(HEL), have been deployed by various nations. Despite widespread successes in the fields of directed energy and adaptive optics, an ability to dispense a powerful space-earth, earth-space CPB or HEL weapons system has yet to be fully achieved due to atmospheric challenges.

With atmosphere-related challenges removed from the equation, many HEL systems could potentially release continuous wave and pulsed outputs reaching into the multi-megawatt ranges. Continued advancements in other subsystem-focused areas, such as beam control and pointing and tracking, will continue to improve overall beam propagation as well. Additionally, it has been shown in years past that it is possible to overpower atmospheric effects by phase-locking multiple DE sources, thus creating a combined energy source. When this is done accurately, the resulting power outputs are drastically increased when compared to a single source DE pulse stream. For this reason, research in refining methods such as this to reduce or eliminate weather-related challenges is rigorously underway.

Many other R&D programs are taking place internationally, across the university, commercial, and military-based scientific communities, to develop ways to improve DEW effects. Constellations of high-strength and thermal-effects-resistant relay mirrors, utilizing advanced nanomaterials, could in 2020 be installed in multiple locations. For example, when mounted to an unmanned aerial vehicle (UAV) or high-altitude airship (HAA), they could accurately direct a beam of energy to any target on earth, thus eliminating line-of-sight barriers. Contrary to the various levels of efficacy provided by such concepts, the deployment of a high-energy, space-based laser or other type of space-based DEW has already been undertaken by as many as three parties that are now capable of space-to-space anti-satellite (ASAT) operations–and, though slightly compromised, space-to-earth attacks. It is also important to note that atmospheric challenges do not degrade space-to-space DEW platforms and their potential. Furthermore, earth-space attacks can be carried out by lasers based on aerial vehicles.

With the help of high-powered supercomputers and AI systems working in concert with ground stations and weather satellites, militaries of the world can now accurately predict weather patterns like never before. Such an ability to predict weather and atmospheric changes allows war planners to accurately diagnose the time, location, and other related information necessary to channel the atmospheric windows of opportunity that would most empower HEL beams. Should these predictive methods be combined with long established research into weather modification techniques and advanced adaptive optics, it will not be long before many countries can unlock the full potential of DEWs.

Not only can EMP effects now be employed anywhere in the world without the need for a high-altitude nuclear detonation, the delivery of these effects can also be achieved with a reasonable level of accuracy. These non-nuclear electromagnetic pulse (NNEMP) generators, which have for decades been used to test hardened military and commercial equipment, have become yet another benefactor of the trend towards increased miniaturization of military systems. As a result of such size reductions, NNEMP systems can now be based terrestrially on mobile units, tactical aircraft, UAVs, space-based systems, and as fixed ground stations.

Ground Segments

The role of ground-based installations in the pursuit of space dominance has never been so significant. In 2020, attacks against the ground segments of a capable space nation are just as destructive as those committed against satellites in space. Cyber, Space, Air, Land, and Sea operations are equally vulnerable to these attacks, though for many nations, such a distinction no longer applies. Joint warfare is no longer a doctrine, it is no longer a practice or a military strategy-it is a constant; it is the only option. From special operations to ground forces, from space command to naval forces, there is no mistaking that there is only a military now–a singular, integrated, and fully-networked military force. And there is no denying the integral role played by ground segments in future wars.

Military space systems and related operations consist of three key components: the space-based segment (satellites), the ground segment (systems operations), and the electromagnetic links, which connect the two. These ground stations house information processing, fusion and dissemination facilities, command and control centres, and many other components that support essential military and intelligence functions. In the years leading up to 2025, advances in the fields of nanotechnology, AI, and DE will begin to redefine everything we thought we knew about the ground segment as the process of technological convergence continues.

Evolved Unmanned Aerial Vehicles & Launch Services

Developmental efforts in the field of unmanned, autonomous, high-endurance, near-space vehicles are coming into fruition as these systems are nearing full-scale production with various concepts having been proven flight worthy and even deployable. This revolutionary platform may feature: supersonic capabilities, quantum-encrypted data transmissions, and advanced nanomaterials that deliver superior ballistics protection, stealth capabilities, and integrated power generation. Weapons capabilities may include: near-space to space DEWs, RF munitions, electromagnetic pulse generators and various ASAT capabilities. It is not expected that such a system would require in-flight refueling, since various energy-generating and conversion methods may be applicable during this time frame; should such a technology not be available until 2025, hybrid propulsion systems would instead reduce the need for in-flight refueling. Such a system can also return back to its point of origin or change flight plans to another location in-flight, depending on the needs of the warfighter.

Other deployable configurations have also now appeared, such as unmanned, autonomous, high-endurance global strike platforms, which are delivered into orbit on a responsive launch system, maintain a stand-by position, and, when called upon, can reach hypersonic re-entry speeds to deliver a variety of weapons payloads.

Subsonic high-altitude, ultra-long-endurance, low-observable unmanned systems have now been deployed by multiple nations and are being used for various military operations, with multiple integrated weapons options. These autonomously-assisted strike platforms provide increased versatility compared to their predecessors. These applications, much like microsatellite systems, have been significantly enhanced in many other areas. Improvements in materials sciences, miniaturization methods, and energy-generation techniques have also improved reliability and survivability, while extending mission duration. It is now also possible that such systems have begun to receive integrated HEL weapons for military operations such as those related to: space asset attack and protection, air-to-ground engagement, and missile defence.

Caveats

As a result of widespread technology exchanges pertaining to space launch systems and the proliferation of long-range ballistic missile technology, coupled with the widespread availability of commercial launch services, virtually every nation on earth now has the potential to place military satellites into space. At the same time, an increasing number of nations now have indigenous ballistic missile and launch capabilities, which have dramatically increased their potential to commit offensive space systems attacks against blue-shirt assets. Additionally, the continued trend toward cooperative space security has combined the launch capabilities of many national space programs. Such an outcome is due to: consolidation of the commercial launch and space systems industry on an international level, decades of abundantly available open-source technical information, loosely monitored multi-tiered collaborative environments, and industrial and military espionage. These influences mentioned above also apply to nearly every area of the military space systems industry, and are responsible for immeasurably enhancing red-shirt military space capabilities. Adding to this, by 2020 emerging technologies have dramatically reduced the overall size of space systems and increased affordability while simultaneously improving upon strategic initiatives such as systems redundancy and interoperability. The resulting widespread access to military space technology has led to an exponential increase in the number of satellites, which has, in turn, heightened the potential for an act of space warfare.

Internationally, the convergence process is continuing as the standardization of space and related technical protocols among allies is ensuring that each nation involved in cooperative space security is on the same page.

This process will also begin to become a polarizing force, making the existence of a red shirt-blue shirt space dynamic more clearly defined. In 2020 space access is power and not solely of the military sort. Now that we rely on space systems for trade, communications, imaging, intelligence gathering, military targeting and navigation, and other functions, the objectives of war planners are being achieved by attacking, compromising, or temporarily rendering inoperable a nation's space assets – and by doing so, economies and societal functions of the targeted nation or nations could as a byproduct be brought to a grinding halt. Given this unprecedented level of space access, combined with smaller payload weights, advanced satellite development programs, and proliferation of military space systems, one can be reasonably confident that most conflicts between industrialized nations will incorporate some methods of space warfare, even if in a limited, nondestructive fashion.

Regardless of the level of taboo associated with such an act, countries that are engaged in conflicts against a more advanced military space power will have to either accept defeat or commit to attacking the systems that are devastating their forces. As with other space warfare scenarios, the probability an attack against a nation's space systems increases as the deterrent decreases; this deterrent factor is greatly reduced in the case of nations with a minimal space presence, especially when under attack or in a position of desperation.

There are very few reasons not to incorporate space warfare attacks in an attempt to deliver lights-out warfare effects that would avoid unnecessary death and destruction while also potentially reducing the duration of the conflict. Such an action would be an extraordinary and irreversible step towards space warfare tactics becoming an acceptable force multiplier. Such a sense of acceptance could be further compounded by internationally-approved military space operations conducted under the banner of peace keeping and sanctions employment and enforcement. Space warfare could become a means to reduce the probability of war–to be able to silence and deafen a military before the first human casualty takes place.

To imagine such a scenario, however, one must ignore a world armed with thermonuclear weapons and the potential for space warfare to result in a debris field so dense that it could serve to preclude the possibility of future space colonization. And as the approach of Strong AI systems looms on the horizon, perhaps a more immediate concern would be this: In an era of increasingly seamless, high-speed military operations and a reduced human presence in the data stream, will this ever-evolving computational capability reduce or increase the probability of accidental nuclear warfare?

2025

By 2025, space warfare systems have been used numerous times both covertly and overtly by various nations, during limited space-specific attacks and in support of larger military operations. These technologies can deliver destructive effects that are physical, societal, and/or economic, in many cases with varying levels of overlap. Such space-specific attack scenarios are conducted in a space-to-space, space-to-ground, and ground-to-space fashion. What has not occurred and is highly unlikely to occur for many decades, if ever, is a dedicated war in space or space war. This is a direct result the intrinsic inability for modern militaries, regardless of partial or complete command of space, to separate military space functions from other areas of military operations. Space has been and will continue to be used as a force multiplier and as part of a larger military operation. Should a nation pursue a dedicated space war scenario, it likely would be capable of only an individualized or limited act of war against space systems, an act that, if committed, would require supplemental attacks and support provided by the remaining four theaters. Therefore, the phrase "space war" is more of a cultural term, describing a scenario that could not in reality be conducted between nations, as either a war of space systems attrition or as a means to achieve a decisive victory against a nation or nations alone. Wars per se can not be fought and won solely in space, though for nations engaged in conflict against a capable space adversary, they are nearly impossible to win without some act of space warfare.

Military space systems, which were once viewed as consisting of distinct or virtually independent elements, are in

2025 progressively appearing unified in many fundamental ways as the converging trajectories of various scientific fields drive the space industry forward. Over the years, technologies that were once referred to by many as merely emerging concepts and theoretical possibilities have by a rapid and consistent pace of development challenged contrarian expectations; today, they transcend and defy their once predefined and now abandoned limitations. We witness this phenomenon in a similar light to what unfolded in the previous century with computer processing technologies. As computational demands increased, relays became vacuum tubes, then transistors, and on to semiconductors. In 1965 Moore's Law charted an exponential growth pattern in the complexity of integrated semiconductor circuits and computer processing. The unprecedented explosion of computational potential, and, in turn, affordability that Moore accurately predicted drove widespread discoveries in the field of computer science, such as the creation of the Internet.

In 2001 Kurzweil's Law of Accelerating Returns extended the growth pattern described in Moore's Law to transcend computers and reach into many other areas of science. Most remarkable is that this scientific and technological growth, which Kurzweil revealed, is not linear but exponential; and it is not limited to the technological, as humanity accelerates its potential in cadence. The way that one technology seems to max out and then suddenly converge with another to become something greater was also observed with the marriage of early of genetics research and advanced computer processors. According to Kurzweil's Law, this would constitute an example of two technologies having pushed and pulled with one another, engaging in almost evolutionary fashion to become more than just the sum of their parts, but rather something superior. The result in this case was the mapping of the genome, improved health care, and longer human life expectancy.

Converging technologies driving one another in parallel as humanity realizes a collective need to meet the next challenge – in 2025 this phenomenon has now set its sights on military space technology. Due to the nature of the sciences that will drive future military space systems advancements, the military space systems industry is now experiencing its exponential growth cycle. The primary influence leading to advanced arms racing and evolved methods of warfare that reach destructively into space is the integration of nanotechnology, robotics, and artificial intelligence technologies (NRai).

Nanotechnology/Robotics/Artificial Intelligence (NRAI)

As the arrival of Strong AI draws ever closer, along with it comes the realization that computing on such a scale and breadth is beyond our human ability to maintain and monitor, even with the assistance of the machines themselves. We will begin to turn over keys to the IT department to the computer within it, as the pending arrival of Strong AI will drive its own evolutionary cycle, with human oversight existing from afar, at specific points in the data stream. This is the liftoff for military space systems, and our final approach towards a victory over the Turing Test.

During the span of this analysis we have seen the devices for human involvement in netcentric warfare leave the point-and-click mouse behind in exchange for voice-command and evolved human-computer collaboration, under the banner of intelligent and Human-Machine Interfaces (HMI). In 2025 HMI takes a step further towards Brain-Computer Interfaces (BCI), also known as Brain-Machine Interfaces (BMI). Working, but limited, examples of this technology, such as the Berlin Brain-Computer Interface (BBCI) have exhibited proven results as far back as 2002. Such technologies to command cyberspace and, as a result, the five theaters of combat including space have been driven by AI. This is specifically through advances in the field of neural networks, a computational data-analysis method that is based upon the architecture of the neuronal connections within the human brain. Such a system will eventually allow human integration into the data stream and in time will not only allow interaction via one single human function, but instead BCIs will be comprised of central nervous system connections, alpha and beta brainwaves, eye movement, and voice and facial recognition. The first manifestations of this technology have been dual-use and have led to tremendous improvements in freedom and mobility for the severely disabled; additional limited civil applications are mostly in the area of video gaming. Military and national security applications of

BCI in 2025 include the control of logistics, supply chains, terrestrial-based weapons systems, unmanned aerial platforms, and space systems.

BCIs will exist in parallel with a virtual world, though they will not be the virtual boxes developed many years prior such as Cave Automatic Virtual Environments (CAVEs). BCIs have combined with a technological ability to create 3-D stereoscopic images direct to the eye, located in interpupillary distance of the warfighter. These virtual domains when fully integrated with Strong AI and connections to the central nervous system, alpha and beta brain waves, and voice and facial recognition, will provide far more than virtual theaters for war gaming and interactive displays for pilots and troop training–we will have effectively and irreversibly fused human intelligence (HI) and AI.

To play ping-pong on a personal computer utilizing a BCI interface that reads alpha and beta brainwaves is impressive in 2009, however in 2025 when BCIs are integrated with optical interpupillary interfaces that transmit a netcentric warfare systems display, combined with central nervous system connections, and voice and facial recognition, we begin to realize its optimal potential. Such a system could ultimately combine with real-time, secure uplink and downlink data transmissions to a satellite in space which, in turn, could direct a small scale UAV or unmanned ground vehicle (UGV) utilizing advanced MOEMS/MEMS-derived sensors and optics delivering streaming video of the battlefield. The truly transformational role of these merged technologies will be difficult to imagine until we first witness the warfighter speak, think, or signal the fire command and neutralize an enemy target.

A specific military application of these technologies that is more likely to be available in 2025 would be those which are used to automatically target objects on the ground from space with hyperspectral imaging integrated into a microsatellite platform. This imaging capability would be combined with principal component analysis (PCA), used to reduce the volume of data to a manageable size for analysis, and a multi-layer perception (MLP) neural network, which uses multiple layers of neurons to turn vast amounts of data into a consolidated form. This could lead to a system capable of educating neural networks on how to execute a specific task, such as delivering strike options in real-time to the war planner via satellite communications to a comprehensive BCI interface.

On a much smaller physical scale, military robotics programs have been enhanced by advances in the field of molecular nanotechnology (MNT), resulting in devices such as molecular motors. This development has spawned numerous concepts which are in the R&D programs of leading NRai nations. These concepts, with molecular scale systems that measure less than a few centimeters, might range from miniature flying vehicles with numerous applications to ground-based robots, both of which, with the help of AI can collectively combine their effects in a swarm-like fashion.

The continued reductions in the size of technology will span all industries and countless military systems, including space systems. For instance, such small flying devices could be contained within a relatively larger rendezvous capable satellite, which would then release the smaller molecular devices or bots to execute acts of sabotage against rival space systems, with a reduced chance of being detected or targeted. Advancements in the field of MEMS-driven micro-thrusters would provide propulsion as reductions in the size of computer systems would allow for control of the devices, either autonomously or remotely via downlink to a ground segment, then onto the device itself.

Microscale and nanoscale UGVs acting alone or in swarms, could eventually mimic biological entities such as insects through MNT processes and be used in military-or intelligence-related operations–as will also be the case with the flying systems. Like nearly every program contained in this analysis, this forefront technology is being pursued by various nations, in multi-tiered collaborations that may include military researchers, university students and professors, and private companies. Such systems would someday be available for deployment as military off-the-shelf (MOT) systems and as commercial off-the-shelf (COT) systems. Additionally, each platform would be field programmable and exhibit Strong AI characteristics. Such technology could be powered by one of a myriad of emerging, nanotechnology-generated energy systems, such as those that use: electromagnetic force, solar energy, microwaves, electricity, magnetism, transistors, and lasers.

Furthermore, developments made to gyroscopes for navigation systems also will be realized.

Other combinations of MEMS/MOEMS, (which it should be mentioned, offer features and benefits which at times overlap one other so much so that the individualized acronyms may in time become integrated under a single designation,) can also be used as sensors, inputs, outputs, or serve other internal processing functions in larger space systems. Such far-reaching technology is leading to entire computer systems on a single chip that could potentially replace silicon chips, adding a further dimension to the forecast beyond 2025. In the more immediate future, innovations in the field of lithography and multi-gate processing, such as double-and tri-gate transistors, may also contribute to dramatic increases in processing speed, especially when compared to the traditional and increasingly more archaic silicon chip.

The role of ground segments in 2025 continues to remain a critical area of military and national security operations. In corresponding fashion with the steps forward witnessed by many other areas of military space systems, the ground segment is reaping the benefits of NRai as well. The vulnerabilities that weakened this bridge between earth-and space-based military functions have been significantly reduced, thanks to improvements in the areas of: miniaturization, maneuverability, survivability, and redundancy. The ground segment of the past has become the unattended ground sensor (UGS), a transportable and affordable, small box-on-the-ground. Deployable in large numbers, providing multiple layers of redundancy, and effective terrestrial-based communications and space-to-earth uplink/downlink, this device has effectively mitigated the threat to ground stations, for now.

DIRECTED ENERGY: WEAPONS AND NEXT GENERATION LAUNCH SYSTEMS

Ground-based (GB) DEWs are in 2025 abundant and can be found in the arsenals of many nations, as they have by now achieved adequate power levels and have clearly demonstrated an ability to strike space assets. For the few nations that have the ability and choose to deploy in space (covertly or overtly), ground targets can be reached from the heavens as well. DEW has redefined warfare, with speed-of-light attack capabilities and a psychological factor second only to nuclear, biological, and chemical (NBC) weapons.

It can be expected that the number of nations with deployed DEW weapons will continue to grow exponentially, as the methods to develop such tools of war and the means to reduce the challenges that hamper development-ready systems will find their way to virtually any nation that seeks to acquire their awesome power.

A thought-provoking combat scenario surrounding GB-DEWs in 2025 begins with the fact that many GB-DEW installations are fixed stationary systems with a large foot print. These fixed systems will likely require massive amounts of energy to provide an effective beam strength that can be capable of sustained offensive and defensive effects.

Because of such constraints, many GB-DEWs are directly wired into nuclear plants and municipal power stations. Accordingly, it should be noted that in 2025, should a nation be faced with a threat to their military forces or space systems by GB-DEWs, there will be few options but to attack these power sources. Clearly then, it is difficult to deny that DEWs powered by fusion sources place a very unique set of challenges upon the war planner.

By 2025 military DE efforts are not only limited to directly improving weapons effects, but rather innovations in the field of DE are also advancing areas such as propulsion. Examples of promising systems in this field include, solar thermal propulsion (STP), which could provide a highly efficient alternative to hydrazine for micro-scale (and larger) space systems that require high Delta-V maneuvers. Another method is based on the concept of using energy generated by a laser to heat a gas, such as hydrogen for example, to a very high temperature.

As a result of this interaction, the gas then rapidly expands and delivers thrust. At this time, lasers have a demonstrated ability to reach the power levels required to deliver this concept to the military in a truly beneficial sense. Just as affordability, reductions in weight, and sheer innovation drove the satellite industry forward in prior decades, those same satellites and their dramatically reduced size and cost has, in turn, provided new opportunities for discovery in the field of space exploration.

In keeping with this spirit of innovation, other methods of propulsion that have been in the R&D stream for many years, such as the Lorentz force ion thruster, are now coming into full fruition. This method delivers a lift capability via the energy created when an electric current is combined with magnetic energy to generate thrust. In 2025, this concept may be already integrated into various space crafts. Other DE propulsion methods such as plasma-based, pulse-detonation engines (PDE), which received much attention in the past, may now be seen regularly preparing for take off.

The rapidly growing threat spectrum against space systems is further expanded by the increasing number of nations and non-state actors with access to ballistic missile technology. At the same time, the ballistic missile defence (BMD) methods deployed in decades past are in some cases now seen as unable to fully respond to the challenges presented in 2025 and beyond. In particular, BMD systems such as the kinetic energy interceptor (KEI) and the miniature kill vehicle (MKV) require elaborate sensor suites, such as infrared, radar, and optics to ensure an accurate trip to the threat. Additionally, components that add weight and systems complexity such as thrusters and guidance systems can now be avoided with the aid of DE missile defence solutions.

Other methods for ballistic missile intercepts such as ground-based lasers (GBL) and space-based laser (SBL) programs have now existed for many years and have proven to be successful for the few nations that possess the resources to employ DE as a BMD system. Though also welcomed are complementary alternatives that help meet the increasing challenges while at the same time preventing threat leakage caused by advanced countermeasures, maneuverable in-flight warheads, and hypersonic global-strike platforms.

One such DE system that may emerge as a complementary BMD application involves a laser-propulsion system named Lightcraft, which could by 2025 deliver a Kinetic Kill Vehicle (KKV) to a target at hypersonic speeds. Such a KKV could be ground, air, or space launched, though its effectiveness is reliant on the overall quality of the DE source that propels it. The structure of the KKV resembles a parabolic-like shape, with an interior consisting of highly reflective mirrors that channel heat away from the laser, resulting in explosive energy that ultimately generates thrust. Such a technology could theoretically be used to deliver lightweight space systems into LEO, without a launch vehicle, resulting in immeasurable cost reductions.

INTEGRATED SATELLITES & CONVENTIONAL LAUNCH SERVICES

Over the past ten years there has been a steady progression towards integrating asset-attack/defence systems, maneuverability-enhancing technology and redundancy measures into individual military and commercial satellites with distinct strategic operations and industry roles. The threat environment, regardless of whether ASAT strikes are common or highly uncommon, dictates that such measures should be integrated into all spacecraft as the potential security and economic effects of downed networks and partial netcentric blackouts outweigh the cost of this integration process.

As large satellites are now perfectly placed in an era that will complete their descent into obsolescence, autonomous formation-flying microsatellite constellations continue to be seen as the most ideal and reliable space-asset platform of choice in an environment plagued with risks directed at space-based operations. Microsatellites such those described in 2020 will continue to be a primary method to ensure netcentric continuity, though the most remarkable advancements are now centred on nanoscale systems. Nanosatellites integrated into microsatellite platforms are in 2025 capable of supporting asset defence and committing acts of sabotage via stealth attack to permanently or temporarily disable a larger satellite or weapons platform. These systems deployed in swarm formations in LEO could provide excellent levels of coverage, with revisit times as good as or better than their larger hosts and counterparts.

This trend towards size reduction and redundancy is setting another revolution into motion as the unmanned, autonomous high-endurance near-space vehicle begins to perform military space roles, and not just in a backup capacity, but one that overlaps and empowers the services delivered by assets in space. As space continues to become an increasingly dangerous place during times of international tensions, the UAV and the satellite will begin to work together regularly to meet the threat. It can be expected that from this trend of satellites and UAVs working together, that a hybrid UAV/Satellite system will emerge. This would be made possible with the help of integrated power generation and compact DE propulsion systems. The first manifestation of this may be satellites launched into orbit from near-space UAV platforms. What is most remarkable though is that through further technology convergence, we in 2025 may be the first to witness a satellite launching itself into space.

4

Conduct of Information Warfare and International Law

THE LEGALITY OF INFORMATION WARFARE

Perhaps because of the newness of much of the technology involved, no provision of international law explicitly prohibits what we now know as information warfare. This absence of prohibitions is significant because, as a crudely general rule, that which international law does not prohibit it permits. But the absence is not dispositive, because even where international law does not purport to address particular weapons or technologies, its general principles may apply to the use of those weapons and technologies. Nevertheless, existing international law leaves space for many types of information warfare techniques in many circumstances.

International Telecommunications Law

Any attack involving networks and telecommunications may implicate the International Telecommunication Union (ITU) and its underlying charter, the International Telecommunication Convention (ITC), which apply to international wire and radio frequency communications. In practice, the ITU may not substantially limit information warfare activities, particularly by the United States and especially in a wartime context.

The primary concerns of the ITU are interoperability and interference. Its predecessor organization, the International Telegraph Union, was established in 1865 to facilitate international telegraph traffic, mainly within Europe. One of the Union's early sets of regulations for radio required interoperability of maritime radio systems, after several dangerous naval incidents occurred because the Marconi Wireless Company, which held the exclusive right to install and operate shipboard radio equipment, refused to permit its operators to communicate with any station that did not use Marconi equipment.

The ITU and the regulations promulgated under it do have some applicability to information warfare attacks that use the electromagnetic spectrum or international telecommunication networks. First, broadcasting stations from one nation may not interfere with broadcasts of other states' services on their authorized frequencies. The International Frequency Regulation Board (IFRB) of the ITU allocates the electromagnetic spectrum to prevent interference. Even military installations must observe the noninterference requirement. Additionally, offshore radio stations are banned, and states may not carry out the transmission of false or misleading signals. Finally, governments must protect the secrecy of international correspondence, although they retain the right to stop radio or wire transmissions for national or domestic security purposes.

The aforementioned provisions would seem to block the disruption or spoofing of adversaries' telecommunications, but in practice they may not. First, the rules against interference do not apply between belligerents, so wartime communications are fair game. Secondly, even in peacetime, violation of the ITU rules and regulations may have limited repercussions, especially for a country as significant in international telecommunications as the United States. The IFRB is more of a coordinating body than a regulatory agency, and it has no actual authority to enforce its decisions; rather, countries respect its edicts against interference so that their own communications will be similarly protected. Even if international sanctions appeared likely, the United States might decide that the risks it faced from external interference would not outweigh its need to conduct operations against a particular adversary. Finally, it is important to note that even where information warfare activities do violate the ITU or its regulations, mere violations are more likely to be considered breaches of contractual obligations under treaty than acts of war justifying forceful responses. Interestingly, the Charter of the United Nations, drafted 50 years ago, appears to contemplate such interference with a country's communications as "infoblockades." Article 41 provides that in its effort to address breaches of the peace, the UN Security Council may call upon UN members to disrupt an aggressor's "rail, sea, air, postal, telegraphic, radio, and other means of communication."

Space

Because of the importance of satellites for international telecommunications, as well as for military (especially U.S.) command, control, communications, and intelligence, many information warfare attacks (including jamming or spoofing of communications or efforts to overcome them) may involve orbital assets, and thus implicate space law. Space law, though, leaves ample room for information warfare.

The fundamental document of space law, the multilateral 1967 Treaty on Principles Governing the Activities of States in the Exploration and Use of Outer Space, Including the Moon and Other Celestial Bodies (the "Outer Space Treaty"), provides that all states shall be free to explore and use outer space on a basis of equality and that no state may place into Earth orbit any objects carrying nuclear weapons or any other kind of "weapon of mass destruction." The 1979 Agreement Concerning the Activities of States on the Moon and Other Celestial Bodies (the "Moon Treaty") applies similar prohibitions to the moon, and also states that the moon shall only be used for peaceful purposes. The 1971 Agreement Relating to the International Telecommunications Satellite Organization (INTELSAT) and the 1976 Convention on the International Maritime Satellite Organization (INMARSAT) also affect telecommunications and the use of space, but their relevance is limited to principles of nondiscrimination among nations using the relevant satellites.

None of these conventions bars information warfare activities that make use of satellite assets. First, although some might argue that state practice and such agreements as the Moon Treaty have created a legal norm of peaceful use of outer space or the avoidance of orbital arms races, it is unquestionable that space can be, and has been, used for military purposes. Orbital surveillance is legal and common, and space is routinely used for military communications, navigation, and weapons guidance. In any event, the meaning of "peaceful use" of outer space is unsettled, and, with its often nonlethal, physically nonintrusive character, it is possible that much of "information warfare" could be considered "peaceful."

Second, for the Outer Space Treaty's prohibition against orbital weapons of mass destruction to apply, it would first have to be determined that the weapons used in an information warfare attack, particularly an electronically based one, were weapons of mass destruction. Many information warfare attacks, which may have no direct physical effects, cannot easily be considered to cause mass destruction in the same way as would, say, an atomic bomb. Furthermore, assuming that the weapons of information warfare could constitute "weapons of mass destruction," those weapons, even when they use satellites, might not be considered to be in space. For example, when a satellite is used to transmit a signal for computer intrusion or sabotage or in communications spoofing, the ultimate "weapon of mass destruction" (the originator of the signal) may actually be on the ground, and the satellite only a conduit for the attack, just as satellites used for guidance of intercontinental ballistic missiles would not be "weapons of mass destruction."

State Practice

State practice, itself a major source of customary international law, seems to permit much of what would go into information warfare. First, espionage, although universally criminal under domestic laws, does not, by itself, violate international law. Furthermore, orbital remote sensing, which may include the bombardment of a country's territory with radar or other forms of electromagnetic radiation, is permissible during war or peace. Second, an adversary's communications are recognized as legitimate targets for disruption during war. Undersea cables, including those connecting belligerents with neutrals, have been interfered with during all naval wars since the Spanish-American War, as Article 15 of the 1884 Convention for the Protection of Undersea Cables exempts belligerents. For example, as World War I began in August 1914, the British cableship Telconia cut Germany's undersea cables, and reeled in the loose ends to prevent repair. Governments have conducted radio jamming in both peace and war for over 60 years, beginning with Austria's efforts to block propaganda broadcast from Nazi Germany in 1934. Finally, ruses have been part of warfare for millennia and their legitimacy has been explicitly recognized; just as the original, ancient Trojan Horse was legal, so too might be some "Trojan Horse" pieces of software.

MAJOR LIMITATIONS ON INFORMATION WARFARE

Despite the novelty of some information warfare techniques, international law poses some constraints on the conduct of information warfare, just as it does on the traditional forms of warfare that use kinetic force for their impact. Nevertheless, characteristics of information technology and warfare pose problems to those who would use international law to limit information warfare, and leave legal space for those who would wage such warfare.

Neutrality and National Sovereignty

By treaty as well as by longstanding customary law, the territory of neutral states is supposed to be inviolable by the forces of belligerents. Apparently, then, an attack through a network that crosses neutral territory, or using a neutral country's satellites, computers, or networks, would infringe upon that neutral's territory, just as would an overflight by a squadron of bombers or an incursion by armed troops. The attack would thus be considered illegal and, perhaps, an act of war against the neutral. Conversely, a neutral's failure to resist the use of its networks for attacks against another country may make it a legitimate target for reprisals by the country that is the ultimate target of the attacks.

Although the argument that electronic incursion would violate neutrality is strong, a counter-argument exists. The encroachments beyond a nation's borders that may violate its neutrality have, in the past, been physical intrusions by troops, ships, or planes. Attacking a neutral's networks, satellites, or computers might not violate the state's neutrality because it might involve no physical encroachment (and might not even constitute an "attack" in the first place). Significantly, although neutrals must not allow any belligerent to move troops or supplies through their territory, or to erect military radio stations there, neutrals have no such obligation to prevent belligerents from using their publicly accessible communications equipment.

Further, as a practical matter, despite an unambiguous rule to the contrary, belligerents have quite significantly violated prohibitions against the erection and use of non-public military communications facilities in neutral territory for military purposes. Thus, the vitality of rules regarding neutrals and telecommunications may have been weakened, as countries have acted as if those laws did not, in fact, have legal force. During World War II, for example, belligerents on both sides took advantage of the neutrality of Portugal, as well as perhaps Turkey and Switzerland, by constructing and using telecommunications facilities for military purposes within those states. In sum, it is not obvious whether the use of a neutral nation's computers, networks, and communications facilities would violate that nation's neutrality, or open that nation up to belligerent reprisals.

International Humanitarian Law

International humanitarian law would seem to welcome the nonlethal "combat" that information warfare promises, but that body of law, which is a combination of conventions and longstanding customary law, may constrain information warfare activities as it does traditional warfare. The fundamental principle of this body of law is that the permissible methods of hurting an enemy are not unlimited, and that the cruelty of war must be mitigated and circumscribed. Nevertheless, although that principle unquestionably survives, even if it is sometimes honored only in the breach, it is not obvious that all types of damage that information attacks would inflict are the kinds of injuries against which humanitarian law endeavors to protect.

Although humanitarian law protects combatants as well as noncombatants, the most significant relevant general tenet of humanitarian law is the protection of civilians. This principle was codified over a century ago in the St. Petersburg Declaration of 1868, which recognized that the only legitimate object of war was to weaken an enemy's military forces. Civilians, as such, may not be the object of an attack. Much of the law addressing the fate of civilians stems from concern over artillery bombardment, and later aerial bombing, as that was how civilians, unless they were loitering near a battlefield, were most likely to come under fire, and it consistently places civilians off limits for attack. Under the Hague Convention (IV) of 1907, military forces could not attack or bombard "by whatever means" undefended towns, dwellings or buildings, a provision that has carried over into the charter of the tribunal considering war crimes in the former Yugoslavia. Similarly, the Charter of the Nuremberg Tribunal condemned wanton bombing of civilian targets.

Despite such legal protections, the reality is that civilians are often victims of modern warfare, without legal consequences for those who hurt them. Nevertheless, when attacks are planned and executed, attackers are supposed to try to avoid injuring civilians, even collaterally. Attacks are to be directed solely toward "military objectives," which have been defined (to the extent such a definition is meaningful) as "those objects which by their nature, location, purpose, or use make an effective contribution to military action and whose total or partial destruction, capture or neutralization, in the circumstances ruling at the time, offers a definite military advantage." To the end of confining attacks to military objectives and limiting civilian casualties, nations may not use weapons that make it impossible for their targeters to distinguish between civilian and military targets (and of course, the targeters must make such distinctions).

The planning and execution of attacks must also include considerations of "proportionality" between civilian damage and the military objective attained. Proportionality is a dual doctrine, arising from customary international law. It applies to both whether a given level of force is appropriate in response to a particular grievance (as part of the law of the use of force, or jus ad bellum), and whether a given action is appropriate in light of its objectives and the casualties that will result (as part of the law of armed conflict, or jus in bello). In the context of humanitarian concern, proportionality derives in part from the Christian "just war" doctrine. Commanders must minimize civilian casualties, subject to the need to accomplish a particular military mission, and they must weigh the cost of civilian lives against the benefit to be gained by the mission. On its face, international humanitarian law anticipates technological change relatively well. Even though some information warfare weapons and techniques could not even have been contemplated when the humanitarian legal principles were developed, those principles can still apply. The "Martens Clause," which has been a part of major humanitarian conventions since 1899, asserts that even in cases not explicitly covered by specific agreements, civilians and combatants remain under the protection and authority of principles of international law derived from established custom, principles of humanity, and from the dictates of public conscience, and that they are not left to the arbitrary judgment of military commanders. In other words, for purposes of humanitarian law, attacks will be judged largely by their effects, rather than by their methods.

Despite its apparent flexibility in coping with technological change, international law may not easily deal with information warfare. It seems obvious that information warfare attacks that were the direct and intentional cause of noncombatant death and destruction-such as disruption of an air traffic control system that caused a civilian airliner to crash, or corruption of a medical database, causing civilians or wounded soldiers to receive transfusions of the incorrect blood type-could violate the laws of war. It is less obvious that attacks with less tangible results, such as the disruption of a financial or social security system, or the disclosure of confidential personal information, constitute the sort of injury against which humanitarian law is supposed to protect civilians, even though for some victims, the consequences of disruption of, say, the banking system, could be more painful than a bombing that damaged a dwelling.

In considering whether information attacks against civilians may violate humanitarian law, it is important to remember that all wars cause suffering for civilians, ranging from deprivations as resources must be diverted to military purposes, to disruption of government services, to destruction of buildings and loss of life, to outright mass starvation, without apparent legal consequences, and often with the law's blessing. Indeed, although the legality of such a strategy might now be questioned, the starvation of the Japanese population was part of the U.S. naval strategy in World War II. Similarly, the hardship imposed on Iraqi civilians by the U.S. and UN embargo against Iraq was supposed to either influence Saddam Hussein or convince the Iraqi people to overthrow him.

The dual-use nature of many telecommunications networks and much equipment further complicates the questions of the applicability of humanitarian law as a constraint on information warfare. These dual uses contribute to the blurring of the distinction between military and civilian systems and, consequently, between military targets, which are legitimate, and civilian ones, which are not. Some information weapons may thus not permit their users to distinguish between military and civilian targets. In the United States, for example, it has been estimated that 95% of the telecommunications of the Department of Defence travel through the Public Switched Network, and during the Persian Gulf War, commercial communications satellites reportedly carried almost a quarter of the U.S. Central Command's transcontinental telecommunications. Additionally, U.S. military forces are particularly dependent upon non-military systems for deployment and logistics. Attacks with military objectives might thus necessarily be directed at predominantly civilian systems, with corresponding injury to the civilians who depend upon them. As Vice Admiral Arthur Cebrowski stated in 1995, "There is no logical distinction...between military or civil systems or technologies. [Therefore] there is also no technical distinction between exploitation, attack or defence of the information warfare target set."

The interdependence and interconnectivity of civilian and military systems may further exacerbate the difficulty in distinguishing among civilian and military targets. Attacks directed at predominantly military targets may cause civilian systems that are connected to those military systems to fail; alternatively, a virus that is directed toward an adversary's military systems may spread, inadvertently or otherwise, into civilian (and even friendly) systems. Furthermore, attacks on systems that would otherwise be legitimate targets may be impermissible because of the danger to civilians that system malfunctions might cause. For example, an attack on a military power facility might pose problems if that facility's failure could release dangerous materials into the atmosphere.

MANIPULATING ENEMY PERCEPTIONS

Spurring Internal Turmoil. Techniques such as video morphing and communications spoofing may make it possible for a country to manipulate the perceptions of its adversary's leaders and populace. The country may spread confusion or disaffection by covertly altering official announcements or news broadcasts, or it may confuse or frighten leaders by spoofing intelligence or other government communications. In principle, these actions would not violate the laws of war.

Taken to the extreme, however, manipulation of news or intelligence in certain cases might be considered the proximate cause of genocide or other atrocities. As Colonel Richard Szafranski has suggested, manipulating an adversary nation to the extent that its citizens or leaders become unhinged from reality, especially when the effects cannot be known or controlled, may be no less wrongful than to force another nation into starvation or cannibalism. The potentially dangerous results of perception manipulation are more than theoretical. Some observers believe that "hate radio" contributed to, or even sparked, genocide in Rwanda and the former Yugoslavia. The use of propaganda, "video morphing," or deceptive broadcasts to the extent that they spur unrestrained civil war, or even genocide, may thus be illegal.

Perfidy. Although ruses are unquestionably permissible in war, not all acts of deception are. Certain acts of treachery or "perfidy" are forbidden by longstanding customary law and by several conventions. While ruses (such as the threatened U.S. Marine landing in Kuwait during the Persian Gulf War) are acts planned to mislead an enemy, as by causing him to become reckless or choose a particular course of action, perfidious acts are designed to convince the enemy that the actor is entitled to protected status under the law of war, with the intent of betraying that confidence. Perfidious acts include feigning a truce or surrender, injury or incapacitation, civilian status, or other protected status, such as that of UN or neutral forces, for purposes of attacking the enemy. Similarly, attacking while wearing the enemy's uniform is prohibited.

Information warfare attacks that involve distorting enemy perceptions may be limited by prohibitions against perfidy. For example, manipulating enemy visual, sensing, or other information systems so that enemy forces wrongly believe that U.S. troops are surrendering would certainly seem perfidious, as would causing them to believe that U.S. combat vehicles were medical vehicles or those of neutrals. Similarly, manipulating an enemy's targeting database so that it believed that a U.S. division headquarters was a hospital would be wrong. Less obviously, manipulating identification signals so that a nation's forces believe that the enemy personnel or vehicles that are approaching are actually friendly forces would arguably come under the norm underlying the prohibition against attacking while wearing enemy uniforms. On the other hand, because of the longstanding view that communications may be disrupted, and because, unlike uniforms, information systems are in no way required by the laws of war but are rather combat aids, such tactics might seem less treacherous than would taking advantage of the requirement that troops wear distinct uniforms to set themselves off from their foes and civilians.

"Peacetime" Use of Information Warfare and Problems of Definition

Definitions and Prohibitions. A side-effect of technological change is that the new activities that it enables may not fit within established legal categories. For example, aerial surveillance has historically been restricted by the sovereignty of each state over its airspace. The development of satellite and space technology in the 1950s later enabled surveillance from orbit. Although such orbital surveillance was functionally the same as aerial surveillance, international law has chosen to consider it as a distinct activity, subject to the universal freedom of actions in space. This characterization was not obvious or required by contemporary understandings of international law; more likely, most countries who wanted to apply traditional understandings of sovereignty to orbital surveillance, such as several African states, lacked the capacity to do anything about it. A fundamental threshold question that arises from the development of information warfare techniques is thus the definitional one. Has the development of information warfare technology and techniques taken information warfare out of the existing legal definition of war? Simply, it is not obvious that all information warfare attacks, including some that would inflict serious hardship upon their targets, are what has previously been included within our understanding of "war." Similarly, the "damage" that such attacks would inflict, particularly upon civilians, may not be the sort of hardship that the historical and conventional laws of war were intended to alleviate. Consequently, there may be confusion over what limits may apply to the conduct of information warfare, and when information warfare attacks may be carried out.

War, as we have traditionally understood it, inherently includes armed forces, force, and violence. The efforts of the United Nations to pursue a more peaceful world are instructive on this point. Article 2(4) of the UN Charter, for example, forbids the threat or use of force against the territorial integrity or political independence of another state. This prohibition has been applied only to physical force since the drafting of the Charter. Most relevantly, the United States and its allies have understood the provision as not applying to economic coercion, although many questioned that view during the 1973 Arab oil embargo. Further, during the drafting of the Charter, when Brazil proposed including "economic measures" with "force," the proposal was rejected by a vote of 26-2. Consistently, Article 51 of the Charter recognizes a state's right to use force in self-defence against an "armed attack."

Although lacking some of the formal legal authority of the Charter, the United Nations General Assembly's declaration defining "aggression" also reveals explicit contemplation of armed forces or military might. The declaration defines aggression, which the Security Council is empowered to address, as "the use of armed force by a State against the sovereignty, territorial integrity or political independence of another State, or in any other manner inconsistent with the Charter of the United Nations." The first use of armed force by a state would constitute prima facie evidence of aggression. The declaration sets out the following as a non-inclusive list of those acts that would qualify as aggression:

- The invasion or attack by the armed forces of a state of the territory of another state, or any military occupation, however temporary, resulting from such invasion or attack, or any annexation by the use of force of all or some of another state's territory.

- Bombardment by the armed forces of a state against the territory of another state or the use of any weapons by a state against the territory of another state.
- The blockade of the ports or coasts of a state by the armed forces of another state.
- An attack by the armed forces of a state on the land, sea, or air forces, or marine and air fleets of another state.
- The use of armed forces of one state which are within the territory of another state with the agreement of the receiving state, in contravention of the conditions provided for in the agreement or any extension of their presence in such territory beyond the termination of the agreement.
- The action of a state in allowing its territory, which it has placed at the disposal of another state, to be used by that other state for perpetrating an act of aggression against a third state.
- The sending by or on behalf of a state of armed bands, groups, irregulars or mercenaries, which carry out acts of armed force against another state of such gravity as to amount to the acts listed above, or its substantial involvement therein.

Other legislative practice of the United Nations reinforces the view that "aggression" is limited to the use of force. In 1953 Iran pressed the United Nations for an understanding that any act serving the same ultimate purposes as an armed attack or involving coercion to endanger independence was "aggression," but the United Nations has never adopted that view. Further affirming the kinetic view of war is the definition of "attacks" as enunciated in the 1977 Additional Protocol to the Geneva Convention. That document, which the United States has signed but not ratified, embodies much customary international law. It defines "attacks" as "acts of violence against the adversary, whether in offence of defence."

Some forms of attack under the information warfare rubric fit comfortably within the above definitions of war, force, aggression, and attack. For example, the use of precision-guided munitions against a military communications post could certainly constitute war. Although the disruption of a social security system database through the use of a virus or hacking during hostilities could certainly be part of a war, it is less obvious that such attacks would by themselves constitute acts of war, because of their nonlethal, nondestructive (in a direct, physical sense), non-physically intrusive character. On the other hand, it is certain that a state of "war" can exist in the absence of what we have traditionally understood as fighting. Wars do not always end simultaneously with the cessation of combat; rather they generally may require some sort of closure, both for international and domestic legal purposes. For example, the United States did not give up its status as a belligerent in World War I until 1921, even though fighting ceased in 1918; World War II did not end for several countries until well after 1945; and Israel and its Arab foes have endured years of largely combatless war. Conversely, although formal declarations of war are virtually nonexistent in the modern era, nations could certainly declare war on each other without actually engaging in battle.

Where the applicability of a principle of law is not immediately ascertainable, it is often helpful to examine the intent underlying that legal principle or statute. Unfortunately, that intent is insufficiently instructive.

The fundamental document of the modern international legal system is the Charter of the United Nations, which was signed in San Francisco in 1945. According to the Charter's Preamble, the aim of the United Nations' founders was, in relevant part, "to save succeeding generations from the scourge of war, which twice in our lifetime has brought untold sorrow to mankind." To pursue those ends, the founders resolved to:

- practice tolerance and live together in peace with one another as good neighbours, and
- unite our strength to maintain international peace and security, and
- ensure by the acceptance of principles and the institution of methods, that armed force shall not be used save in the common interest, and

- employ international machinery for the promotion of the economic and social advancement of all peoples.

The stated purposes of the United Nations are:

1. To maintain international peace and security, and to that end: to take effective collective measures for the prevention and removal of threats to the peace, and for the suppression of acts of aggression or other breaches of the peace, and to bring about by peaceful means, and in conformity with the principles of justice and international law, adjustment or settlement of international disputes or situations which might lead to a breach of the peace;
2. To develop friendly relations among nations based on respect for the principle of equal rights and self determination of peoples; and
3. To achieve international cooperation in solving international problems of an economic, social, cultural or humanitarian character.

Members of the United Nations, and the organization itself, are pledged to act in accordance with the following relevant principles:

All members shall settle their international disputes by peaceful means in such a manner that international peace and security, and justice, are not endangered; and All members shall refrain in their international relations from the threat or use of force against the territorial integrity or political independence of any state, or in any other manner inconsistent with the Purposes of the United Nations. The UN General Assembly has set out its interpretations of nations' obligations under the Charter. The Declaration of Principles of International Law Concerning Friendly Relations and Co-operation Among States in Accordance with the Charter of the United Nations opposes all forms of coercion, including economic pressure against a state "to obtain from it the subordination of the exercise of its sovereign rights." In a similar vein, the General Assembly also set out a Declaration on the Inadmissibility of Intervention into the Domestic Affairs of States, which included similar language against the subordination of sovereign rights, and asserted:

No State has the right to intervene, directly or indirectly, for any reason whatsoever, in the internal or external affairs of any other State. Consequently, armed intervention and all other forms of interference or attempted threats against the personality of the State or against its political, economic and cultural elements, are condemned;

The problem in using the fundamental principles laid out in these declarations as tools in interpreting whether the prohibitions on the use of armed force would apply to certain forms of information warfare is that to do so would be to rely upon reasoning that is either circular or demonstrably unrealistic. For example, the UN Charter language about the "scourge of war," "threats to the peace," "respect for...international law," preventing the use of "armed force," settlement of international disputes through "peaceful means," and refraining "from the threat or use of force" is only relevant to nonlethal information warfare attacks if we have already established that the information warfare attacks are, indeed, "war," "force," "unpeaceful means," or whatever other term would apply to something we would be trying to forbid. Similarly, the Friendly Relations declaration's prohibition of the use of coercion to force the subordination of the exercise of a state's "sovereign rights" applies only to the extent that we have determined that the information warfare attack violates those sovereign rights, which are nowhere defined. To read the provision otherwise would be to forbid diplomacy or other forms of inducements.

Finally, the declaration on intervention does not really define intervention, and in any event, does not equate nonmilitary intervention with aggression or the use of force, thus leaving room for attackers to defend their conduct. Indisputably, although virtually all states purport to recognize the norm of nonintervention, intervention of various kinds occurs frequently, without constituting aggression or war. The declaration thus leaves us with no principled way to place information attacks along a continuum of intervention stretching from a nation's leader publicly meeting with one candidate in a neighbouring country's election, to funding of foreign political parties, to bribing government officials, to arming dissidents, to bombing military or police installations.

Reliance upon exhortations to cooperative or friendly behaviour as aids in interpreting the applicability of the prohibitions on the use of force to information warfare would also require circular reasoning and disregard actual state practice, which is itself a source of international law. None of these documents mandates a unified, consistently harmonious world. Because the United Nations was established to promote the peaceful resolution of conflict, it implicitly assumes that conflict will arise, and that nations will use various means to resolve them. Information warfare techniques are thus inappropriate to resolve conflicts only if it is determined that they are not peaceful means, the very determination the provisions should help us to make.

The Ability of States to Hurt Each Other. It is important to remember that merely because a government action weakens another country's military forces or hurts its people, does not make that action an act of war, aggression, or force. Longstanding international practice recognizes that nations may inflict great hardship upon each other and their respective citizenries without such infliction constituting the use of force or a violation of international law. In the absence of any international agreement, nations have no underlying legal obligation to deal with each other. A government may thus legally withhold a resource, such as fuel, food, or even medicine, without which the population of another nation might suffer severely. A country may even pressure others not to deal with a third country.

Economic boycotts, embargoes, and other sanctions have been common tools of international coercion in the twentieth century, especially after World War II. Countries of virtually all political persuasions have tried to use the infliction of hardship as a way to convince governments to amend policies. For example, in 1908 the Ottoman Empire boycotted all goods from Austria-Hungary in response to that nation's annexation of Bosnia and Herzegovina. In 1948, the Council for Mutual Economic Assistance (COMECON) imposed a boycott on trade with Yugoslavia after the rift between Marshals Stalin and Tito. The United States and United Kingdom organized an international boycott of Iranian oil after the short-lived government of Mohammed Mossedegh nationalized Iran's oil industry in 1951. Finally, in the decades following the 1948 Arab-Israeli war, the Arab League instituted primary, secondary, and tertiary boycotts against Israel, against companies that did business with Israel, and against companies that did business with companies that did business with Israel.

Similarly, where it has not internationalized a canal, the country through which a canal travels may close that waterway to other nations, even when doing so would hurt those who depend upon the shipping that must travel through it. Furthermore, states have routinely practiced "dirty tricks" against each other, ranging from economic espionage to sabotage of exports and imports and beyond, with few, if any international legal repercussions.

The Significance of Armed Force. Comparison of information warfare attacks and naval blockades may be instructive for understanding the possible place of information warfare under international law. It is not obvious whether nonlethal attacks that are neither physically intrusive nor physically destructive would constitute acts of "war," "force," or "aggression." Naval blockades, in contrast, are recognized as forceful and potentially aggressive acts, even though some effective blockades may be nonviolent, as ships either avoid the blockaded ports or are diverted peacefully.

The effects of naval blockades and information warfare attacks can be similar. Naval blockades prevent the transport of people and products into the target country or area, and may paralyze an economy. In the past, where intercontinental communication was largely by ship, a blockade would keep out information as well. An information warfare attack may also make transport of people and products impossible, paralyzing an economy, and it too may block the spread of information (especially as in an "infoblockade").

The primary distinctions then between a naval blockade and some information attacks might be that the blockade is executed by military forces and includes the threat (or actual use) of physical military force, while the information warfare attack may be executed by military or civilian personnel and contains no physical component or threat. The relevance of these distinctions will be significant for the treatment of information warfare under international law.

In sum, international law seems to draw a strong distinction between traditional, kinetic force and the infliction of hardship or suffering on a government or population. Without getting overly philosophical about the meaning of "violence," the experience of the United Nations and United States in Iraq is instructive. The United Nations has enforced an embargo against Iraq since 1990, with reportedly devastating effects on the Iraqi population and economy. During that time period, the armed forces of UN members, mostly the United States, have taken military action on several occasions, but only in response to specific perceived Iraqi provocations, such as the planned assassination of former U.S. President George Bush or the launching of missiles at U.S. planes enforcing a no-fly zone. If this distinction between the use of physical force and the infliction of hardship is legally valid, nonviolent information attacks may not be considered to be "war," and thus might not be subject to the legal constraints that govern warfare.

The Importance of Categorization

The issue of how to categorize information warfare attacks is of more than academic interest. First, whether or not an information warfare attack can be considered an act of "war," "force," or "aggression" is relevant to whether a forceful response can be justified as self-defence, as well as to the issue of whether a particular response would be proportionate to the original attack. Conversely, whether an information warfare attack can be considered the use of force goes to the attack's legality as a coercive measure in "peacetime." If a computer or communications intrusion or manipulation is considered the use of force (as in, say, a naval blockade or the bombing of a radar facility), then it could be an illegitimate tool of international coercion. But if it is the rough equivalent of, say, trade sanctions, then it might be appropriate in a peaceful context. Additionally, characterization of an action as "war" would affect the rights and responsibilities of nations that are neutral in the ongoing conflict.

Finally, characterization of attacks and the damage they cause is relevant to the status of those attacks under international humanitarian law, specifically those provisions that protect noncombatants from attacks and the consequences thereof. First, if an information warfare attack is not considered to be an act of "war," then humanitarian law may not apply; the attack could be considered to be equivalent to such measures as closing a canal, or refusing to trade, the sort of act that nations appear to have the legal right to commit. Second, it is not settled that the non-physical or indirect damage that some information warfare attacks could cause are the sort of effects against which humanitarian law protects noncombatants. If humanitarian law does not apply, then countries may legally pursue information warfare without (legal) concern for the harm that civilians might suffer.

Difficulty in characterizing certain forms of information warfare as "force," "war," or "aggression" under international law does not mean that international legal institutions cannot respond to such attacks, though. For example, Chapter VII of the UN Charter gives the UN Security Council the authority and responsibility to determine the existence of any "threat to the peace" or acts of aggression, and the Council can recommend and lead responses thereto. Many information attacks that may not constitute "force" or "aggression" could certainly be considered threats to the peace and thus subject to Security Council action, perhaps including the use of military force. After all, anything that would anger a government to the point that it might feel the need to resort to military action could thus "threaten" the peace, even if the provocative action was not technically illegal. Nevertheless, because any Security Council action would be subject to international political negotiation and maneuvering, as well as a veto by one of the permanent members of the Council, such a response would likely not be quick, sure, or a significant deterrent to a state or non-state entity that was considering an attack, nor might it provide solace to the attack's target.

THE DEVELOPMENT OF INFORMATION WARFARE

As the worldwide explosion of information technology, including computing, telecommunications, and networks, is changing the way we conduct business, government, and education, it promises to change the way we fight. Information technology is diffusing into virtually all military weapons, communications, and command and control systems, as well as the civilian systems that support modern industrial (or post-industrial) economies and their military efforts. Some of the new ways of fighting have been labelled "information warfare," which has been broadly defined as "any action to deny, exploit, corrupt, or destroy the enemy's information and its functions; protecting ourselves against those actions; and exploiting our own military information functions." As such, information warfare includes both new techniques, such as computer intrusion and disruption and telecommunications spoofing, and old ones, such as ruses, camouflage, and physical attacks on observation posts and lines of communication. Some have suggested that information warfare could usher in an era of largely bloodless conflict; battle would occur in "cyberspace," as U.S. "information warriors" would be able to disable important enemy command and control or civilian infrastructure systems with little, if any, loss of life. Others have projected futures of conflict in which the bloodletting is only enhanced by improved and broadened communications. Still others have suggested that information technology may contribute to the development of new forms of social organization, along with new forms of conflict.

Whatever the development and diffusion of information technology mean for the future of warfare, it is apparent that some of the new forms of attack that information technology enables may be qualitatively different from prior forms of attack. The use of such tools as computer intrusion and computer viruses, for example, may take war out of the physical, kinetic world and bring it into an intangible, electronic one. These newer forms of attacks, some of which may seem to be the products of science fiction, range along continuums extending from those with no physical impact on the enemy to some that would cause grave destruction or loss of life, from those with no physical intrusion beyond national borders to those requiring traditional, military invasions, and from those affecting purely civilian targets to those hitting purely military ones. Attacks could be conducted from a distance, through radio waves or international communications networks, with no physical intrusion beyond enemy borders. Damage could range from military or civilian deaths from system malfunctions, to the denial of service of important military or governmental systems in time of crisis, to widespread fear, economic hardship, or merely inconvenience for civilian populations who depend upon information systems in their daily lives.

The following are examples-some likely, some perhaps farfetched-of attacks that countries or nongovernmental entities might pursue, or suffer, as they wage warfare in the Information Age.

- A "trap door" might be hidden in the code controlling switching centres of the Public Switched Network, causing portions of it to fail on command.
- A mass dialing attack by personal computers might overwhelm a local phone system.
- A "logic bomb" or other intrusion into rail computer systems might cause trains to be misrouted and, perhaps, crash.
- An enemy's radio and television network might be taken over electronically, and then used to broadcast propaganda or other information. Advanced techniques such as "video morphing" could make the new broadcasts indistinguishable from the enemy's own usual broadcasts.
- A computer intruder might remotely alter the formulas of medication at pharmaceutical manufacturers, or personal medical information, such as blood type, in medical databases.
- A concerted e-mail attack might overwhelm or paralyze a significant network.
- Computer intruders might divert funds from bank computers, or corrupt data in bank databases, causing disruption or panic as banks need to shut down to address their problems.
- Computer intruders might steal and disclose confidential personal, medical, or financial information, as a tool of blackmail, extortion, or to cause widespread social disruption or embarrassment.
- A "computer worm" or "virus" could travel from computer to computer across a network, damaging data and disrupting systems.

- An "infoblockade" could permit little or no electronic information to enter or leave a nation's borders.
- A nation's command and control infrastructure could be disrupted, with individual military units unable to communicate with each other, or with a central command.
- Stock or commodity exchanges, electric power grids and municipal traffic control systems, and, as is frequently suggested, air traffic control or navigation systems could be manipulated or disrupted, with accompanying economic or societal disruption, physical destruction, or loss of life.

INTERNATIONAL LAW—THE LAW OF NATIONS

Law attempts to govern war, as it does most human endeavors. International law governs interaction among nations. International law primarily consists of "conventional" law and "customary" law. Conventional law is that made by treaty or other explicit agreement among nations, who are bound to their agreements under the principle of pacta sunt servanda, or "agreements are to be observed." Examples of conventional law would include the Paris Peace Treaty of 1783, which ended the U.S. War of Independence and fixed the borders of the new republic, the 1968 Treaty on the Non-Proliferation of Nuclear Weapons, and the General Agreement on Tariffs and Trade (GATT).

Customary law results from the general and consistent practice of states' opinio juris, or with the understanding that the practice is required by law, not just expedience. Customary law may develop from understandings reflected in treaties or other agreements, even if they have not been ratified, declarations or votes of international bodies such as the General Assembly of the United Nations, or the statements and actions of governments and their officials. There is no universally accepted way to determine whether a customary international legal norm has been established. To a great extent, customary international law must be like obscenity to the late U.S. Supreme Court Justice Potter Stewart-something we know when we see it. Examples of customary law include the traditional protected status of diplomats and the historical three-nautical mile claim to coastal territorial waters. Even when legal norms seem well-established in theory, patterns of contrary state practice may contribute to the decline or alteration of the principles. Just as popular disregard for a trademark, such as cellophane, aspirin, or thermos, can result in that trademark losing its legal force and becoming a generic term, violation of an ostensible customary legal principle can cause its demise. Law based upon actors' recognition that it is indeed law loses force when those actors no longer recognize it.

In considering international law, particularly in the context of national security, it is important to stress some distinctions between international and domestic law. Unlike most nations' domestic law, international law is not a body of law created by legislatures and courts and enforced by police through a court system. Rather, international law is generally established by agreement, either explicit or tacit, among the parties who will be bound by it, much as private parties enter into contracts with each other. Although international legal forums, such as the International Court of Justice, do exist, their enforcement mechanisms are limited at best; no international police force walks the world beat. Consequently, a country that is willing to accept the political and diplomatic consequences that may ensue when it defies international law may do so. As a crude example, the Revolutionary Islamic government of Iran blatantly disregarded the traditional sovereignty and sanctuary of the U.S. Embassy in Tehran in the late 1970s and early 1980s, but if it had any concerns about external reactions, those concerns seemed more directed at the threat of economic sanctions or U.S. military action, not at some global police force. It seems likely that nations will be least likely to follow the dictates of international law where those dictates endanger or conflict with the pursuit of their fundamental interests, including national security.

The Legal Challenges of Information Warfare

From a legal perspective, the older forms of information warfare pose few unanswered questions under customary or treaty law. For example, the use of camouflage to elude enemy observers was old even when Macduff and his men brought Burnham Wood to Dunsinane; ancient Greek soldiers blinded their foes by reflecting the sun off their shields; and both sides attempted to cut each others' telegraph lines during the U.S. Civil War, and there is little doubt of these actions' propriety. Similarly, wartime physical attacks against military observation systems, from lookout posts to radar stations, are unquestionably acceptable under international law.

But the development of information technology, specifically computers, telecommunications, and networks, makes it possible for adversaries to attack each other in new ways and with new forms of damage, and may create new targets for attack. Attackers may use international networks to damage or disrupt enemy systems, without ever physically entering the enemy's country, and countries' dependence upon electronic or other information-based systems may make those systems particularly attractive targets. Furthermore, the dual-use nature of many information systems and infrastructures may blur the distinction between military and civilian targets.

Such new attacks may pose problems for international law because law is inherently conservative; technological change may enable new activities that do not fit within existing legal categories, or may reveal contradictions among existing legal principles. Information warfare challenges existing international law in three primary ways. First, the sort of intangible damage that such attacks may cause may be analytically different from the physical damage caused by traditional warfare. The kind of destruction that bombs and bullets cause is easy to see and understand, and fits well within longstanding views of what war means. In contrast, the disruption of information systems, including the corruption or manipulation of stored or transmitted data, may cause intangible damage, such as disruption of civil society or government services that may be more closely equivalent to activities such as economic sanctions that may be undertaken in times of peace.

Second, the ability of signals to travel across international networks or through the atmosphere as radio waves challenges the concept of national, territorial sovereignty. Sovereignty, which has been a fundamental principle of international law since the Treaty of Westphalia of 1648, holds that each nation has exclusive authority over events within its borders. Sovereignty may not be suited to an increasingly networked, or "wired" world, as signals travelling across networks or as electromagnetic waves may cross international borders quickly and with impunity, allowing individuals or groups to affect systems across the globe, while national legal authority generally stops at those same borders. Furthermore, the intangible violation of borders that signals may cause may not be the sort of violation traditionally understood to be part of a military attack.

Third, just as information warfare attacks may be difficult to define as "peace" or "war," it may be hard to define their targets as military (and thus generally legitimate targets) or civilian (generally forbidden). Furthermore, the intangible damage the attacks cause may not be the sort of injuries against which the humanitarian law of war is designed to protect noncombatants.

The Importance of International Law for U.S. Policy

The United States has a particularly significant stake in understanding how international law will apply to these new forms of conflict. First, as a matter of domestic politics, the United States has a largely legal culture. The U.S. Government is described as one of laws; in public political rhetoric acts are routinely described and discussed in legal terms, and characterizing an act as illegal can be a harsh and politically damaging criticism. Second, as a matter of domestic law, international law is as much a part of the "law of the land" as are the statutes that Congress enacts. Third, given the U.S. Government's apparent preference in the post-Cold War era (and even before) for acting militarily under the auspices of international coalitions or the United Nations, its prospects for obtaining such auspices are greater when it can persuade other nations that its actions are legal and those of its foes are not. Finally, as the preeminent world power, and one particularly dependent upon information systems, the United States has a stake in the international status quo. To the extent international law helps to provide stability and protect critical information systems, it may benefit U.S. interests.

5

The Future of Warfare: Small Arms are the Big Challenge

INTRODUCTION

This was Henry Dunant, writing in "Un Souvenir de Solférino" about the experience that motivated him to form the Red Cross. He eloquently expressed the mixed feelings on the subject of war that still persist in our world today. He speaks of the apparent glory of armies, the excitement of battle, the reality of the horror of what man can do to man, and the desperate need to alleviate the suffering. As a consequence of his book, and his description of the unimaginable suffering after the battle, he helped us move towards what many of us feel today: war is at best a necessary evil and, at worst, it is hell on earth.

War is something that should first be prevented, and if not prevented, then controlled and mitigated. Eventually this cruel, barbaric institution should be abolished entirely. We can only hope that someday it will follow in the footsteps of other abhorrent human practices that were more or less successfully banned, like slavery, duelling, public executions, and torture. But for the moment, to minimize war, it must be studied: its development analysed, its methods and tools understood, and its future threat assessed.

HIGH TECHNOLOGY IN WARFARE

Dunant, in his "Souvenir de Solférino", also provides insights into the tools and technologies of war: "... since new and more terrible methods of destruction are invented daily, with perseverance worthy of a better object, and since the inventors of these instruments of destruction are applauded and encouraged in most of the great European States, which are engaged in an arms race... future battles will only become more and more murderous."

For an article written in 1862, it was remarkably prescient. Soon the machine gun was introduced as a much more effective killing machine than the black-powder cannon and the infanteers' bayonet. WWI heralded the eerie arrival of chemical weapons, the tank, and aerial warfare. At the end of that war, called the Great War, US President Woodrow Wilson predicted another world war within 20 years, saying that the weapons the Germans had used in the Great war would be like "toys" compared to those used in the next. Hitler's V-2 rockets, Panzer tanks and Stuka dive-bombers all showed that to be true. In the Cold War after World War II, there was steady and immense improvement in the tools possessed by modern armies. We witnessed more than one "revolution in military affairs" or RMA, to use the buzzwords which are currently very popular in military circles to describe what happens when a powerful new technology is integrated into a deadly new strategy. Examples include nuclear deterrence under the strategy of Mutually Assured Destruction (appropriately called MAD) using Intercontinental Ballistic Missiles (ICBMs), precision bombing with guided missiles, etc.. In order to accomplish these RMAs, scientists and engineers became an integral part of the "military-industrial" complex.

The US alone, which led virtually all the RMAs in the past half century, spent about $30 billion dollars annually (in constant 1998 dollars) during the Cold War on science and technology for military purposes. It even spends more than that now! This is also more than half of what the world as a whole spends on official development assistance to the developing world. The direct relevance of this comparison will become even more clear later in this presentation. It was none other than President Eisenhower who said: "The world is spending the sweat of its labourers, the genius of its scientists...." (paraphrased) and "Every gun that is made, every warship launched, every rocket fired signifies, in the final sense, a theft from those who hunger and are not fed, those who are cold and are not clothed." The results of this scientific work have been an incredible increase in destructiveness, precision and war-fighting capability for the advanced militaries. These technologies have their severe drawbacks, as we will note, but they have resulted in a significant changes in the "modern" military thinking and capability, especially in the West.

Destructiveness. This capacity is most dramatically illustrated with nuclear weapons. In 1945, the two nuclear bombs detonated at 10-20 kilo-tonnes of TNT. Within twenty years, there was a one thousand fold increase in explosive yield. The Soviet Union, under Khrushchev, detonated a nuclear device of 50 mega-tonnes in the Arctic in the early 1960s. By comparison, the cumulative explosive yield of all bombs in World War II was less than 5 mega tonnes. The explosive power of non-nuclear arms also increased. In the 1991 Gulf War, the Americans hammered into Iraq more explosive power in one hundred days than it used during all of World War II. This means the militaries have gained "more bang for the buck" or, in the humorous Russian equivalent, "more rubble for the ruble." The second RMA in advanced modern militaries, especially the US, is precision targeting: the ability to detect a target from long distances, including from outer space, and then deliver the munition with virtually pinpoint accuracy. The Chief of Staff of the US Air Force in 1997 even predicted that: "In the first quarter of the 21st century you will be able to find, fix anything+in near real-time +or track and target of consequence that moves upon or is located on the surface of the earth."

Behind the increase in precision, lies an even broader phenomenon: an information revolution. "Smart" weapons are tied into vast information systems with vast databases, interconnected using global military/civilian telecommunications systems. Firing systems of missiles operate far from their intended targets thus ensuring greater safety to the user. The "fire and forget" missiles can be heat seeking, object identifying or precision guided, and some can hug terrain to avoid radars.

In spite of the immense technical progress and "Gee Wiz" value of these technologies and "revolutions", they are not all that they are cracked up to be. Each technology has limitations that reduce their effectiveness while increasing the danger to the world.

Destruction. Stated simply, nuclear weapons, which represent the apex of destructive power, cannot be used by any nation with ethical principles. As they would kill civilians, perhaps millions of them, indiscriminately their use would be contrary to international humanitarian law (IHL) as well as to all codes of morality. Thus, they are not practical. Since no sane person would authorize a nuclear attack, nuclear weapons are at best a bluff that one hopes no one ever calls. The use of nuclear weapons would be suicidal whether against another nuclear power or a non-nuclear one, given that the precedent would be so dangerous for the future of the world, not to mention the problem of radioactive fallout! Similar destruction on grand scale, with or without nuclear weapons, though technically possible, is not politically, legally or morally justifiable.

While the advent of precision targeting reduces the need for more powerful explosive yields, these systems which rely on modern information databases can go terribly wrong, as we witnessed in the bombing of the Chinese embassy in Serbia, the erroneous shooting down of an Iranian airbus (killing 290 civilians) by the US warship *Vincennes* whose Aegis high tech missile system misidentified the commercial aircraft, or the friendly (at the time) fire by an Iraqi aircraft on the USS *Stark*, whose defensive systems failed to stop the oncoming missile. All of these examples show that missiles can reach their targets but the information used to determine the targets may be incorrect. Detecting and tracking a target may be easy on open land, the ocean or in the air but it is much more difficult in dense areas, such as cities or jungles. In guerrilla warfare, it becomes almost useless. Witness the need for virtual "carpet bombing" of Grozny in the current Chechnia war. Earlier, in the US operation in Mogadishu, Somalia, only 2 of 60 mortars fired upon in Mogadishu were successfully destroyed. Also, less than half of Iraq's SCUD missiles were destroyed during the Gulf War, which was the most high-tech international war yet fought (one-sided as it was).

There are also some benefits for peace of technological innovation in these areas, namely the positive applications in peacekeeping (which I, as a scientist, have in recent years been examining): (1). Non-lethal Weapons: A spectrum of non-lethal weapons (e.g., sound, stun, slick'n or stick'ms, blunt munitions) are becoming available which will give peacekeepers a wider range of options to apply force. (2). Precision monitoring: Here the goal is not to target for hostile purposes but for verification and confidence-building. Sensors include passive infra-red with illuminators, permanent (invisible) markers (similar to those used by the UN in East Timor to blot a finger) to mark a thief or transgressor for ease of later identification and apprehension. Tamper-evident seals and trackable tags using GPS can be useful for disarmament and the movement of goods, as in aid convoys. (3) In the third category, the information revolution, there are a range of benefits for early warning and conflict management. The "CNN effect" was pioneered by my co-panelist, General Lewis Mackinzie, to great effect in Bosnia.

WAR IN THE 21ST CENTURY: A SURVEY

Having reviewed some major RMAs in advanced armies, we have to ask ourselves, will this new technology really matter? As it turns out, to answer the question of future warfare, we have to look more at politics and less at technology. To assess the future of warfare, it is most important to determine *WHO* will be fighting. Certainly those who met in the battleground in Solférino (the Austrians and French) won't be fighting. A Europe moving towards unification has removed any threat of armed conflict. Conflict will be handled politically and legally, not militarily (as seen by the recent European Union reaction to the inclusion of Dr. Haider in the Austrian government). In fact, Germany and France (mortal enemies for so long) no longer even guard their mutual borders, and travellers have a hard time even telling where these borders are as they cross them. Now they have created a virtually borderless market, they are utilizing a common currency, the Euro, and even sending soldiers to a common force, the Eurocorps. From this European experience we can support some generalizations about future war.

In examining potential wars, we can exclude one broad category of war: those fought between democracies. The "democratic peace", the notion that democracies do not fight wars against each other. History has yet to show exceptions to this theory, and the "democratic peace" theory is the closest equivalent that political scientists have to a "physical law."

For me, the basis of the Democratic Peace, is two-fold: First, democracies tend to respect each other (even when they quarrel) because they respect more the freedom of action of other democracies and their right to choose their leaders and policies, certainly enough not to impose militarily on them. This is analogous to the feelings expressed more sublimely by Gandhi: "I love my liberty so much that I would not want to do anything to limit yours" (paraphrase). Secondly, the democratic nations are becoming increasingly interdependent, with information refusing to be bound by the traditional notions of sovereignty. The world is shrinking in terms the ability of information, people and goods to travel to other lands. Communication with the far reaches of the globe is becoming cheaper, faster and easier. Also new moral and legal norms and standards, including the Geneva Conventions, are being widely known and adopted.

The consequence of the "democratic peace" is fantastic. Freedom House reports that, at the turn of the century, 120 of some 190 nations are democratic, the largest percentage ever. [Footnote or endnote: Democracy Momentum Sustain As "Freedom Century" Ends: Freedom House Reports Rands 120 Countries as Democratic, Largest Number Ever", 21 December 1999, press release available at]. Three-fifths of the world`s people live under democratically elected governments. However, democracy means more than just elections. A closer look reveals that of these 120 nations, 85 are called free and 59 partially free. Forty-eight are said to be "not free". The "worst of the worst" tend, not surprisingly, to be countries with internal armed conflict, like Afghanistan, Burma, Iraq, Libya, Somalia and Sudan.

Wilson proclaimed that US entry into the First World War was "to make the world safe for democracy." It now appears that democracy itself is making the world safe. We can now consider each of the other categories of war, having excluded wars between democracies. We start with the most catastrophic of all wars, the World Wars.

International enforcement (police) actions

Another threat to the peace, much less discussed, is actually the misuse of the means designed to keep the peace, i.e., enforcement actions. There is a tendency in our superpower neighbour who is leading the charge in enforcement operations and has, for better or worse, become the world's lead policeman, to resort to the early use of force, like the sheriff in the wild west. There is, unfortunately, no court to penalize the "police brutality" on the world stage. The aggressive instinct is more subtle today than in the past, but it is nevertheless still present. Whether it be the evil Red Russians of 20 years ago, the "Redskins" of 200 years ago, or the pseudo Reds (like Milosevich), there is a tendency for the US to use force in the form of weapons and threats against those elevated to the status of enemy. According to some conservatives, Red China is the next enemy to hate and, even more unfortunate, to threaten.

In my opinion, the US is not exercising "imperial power" but its unilateralism borders on pseudo-imperialism. Under the guise of international enforcement action, aggression and other atrocities have been committed, most recently in the former Yugoslavia. The difference between true enforcement and aggression is not only who you target and what authorization you get, but in the degree of damage inflicted. While war necessitates surrender no matter what the cost to the victim, law calls for proportionality of force. This is the dilemma which the international community faces time and again as the US uses "all necessary means" to accomplish its military aim.

Another danger is the use of the concept of peacekeeking as a cover for intervention. Thirty thousand Russian soldiers are stationed in Georgia, Moldova and Tadjikistan since 1990 under the guise of peacekeeping. This is a dangerous practice, which has spread to other regions of the world, as we see with the Nigerians in West Africa.

It is my belief that a major obstacle to world peace is the undemocratic and unequal status given to the major powers in the Security Council, especially in the form of the unrestricted veto. With the creation of the UN after the second World War, the world witnessed the use of the Russian veto over 120 times before the first US veto was cast. It was common to talk about the paralysis of the UN by the veto and the US was looking sincerely for a means to avoid or change the practice that was so often used by the Soviets. It is in times of peace, such as today, that we should modify the rules for using the veto, before it is again subjected to continuous abuse.

Since wars have become and will remain mostly internal, we can expect that they will not be waged between battle groups or armoured divisions, but with one side at least being guerrilla forces using small arms. The guerrillas will fight from mountain or jungle bases, staging "hit and run" attacks before seeking cover. Ethnic warfare may also be fought in cities "block by block" as was the case in Grosny and Mogadishu. The worst part of this picture is that these types of wars take a long time to end, and usually they do not end cleanly. In addition, the parties will use crime as a means of revenue. In Africa especially, crime and war will be mutually reinforcing. Thus, the major threat to human beings in the twenty-first century will not be ICBMs rocketing through the outer atmosphere across oceans, but streams of AK-47 bullets in gang war fought across streets within states.

Small Arms are the Big Threat

The greatest man-made threat in practice to human security in our world. Nuclear weapons may have the capacity to annihilate populations (and are therefore called the ultimate evil), but they are not used daily to take hundreds of lives in communities in virtually every country, as is the case with small arms. The fact remains that most killings in our world are carried out with small arms, those weapons that can be carried and used by a single person. Small arms are the preferred tools of violence in most internal wars, coups, militia and gang violence, government oppression and human rights abuses, as well as for domestic and transnational crime. Even in international wars they play a major role, and in some cases a predominant one. Though not categorised as weapons of mass destruction, today they are truly the premier instruments of mass murder.

Even long after an armed conflict is over, these weapons continue to exact their toll on vulnerable populations. The ICRC estimates even a year and a half after the formal end of conflict, the weapons-related casualties remain at 60-80 percent of the rate during the conflict. Unless strong disarmament measures are instituted as part of a peace agreement, the weapons remain available to promote criminal, communal and family violence.

In cultures of violence and gun-ownership, often created initially by armed conflicts but remaining ingrained long afterwards, these instruments become a symbol of power and pride (and even the subject of affection!). In times of tension, such an unnatural status promotes an increase in boasting, intimidation, threats of violence and the inevitable demonstrations of force. Finally, the result is all too often widening lethality as the spiral of retribution and revenge is reinforced and fuelled, leading to social disintegration.

The statistics are alarming. Small arms have caused more than 3 million deaths in the past decade, with the vast majority of victims being civilians, 8 out of 10 being women and children, according to UNICEF. It is estimated that there are 500 million arms in the world, an average of one for every 12 inhabitants.

Arms producers, brokers and dealers (sometimes called the "merchants of death") continually look to new markets in search of increased profits, thereby helping to proliferate both arms and conflict. The result is that weapons end up where they are the least controlled and do the most damage. Clearly there is a need to combat this menace to human security. The widespread distribution of small arms in the world leads to a horrendous global tragedy that every national and international authority has a responsibility to help mitigate. The human tragedy of small arms alone provides compelling reason to motivate the international community to participate in efforts to solve, or at least mitigate the global arms threat.

In some of the poorest countries of the world, there is easy access to inexpensive firearms. In Uganda, an AK-47 could be purchased for the cost of a chicken. Before the genocide in Rwanda, a grenade could be obtained for two beers. The value of arms deliveries nearly doubled to Sub-Saharan Africa in 1998 though it remained steady in East Asia and Austalasia

A strong International Code of Conduct on Arms Transfers is needed, such as the one proposed by a group of Nobel Peace

Laureates led by former Costa Rican President Oscar Arias. Recipient countries must accept democracy (defined in terms of free and fair elections), the rule of law, civilian control over military forces, and abide by the accepted conventions on torture, civil rights and international aggression. Another provision requires that the military spending of recipient governments must not exceed the combined budget on health and education. In addition, states must report their arms purchases to the United Nations.

Conclusion

Henry Dunant, feeling his "own utter inadequacy" in the face of a screaming need to ameliorate the condition of the wounded in the field, was moved to suggest that new societies be organized in times of peace to prevent the reoccurring disaster of unattended wounded. His plea led directly to the formation of the Red Cross, the first Geneva Convention of 1864 and, indirectly, to the Geneva Conventions of 1949 and the additional Protocols of 1977 over a century later.

Today we face similar distress as Dunant felt in 1859, with "so much to do and so little means to do it" in our goal of continuing to reduce the barbarity of warfare and to eventually abolish the institution altogether, whether it be between or within nations. But we can take heart from the progressive and ongoing work of the Red Cross. The 1980 Excessively Injurious Weapons Convention, championed by the Red Cross, expanded on earlier agreements to ban so-called dum-dum bullets, as did the Protocol to ban laser anti-blinding weapons. The 1987 Ottawa Convention on Antipersonnel Mines, which was urged and backed by the Red Cross movement and many other members of our global civil society, was another step along the road of sanity and morality. The next step, in my mind, is to develop new mechanisms to limit the proliferation and use of small arms. With a world in which wars are increasingly internal, international humanitarian law (IHL) is now more difficult, but as important as ever. The two major challenges in my mind are (1) finding the means to "bind" non-state parties (i.e., to gain their acceptance and find the means to support their compliance) and (2) measures to reduce the presence of the most common killers-small arms. Fortunately, we have important organizations, such as the Red Cross to help in both areas.

The Red Cross has played a vital seminal role in the past not only in the development of new international humanitarian law (IHL) but also in its dissemination and implementation. With this in mind, it is a pleasure to participate in this Symposium on "IHL in the New Millennium." It seems to me that the Red Cross is needed as much as ever (instead try "more than ever"?) in this new millennium, and its age-old motto is more applicable than ever: "Above all—humanity."

6

Responding to Information Warfare Attacks

ATTACKS AGAINST INFORMATION SYSTEMS: METHODS AND MOTIVES

Although the United States is believed to lead the world in information warfare capability, other countries are pursuing such capabilities, as perhaps are transnational criminal organizations or terrorist groups. Because of the perceived overwhelming traditional military might of the United States and its allies, and because international networks may offer a way for adversaries to strike at the U.S. homeland without needing the sort of logistical and military capabilities that a traditional attack would require, it seems likely that the United States or one of its technologically and economically developed allies will suffer some sorts of serious information warfare attacks. If such an attack comes, the United States (or any other victim) may find its response hindered, as it may find both that the norms arising from traditional concepts of the international system of sovereign states may conflict with the physical reality of the newly wired world, and that the international legal system may not yet have arrived at rules applicable to such attacks. The United States may thus face difficulty in tracing an attack across national boundaries, gaining authority over the attackers, and determining the appropriate responses the attack.

Other observers have laid out in detail the types of information warfare attacks that adversaries may conduct against U.S. security facilities, the U.S. homeland or infrastructures, or the facilities of other countries. These adversaries may include foreign governments, including those of some "friendly" countries; state-supported or independent terrorist organizations, which may be international in composition or aim; transnational criminal organizations, such as the Russian mafiya or Latin American drug cartels; foreign competitors of U.S. companies; domestic terrorists or other criminals; or "hackers," who conduct mischief of varying severity using computers, telephones, and networks.

Such attacks may be part of armed conflict or a prelude to war. They may constitute a warning or threat to influence a government's decision makers as they contemplate particular courses of action. They may be part of an economic conflict, either between nations or between corporations (and in many countries, such a distinction is blurred). They may be terrorism, or part of other efforts to attract attention to a cause. They may be part of crime, as a mechanism of theft of funds or valuable data, as part of extortion, or as part of an effort to hinder law enforcement. Finally, the attacks may be motivated by perversity, as individuals or groups attack systems because they can, or to show off, or because of various personal shortcomings.

Identification of an Attack

The first dilemma that a country that has suffered an information attack may face in responding to the attack may be to identify an event as an actual attack. Especially when an attack does not come during a period of heightened international tensions, it may be difficult for investigators to distinguish a catastrophe resulting from a "natural" or "accidental" computer error from one stemming from malice.

Physical attacks should be distinguishable from accidents or malfunctions, as the culprits must come into some proximity with their target, and they may leave some physical evidence behind. As Aristide Briand said, "A cannon shot is a cannon shot; you can hear it and it often leaves traces." But even so, the causes of catastrophes may be hard to ascertain, especially when they involve complex systems that may not be fully understood. For example, despite exhaustive investigations, the separate but similar crashes of two Boeing 737 passenger jets remain unexplained. Furthermore, and most dramatically, the mystery of the July 1996 crash of TWA Flight 800 into Long Island Sound, which some immediately assumed was a terrorist incident, remains unsolved, and investigators did not publicly rule out the possibility of sabotage until May 1997.

Computer-based attacks may be even harder to distinguish from innocent malfunctions. If the attack is carried out across a network, the culprits may never be physically close to the target (perhaps never entering the same continent), and they may leave no tangible evidence. Attacks or sabotage using viruses, logic bombs, or simply buggy software may be particularly difficult to detect quickly, if at all, because of the complexity of systems and the frequency of unintentional errors in publicly shipped products.

Software errors or conflicts are known or suspected to have caused a number of incidents that might have seemed to be intentional attacks on important systems, products, or weapons by criminals, terrorists, or even enemy nations. Perhaps the most dramatic example occurred on Martin Luther King Day in 1990, when the AT&T long distance network failed for nine hours. Although the actual source of the failure was ultimately attributed to a faulty software update, many believed that hackers had actually caused the system to crash. Perhaps more frighteningly, a software error caused a Canadian nuclear reactor to release thousands of liters of radioactive water in 1990. Similarly, a timing delay in targeting software caused a British Royal Air Force pilot to drop a practice bomb on a British aircraft carrier in 1992, and it has been suggested that the crashes of two U.S. Air Force F-117 fighters in identical, suspicious circumstances were due to a bug in their software. Systems may even be inadvertently sabotaged by their creators. For example, in October of 1994, Adobe Systems, Inc. accidentally shipped a "time bomb" in a version of its popular Photoshop software program. The time bomb, which was to cause the program to stop running after a particular date, had been inserted into the code to force those using a pre-release version of the program to upgrade to the final shipping version, only when it was time to ship the product, nobody remembered to take it out.

An incident during a time of heightened international tensions might seem to present evidence that wrongdoing is afoot. Nevertheless, such evidence might not be compelling alone, as times of stress are also the times when complex, brittle systems may be most likely to break down.

The difficulty in distinguishing attacks from accidents is particularly significant in light of the apparent U.S. preference for acting under the auspices of international coalitions. Unless the United States is prepared to act alone, the evidence it uncovers that an incident was the result of an attack, and that the attack stemmed from a specific source, must be sufficient not only to convince U.S. policymakers, but also to convince foreign governments. There is no set standard of proof for U.S. officials to meet; the deliberations of the UN Security Council, and those of foreign governments, are political rather than judicial. Diplomacy, including carrots and sticks, may be more significant than persuasive, logical arguments. That foreign governments may be skeptical of both U.S. intentions and U.S. technical methods of detection complicates the tasks of investigators and policymakers alike.

After extensive investigation of the explosion of Pan Am Flight 103 over Lockerbie, Scotland, in December 1988, for example, the United States and United Kingdom tried to convince the Libyan government of Muammar Qadhafi to extradite the Libyan agents who were allegedly responsible for the bombing. In their efforts to obtain UN sanctions against Libya for its refusal to extradite the suspects, they presented evidence to the other members of the UN Security Council, which held meetings in camera, with no public minutes taken, to protect the confidentiality of the evidence and the Council's deliberations. Qadhafi refused to extradite the suspects and demanded that the United States provide him with evidence to support its charges, which he mocked. Perhaps to protect intelligence sources and methods, the United States refused to provide Libya with the evidence. Despite ongoing sanctions, Qadhafi has neither acknowledged the value of the U.S. evidence nor complied with the Security Council's demands.

The Problem of Territorial Jurisdiction

Investigators tracing attacks across computer networks

may be stymied by a collision between fundamental principles of physics and those of international law, namely that electrons may flow through networks freely across international borders, but the authority of agents of national governments does not. Simply, an attack may come from a foreign country, or may be routed through computers in several countries, but law enforcement or national security personnel cannot unilaterally launch pursuit into networks in other countries. Under the principle of sovereignty each government has exclusive authority over events within its borders. Investigators will thus need foreign cooperation or help in their investigations or, with proper domestic authorization, they will need to operate covertly.

Historically, foreign agents have not been permitted to operate physically on a state's territory without that state's permission. As the International Court of Justice held in the 1949 Corfu Channel case, when Great Britain wanted to investigate and stop the Albanian mining of the channel, intervention in another state to secure evidence is prohibited.

Although the principles of sovereignty were conceived when international law contemplated only physical intrusions into a nation's borders, national governments would probably try to apply the principles to intrusions into computers, networks, or data banks, and they would probably succeed. Individual governments have already exerted authority over information in domestic systems just as they would if it had physical form; many European governments, as well as the European Union, for example, have enacted data protection codes that forbid the transport or transmission of certain personal data to countries (such as the United States, perhaps) that do not provide sufficient protection for that data. Governments may thus go so far as to consider the act of investigation by foreigners of criminal misuse of their systems to be a form of computer crime, or worse.

The 1994 intrusion into the computers at the U.S. Air Force's Rome Laboratory in New York hinted at the problem of the collision between sovereignty and a wired world. That spring, two hackers, both now believed to have been British, broke into and took control of the operational network at the U.S. Air Force's command and control research facility at the Rome Labs. Air Force investigators were observing one attacker in the Rome computer when he accessed a system at the [South] Korean Atomic Research Institute, obtained all of its stored data, and deposited that data into the Rome Labs system. The investigators, initially fearing that the system belonged to North Korea, were concerned that the North Korean government would interpret the intrusion and transfer of data to the U.S. Air Force system as an act of war, at a time of sensitive negotiations with North Korea over its nuclear weapons program.

Although the stronger view is probably that government agents' intrusion into a foreign computer would constitute a violation of the target nation's sovereignty, it is important to note that not all electronic crossing of boundaries is considered that way. For example, orbital remote sensing, including the bouncing of such signals as radar off a country's territory, is now so universally accepted that it is conducted by private entities, which may sell the products of their sensing on the open market.

Furthermore, particularly where they do not interfere with registered stations, countries have no obligation to keep their radio broadcasts from penetrating others' borders. Weak authority even supports the proposition that the target country may not resist such broadcasts by jamming. Even if the dubious international legality of unauthorized cross-border electronic intrusion by a government's agents were to become accepted, those intrusions could still violate the target country's domestic laws, if any, on espionage or computer intrusion. Just as it would be hard for U.S. authorities to exert authority over foreign computer attackers, though, foreign governments would face difficulty in enforcing their laws against U.S. agents operating from computer terminals within the United States.

The conflict between international networks and national sovereignty is not merely an academic one. The U.S. Government has already had to face the problem of pursuing foreigners who have broken into U.S. computer systems from abroad for malicious purposes, although these attackers have apparently not succeeded in causing, or have not attempted to cause, significant destruction or denial of service. Attackers have complicated U.S. investigatory efforts by "looping and weaving" their attacks through several foreign countries so that investigators cannot follow the trail. For example, to stymie tracing efforts, the attackers who invaded the Rome Labs computers wove their way through phone switches in Columbia and Chile before entering Rome Labs through commercial sites in the United States.

The apparent widespread, inexpensive availability of the technology necessary for international attacks across computer networks, combined with the anonymity that the technology may provide its users, may complicate the efforts of investigators to determine whether responsibility for an attack carried out by an individual or group rests with a foreign government, and would certainly make it more difficult to convince other nations or international organizations of that government's role. This availability could reduce the need for terrorists or similar actors to seek state support. It should also give states that do support terrorism claims of "plausible deniability" that are stronger than those of states that have supported terrorism in the past. Conversely, the inexpensive, small, and ubiquitous technology may make it harder for states to live up to their obligation to prevent their territories from being used for attacks against other states. As Paul A. Strassmann, former Director of Defence Information and Principal Deputy Assistant Secretary of Defence for Command, Control, Communications and Intelligence, has stated, "Info-assassin paraphernalia is booming, and it's gory stuff you can buy....There is also a wide range of people available for hire to carry things out, many of them ex-intelligence agency people."

The tasks of investigators, policymakers, and diplomats are made harder by the uncertainty that arises from the ability of users (or abusers) of computer networks to hide their identities through such techniques as "spoofing" so that others may be blamed for their misdeeds. In fact, absent a credible admission of responsibility, it may be impossible to attribute an attack to its actual source with any degree of confidence. This uncertainty may have ramifications both for national security and for law enforcement.

Cooperation

Further complicating nations' attempts to trace attacks against them is the international investigatory legal regime, or lack thereof. First, in the absence of a treaty, countries have no underlying obligation to cooperate with each other in their law enforcement or national security investigations. The mere fact of noncooperation probably cannot be considered evidence of implication in the attack. Even where they had no involvement in, or sympathy for, an attack, hostile or indifferent nations may be unwilling to assist foreign investigators, whom they may view as spies. Even largely friendly governments may be reluctant to cooperate, often for domestic political reasons.

International law enforcement agreements may not be adequate to support an investigation. For example, treaties of mutual legal assistance, which may institutionalize cooperation between countries' law enforcement agencies, generally contain exceptions that permit parties to refuse cooperation under certain circumstances, such as to protect "sovereignty, security, or similar essential interests." In the context of computers, networks, and databases that may implicate a country's national security interests, its technological development, security of its financial and communications infrastructure, or the privacy of its citizens, and where governments may not feel confident about their ability to monitor foreign (especially U.S.) investigators' activities, some nations may likely at least consider taking advantage of any loopholes they can.

Even where other countries are cooperative, mechanisms of international cooperation, such as letters rogatory, may be prohibitively slow, particularly given the speed of communications and action across networks. Furthermore, and perhaps most significantly, requesting cooperation, even through such an organization as Interpol, would require the substantial involvement of foreign governments' officials and could expose them to information about the victim's intelligence capabilities or the vulnerabilities of the systems and networks they depend upon.

Given the difficulties of international cooperation discussed above, some in the U.S. Government may advocate that it unilaterally pursue its investigation without the cooperation of countries whose computers or networks have been used for attacks against U.S. systems. Although such a course of action seems likely to violate the sovereignty of those nations, and may be inconsistent with U.S. responsibilities under individual treaties of legal assistance, it would not in itself violate international law any further. The investigation would probably be characterized as "espionage," which does not violate international law, although it violates the domestic law of virtually all states. The U.S. Government would need to consider the diplomatic, political, and precedential ramifications that would arise if such an investigation were detected, just as it would have to in the case of more traditional forms of espionage or covert action.

Responding

Obviously, a government cannot respond to an attack successfully unless it can identify the attack's source. If the culprits can be identified, the options available for the victim state are unsettled and potentially unsatisfactory. As discussed above, it may be difficult, if not impossible, to tie the individual culprits to state support. A victim state may therefore need to proceed as if a given attack were a purely criminal matter, and request that the state in which the culprits are present extradite them to its territory for trial. Even where the victim has substantial grounds for believing that state support existed, it may proceed with the extradition request, because denial of the request may be seen in world forums, as well as in its domestic politics, as further evidence of that state's complicity. The UN sanctions against Libya in the wake of the Lockerbie bombing, for example, stemmed not as directly from Libya's involvement in the bombing, as they did from Libya's refusal to extradite the alleged bombers to the United States or United Kingdom, in violation of Security Council Resolution 748. The significance of political considerations in such a calculus is emphasized by the fact that at the time the sanctions were promulgated, Libya, which had claimed to be willing to try the alleged culprits, had not actually violated the procedural terms of the Montreal Convention on the Suppression of Unlawful Acts Against Civil Aviation, which permits a signatory to extradite or try a suspect (although, of course, bombing a plane would, indeed, violate the convention).

The ability of a victim state to gain custody of those who have attacked its systems from abroad is complicated by the collision of the longstanding international state system, the international nature of networks, and the relative historical novelty of computers and networks. For a country to apprehend an alleged criminal in a foreign country and transport the culprit to the requesting country for trial, certain conditions must exist. First, an extradition treaty must bind both countries, as there is no underlying right of extradition under international law. Extradition treaties may be bilateral or multilateral, and they may apply to a broad range or to discrete categories of offenses.

Second, the requesting country must have jurisdiction to prescribe the activity for which it seeks extradition; in other words, it must be within the power of the state to apply its laws to the relevant conduct. States base their claims to jurisdiction over criminal suspects on five general theories: first, and most simply, the territorial theory, by which states claim jurisdiction over those who act within their territories; second, nationality, by which states claim jurisdiction over their nationals; third, protective, by which states claim jurisdiction over those whose activities threaten their security or vital interests; fourth, passive personality, by which they claim jurisdiction over those who might threaten their nationals, even if they are abroad; and fifth, universality, under which all states may claim jurisdiction over those who have committed certain universally condemned crimes, such as piracy. An extended discussion of prescriptive jurisdiction is beyond the scope of this report, but it seems obvious that an attack against U.S. systems would fall within U.S. prescriptive jurisdiction, even if its perpetrators were beyond the reach of U.S. authorities.

Third, virtually all extradition treaties contain a "double criminality" requirement that mandates that the act that is the basis for the extradition request be an offence under the laws of both the requesting country and the one to which the request is directed. This requirement has been a significant obstacle to U.S. efforts to try those who have intruded into sensitive U.S. data systems. In the case of computer hackers from the Netherlands who broke into U.S. Navy and NASA systems during the Persian Gulf War, for example, Dutch concepts of privacy were such that the hackers' intrusion into sensitive systems was not yet considered a crime under Dutch law. Similarly, when Julio Caesar Ardita, a young Argentine, broke into computers containing sensitive information at the Naval Command Control and Ocean Surveillance Centre, the Navy Research Laboratory, and Los Alamos National Laboratory, among others, the United States was unable to obtain his extradition, even though Argentine police cooperated with U.S. authorities, because Argentina's legal system, faced with new technology, had not yet classified such intrusions as criminal.

The dual criminality requirement has, perhaps, also protected U.S. nationals who have been combatants in a different form of information conflict, namely the conflict surrounding the spread of U.S. popular culture. For example, when a Pakistani cleric recently reportedly asked the U.S. Department of State to extradite the entertainers Madonna and Michael Jackson because the lasciviousness of their performances violated Islamic law, the United States had no obligation to comply because, among other reasons, such violations of Islamic law are not criminal offenses in the United States.

Lastly, most extradition treaties contain exemptions for "political offenses," although governments interpret that term differently. Some states will refuse extradition only where the crime for which extradition is sought is a "pure" political offence, one directed at a sovereign political institution, absent the elements of common crime. Others refuse extradition for offenses committed in connection with a political cause or national liberation struggle. Some other states require that the political elements of the offence predominate over the common criminal elements. Finally, the French interpretation of the political offence exception is broader; French courts tend to deny extradition when a state wishes to punish an offender for injuries inflicted upon that state. Whatever interpretation they embrace formally, many states will find rationales to deny extradition for those accused offenders whom they do not wish to extradite.

A country's extradition requests for those who have attacked it from abroad may fail for several reasons distinct from the aforementioned requirements. First, a country that supported an attack will have tremendous, obvious incentives not to extradite its agents and may take advantage of any loophole it can find. Such loopholes may include the requirements, as well as the prohibition in many countries' domestic laws against extradition of their own nationals. For example, in rejecting the U.S. and UK requests that it extradite the agents who were alleged to have carried out the Lockerbie bombing, Libya claimed that its law prohibited the extradition of its nationals and said that it planned to try them itself, fulfilling its obligations under the Montreal Convention.

Second, as has apparently been the case with some terrorists, governments may reject extradition requests out of fear that the alleged criminals' colleagues will retaliate against them for their cooperation. In 1977, for example, France released Abu Daoud, the architect of the 1972 Munich Olympic massacre, despite efforts of the Federal Republic of Germany and Israel to obtain his extradition, apparently because it feared retaliation. Similarly, after two Germans were taken hostage in Beirut, West Germany used the political offence exception in its extradition treaty with the United States and released Mohammed Ali Hamadei, whom the United States had indicted for hijacking TWA flight 847 in 1987. Where information attacks with broad effects may be carried out from a distant sanctuary, the threat of such retaliation would appear particularly grave, especially for Western or other developed nations with significant dependence upon information infrastructures.

Third, the United States and other countries with advanced, vulnerable information infrastructures may exert diplomatic or other pressure to close some of the above loopholes, especially the failure of many countries' legal codes to recognize certain forms of computer intrusions as crimes. Nevertheless, potential incentives exist for countries to refuse to join any such formal or informal regime. First, of course, some countries may wish to use such intrusions or other attacks for their own political, economic, or other ends, and they may value maintaining that offensive capacity more than they do the incremental security that their systems would receive, particularly where their systems are poorly developed or relatively unimportant. Secondly, it is conceivable, although perhaps unlikely, that some nations may have ideological reasons to resist such rules, such as differing conceptions of privacy in electronic systems or data, or distrust of any system that would appear to preserve the advantages of the developed nations. Finally, and perhaps most disturbingly, countries may choose not to criminalize certain conduct as part of a development strategy. In what could be termed a form of "regulatory arbitrage," nations that hope to improve their information technology development may permit the behaviour of hackers or other attackers in the hope that they will relocate to these nations, bringing with them their technical expertise. Such countries may seek the skilled personnel either to deploy them against enemies or to build their own economy or infrastructure.

Although the concept of "regulatory arbitrage" may seem farfetched, it should not be dismissed out of hand. First, it seems likely that countries, as well as transnational criminal organizations and, perhaps, terrorist groups, have sought individuals or groups of foreign hackers to engage in espionage, crime, or other attacks and that such recruitment will occur in the future. During the 1980s, for example, the Soviet Union employed a group of West German computer hackers, who were eventually apprehended after they broke into a series of U.S. civilian and military computers in search of U.S. and NATO defence secrets. Second, "regulatory arbitrage" has taken place in other contexts. For example, in the wake of the U.S. military and diplomatic withdrawal after the Cold War, the Seychelles, hoping to attract foreign capital, enacted an Economic Development Act that granted citizenship and immunity from asset forfeiture or extradition to anyone investing at least $10 million in the islands. Closer to home, the legislatures of several U.S. states have, at times, engaged in a "race to the bottom," weakening their restrictions on the conduct of corporate officers and directors in the hope of attracting corporations to register in their respective states. States and countries have also given special incentives, reducing taxes and regulations or providing other benefits, in the hope of attracting business, including professional sports franchises.

Where a government refuses to extradite those responsible for attacks against another country, the victim state is not without recourse, although some options facing it may not be particularly attractive. First, of course, it may exert diplomatic, economic, or multilateral pressure against an uncooperative state, as has been the unsuccessful case with Libya after the Lockerbie bombing. Second, it may attempt to capture the alleged culprits and bring them back home for trial.

A government may contemplate abductions of criminal suspects from foreign lands when the urgent need to try the suspects outweighs the diplomatic and precedential costs of the abduction, and where such abductions do not violate the government's domestic law (if the government cares about such niceties). Abduction of suspects from foreign lands is not illegal under U.S. law, nor, at least, does it deprive U.S. courts of their ability to try abductees. In 1990, for example, after the Mexican government was unwilling or unable to extradite Dr. Humberto Alvarez-Machain, who had been indicted in a U.S. court for his role in the torture and murder of Enrique Camarena-Salazar, a U.S. Drug Enforcement Administration agent, U.S. agents abducted Dr. Alvarez-Machain and returned him to the United States for trial. The U.S. Supreme Court ultimately held that neither general principles of international law nor the terms of the U.S.-Mexico extradition treaty barred his prosecution, and that forcible abduction does not deprive a court of the ability to consider the case against the suspect. Eventually, though, charges against Alvarez-Machain were dismissed for lack of evidence.

Depending upon the language of the applicable extradition treaty, such abduction will not violate its terms and, under the maxim male captus, bene detentus, international law recognizes the right of a state to try a suspect, even where his capture was technically illegal. Nevertheless, agents operating abroad to capture suspects do violate the sovereignty of the countries in which they operate and risk punishment, perhaps for espionage or kidnapping, if they are apprehended by those countries' authorities. Furthermore, in the wake of the international and domestic furor that followed the abduction of Alvarez-Machain and the Supreme Court opinion permitting the abduction, such abductions seem likely to be extremely rare.

Retaliation

Responding to an "armed attack." Where a state can tie an attack to a foreign government, it may need to retaliate, either to terminate an ongoing attack or to prevent future attacks. The retaliating state would probably justify its retaliation as part of its right of self-defence as set out in Article 51 of the

UN Charter. However, it is not obvious that Article 51 actually provides a basis for military action against a state conducting certain information attacks.

The peaceful settlement of disputes is one of the primary purposes of the United Nations Charter. The Charter forbids the threat or use of force by one state against the territorial integrity or political independence of another state. The only lawful use of force, besides collective action to enforce peace under UN auspices, is in individual or collective self-defence against "armed attack." As the International Court of Justice asserted in its opinion in the case of Nicaragua v. United States, states do not have a right of armed response to acts which do not constitute an "armed attack." A computer network-based attack, or one involving software weapons such as viruses, would not unquestionably qualify as "armed attack" under the UN Charter, and thus might not provide the international legal basis for a conventional, kinetic military response.

The UN Charter does not define "armed attack"; nor has the International Court of Justice (ICJ) laid out any comprehensive definition. To the extent that the term has been construed, it seems to include the use of armed forces, force, or violence, as well as interference with a nation's sovereign rights. Economic coercion does not constitute "armed attack" nor, for that matter, according to the ICJ, did the Nicaraguan Sandinista government's actions in providing sanctuary and support during the early 1980s to the rebels who fought the U.S.-backed government of El Salvador. Even actions using destructive physical force may not rise to the level of "armed attack." Despite repeated requests, the United Nations refused to recognize guerrilla and terrorist attacks by Palestinians against Israel during the late 1960s and early 1970s as armed attacks, rejecting the Israeli position that individual small attacks from bases in Lebanon should be considered on a cumulative basis, as parts of an "armed attack" justifying Israeli incursions into Lebanon.

Such terms as "war," "aggression," and "force" have shown, it can be difficult to predict whether specific actions will be considered to be "armed attacks." Unlike the domestic criminal law, international law sets out no mandatory elements of "crimes." and any determination in such forums as the United

Nations will be inherently political and diplomatic. Nevertheless, it appears likely that an "armed attack" would include some level of actual or potential physical destruction, combined with some level of intrusion into its target's borders, or violation of its sovereign rights. Some attacks, such as aerial bombing strikes against a nation's military command and control centres, are highly likely to be considered "armed attacks," as they involve high levels of both intrusion and destruction. Other attacks, such as propaganda broadcasts, are unlikely to be considered "armed attacks," at least by relatively impartial world forums. Attacks such as computer intrusions or communications disruptions are much harder to characterize. It may be that increases in one variable may make up for limitations in the other. For example, computer intrusions for purposes of stealing data and to disrupt air traffic control may be equally intrusive, but the greater level of destruction and death that the air traffic control system attack may cause may make it more likely to be considered "armed attack" than would the data theft attempt. Furthermore, attacks that are sufficiently destructive may qualify as "armed attacks," no matter what their level of intrusion, and vice versa.

If a target country cannot characterize a computer attack against its information systems as an "armed attack," then it may not be able to respond to the attack with conventional, kinetic force, unless it wants to risk having its response considered the aggressive "armed attack" under Article 51. Presumably, a response in kind would not constitute "armed attack" if the original attack did not, but some potential information attackers, who may be able to hire from abroad the equipment and expertise they need for their attacks, may lack the information infrastructures to make them vulnerable to such attacks.

Proportionality. In addition to the United Nations' requirements that force be limited to a response to an armed attack, customary international law has developed requirements for retaliation. Such retaliation must be in individual or collective self-defence against an attack; it must be necessary to stop the initial, unjustified attack or to prevent further violations; and it must be proportional to the attack to which it is a response. The proportionality analysis applies in two ways. First, under the requirements of the jus ad bellum, the level of force of the response must be proportionate to that of the initial attack-a full-scale blitzkrieg across a broad front accompanied by aerial bombing would generally be disproportionate to a patrol's border raid, for example. Second, as in any other military action, the response must balance the damage it will inflict, especially to civilians, against the military objectives it is intended to accomplish.

Just as it is not obvious that an information attack will be an "armed attack," it is not obvious what would be proportionate to such an attack, especially where the attack inflicts little or no physical destruction or loss of life. Where a computer intrusion disrupts or corrupts a database or denies service for important elements of the electronic infrastructure, inflicting great hardship on the target country, that country must determine what sort of response would be proportionate to the attack. In the absence of real physical destruction or death, such as by the crash of a passenger aircraft through manipulation of the air traffic control system, it is questionable that a conventional military attack would be proportionate. The use of force may be qualitatively distinct from other tools of coercion, as demonstrated by its inclusion in the UN Charter and the UN definition of aggression.

If a conventional response is disproportionate to an information warfare attack, a response in kind could seem likely to be proportionate. However, such a response may require the use of neutral assets, such as networks owned by or passing through neutral countries and thus could run the risk of violating their neutrality. Perhaps more significantly, because of the limited infrastructure and resources necessary to conduct some information warfare attacks, and the potential expertise available for hire or ideological recruitment, an adversary who has attacked the United States or a similarly advanced country may lack sufficient targets for an information warfare response, or may have only targets that are too important to be retaliated against for anything other than a grave attack. It would seem inappropriate to cause aircraft to crash, for example, in retaliation for a limited disruption of a local telephone network, or an intrusion into a military computer. It seems unlikely that the United States would refrain from traditional military retaliation where an information warfare response would be inappropriate overkill or ineffectual underkill. It also seems unlikely that international law would mandate such inaction. Assuming that an information warfare attack is an "armed attack," and an information warfare response were unavailable or excessive, then a kinetic response, appropriately calibrated, would seem proportional even if, as a general rule, the relevant form of information warfare attacks were considered distinct from violence. If the information warfare attack is not an "armed attack" justifying a military response under the UN Charter, then, aside from such measures as economic sanctions, the United States might then assert an underlying, inherent right of national self-defence, which predates and goes beyond the rights contained in Article 51 of the UN Charter, rather than suffering ongoing attacks stoically or petitioning the UN Security Council for help. In considering their responses to such attacks, policymakers must be aware that their actions may establish precedents that other nations may look to in similar circumstances, or draw upon cynically to excuse their behaviour in dissimilar circumstances.

In sum, current understandings of "armed attack," as well as dissonance between international networks and the international system of state sovereignty, may complicate or hinder victims' efforts to respond to information warfare attacks. The United States may need to pursue international initiatives to change that understanding, as well as to alter nations' responsibilities, or lack thereof, to forego such attacks, prevent their occurrence, or to cooperate in defensive or law enforcement measures.

BALANCING CAPABILITIES

The international law has not yet resolved ambiguities over the characterization of information warfare activities, and must face a conflict between the international system of sovereign states and the realities of global networks. International law thus leaves space for the United States and others to conduct information warfare activities, perhaps even in peacetime, without significant legal repercussions. Conversely, international law may permit attacks against the United States, as well as exacerbate U.S. difficulties in responding to attacks against it, particularly in peacetime. The legal status quo may appear satisfactory to U.S. policymakers. As the United States apparently leads the world in information warfare development, an international legal regime that permits information attacks can give it an advantage, allowing the United States to apply its technological strength to international conflicts in ways beyond the capacities of anyone else. In the absence of conclusive legal authority indicating, say, that particular information warfare attacks are "armed attacks," "aggression," or "force," the United States can act with some confidence that its acts will not be held to be so. Given its position in the world, the United States will have the opportunity to begin the state practice that can establish international norms and, perhaps, customary international law. To an extent, then, given the United States' voice in world politics and predominant military might, the United States is in the positions of legislator, sheriff, and (perhaps, to its adversaries) executioner, and it has a lot of influence over the judge.

Despite its freedom to act, the United States should not be sanguine about the state of international law. The "legislator, sheriff, and executioner" may all live together in a large glass house. Just as the United States can attack, it can be attacked, and its actions in conducting attacks may provide precedent for attacks against it and its allies. Furthermore, just as U.S. capabilities may outstrip those of its potential adversaries, so too may its vulnerabilities, as it is perhaps uniquely dependent upon its information infrastructure for both civilian and military needs. If only to increase protection for U.S. systems, then, certain nonexclusive legal, diplomatic, or policy initiatives may be appropriate.

Legal Ambiguities

A first approach would be to clarify the delineation of such terms as "armed attack," "force," and others, so that the status of information warfare attacks under international law is understood. Without knowing the extent of U.S. offensive capabilities or defensive vulnerabilities, it is impossible for us to judge the desirability of limiting information warfare. The United States might support restrictive definitions of those terms, so as to preserve its ability to use its technological advantages, to protect potentially desirable technological developments, and to encourage the use of nonlethal methods of conflict; or it might support broad definitions, to help reduce the lawful methods by which adversaries can exploit its vulnerabilities. Definitions that included nonlethal information warfare attacks within "war" or "force" could give civilians a measure of protection from such attacks during times of peace, as they would increase the diplomatic and political repercussions of such attacks. To protect civilian targets during wartime, the United States could pursue treaties or other international understandings that the financial or other intangible damages caused by certain types of nonlethal information attacks are, indeed, the types of injuries against which humanitarian law should protect noncombatants.

The United States may use several legal mechanisms to achieve the goal it chooses, ranging from a treaty setting out the circumstances in which certain types of information warfare are permissible, to silence on the subject to avoid hindrances on U.S. capabilities. Additionally, the United States could try to influence the development of customary international law regarding the appropriateness of information warfare. It may move for declarations of the UN General Assembly interpreting the Charter as it would apply to information warfare. U.S. statements of its views on the subject would have a significant effect both on the opinions of other states and, ultimately, the emergence of international norms regarding information attacks, or particular aspects thereof. Although customary international law traditionally evolved naturally from state practice over an extended period of time, states have recently pursued efforts to create customary law purposefully. Such efforts have been most visible in international forums, such as the General Assembly, which has passed declarations setting out world opinion as to the state of the law on such topics as the use of nuclear weapons, seabed mining, or the equation of Zionism with racism.

There is no reason, though, that an individual state could not set out to influence the development of customary legal norms, especially in an area such as information warfare, where that state leads the world in the development or application of the technologies and techniques to which these norms would be applied. U.S. efforts to draw world attention to dangers that information warfare poses could be counterproductive, however, as they might spur other countries' efforts to obtain or use information warfare weapons, and those countries may be suspicious of what they perceive to be U.S. efforts to protect its technological advantages or retard the development of others' capacities.

Computer Attacks

Second, to improve its defensive or responsive options, the United States could make efforts to reconcile the system of sovereign states with international networks, through promoting harmonization of laws and cooperation in investigation and prosecution of computer attacks. The first part of such a strategy would include diplomatic pressure and criminal justice advice and assistance to promote the criminalization of computer-based attacks in those nations that do not yet recognize such attacks as crimes, both to encourage other countries to discourage such behaviour by individuals within their borders, and to enable extradition of offenders. Secondly, the United States could support the development of an extradition regime for criminal or terrorist computer attacks, obliging all countries to extradite or try those who have committed specified network-related crimes. Models for such measures could be drawn from the treaties executed in the 1960s and early 1970s to combat hijacking and other terrorism against civil aviation. The Montreal Convention on the Suppression of Unlawful Acts Against Civil Aviation, for example makes it an offence for anyone to destroy an aircraft, place a device likely to destroy an aircraft, destroy or damage air navigation facilities, or communicate information which he knows to be false, thus endangering the safety of aircraft in flight, and it obliges countries to extradite or try suspected offenders. Such agreements, along with diplomatic and other public statements relating to the criminalization of such attacks, could also contribute to the development of a norm that countries cannot support computer-based attacks in peacetime, or that they must cooperate in resisting such attacks. Given the United States' and its allies' ambiguous success in fighting international terrorism, it is obvious, though, that such agreements or norms would not be panaceas.

Critical Systems

Third, just as the aviation efforts were incremental steps in the fight against terrorism, similar efforts could be made for the protection of particular information systems from dangers including crime, terrorism, war, or even natural disasters. Some systems may be so critical that countries can agree that they must be put off limits from attacks, or that all countries must cooperate to defend them. Systems that could be the subject of individual protection regimes include those involved in the command and control of strategic weapons, international financial transfers, individual financial markets or stock exchanges, telephone switches, emergency communications, rail transport, and medical databases. Such arrangements could be pursued under direct UN auspices, or as individual treaties in the context of existing institutions, such as the ITU, OECD, or ICAO, or even, perhaps the World Intellectual Property Organization (WIPO).

Along with providing legal bases for responses and countermeasures, incremental prohibitions against certain information warfare attacks could contribute to the development of broader international norms against such attacks, particularly in peacetime. In the context of nuclear weapons, in comparison, proclamations and regional agreements against the use of nuclear weapons contributed to the legal argument that the use of such weapons had become illegal, although the International Court of Justice did not ultimately embrace that argument.

Arms Control for Information Warfare?

A fourth approach that has been suggested could be to pursue some sort of ban on information warfare attacks or control of the weapons of information warfare. Such an approach would seem to provide clear legal norms to guide future actions, and might seem particularly sensible if the United States were to determine that its vulnerabilities outweighed its technological advantages.

But such clarity would be illusory; the distinction between information warfare and traditional warfare is blurry, at best. An information warfare weapons ban would pose problems because not only do many information weapons have dual military and civilian uses, but their applications are predominantly civilian. Because of technological diffusion, the small size of much information technology, and its primary incorporation into consumer goods, an arms control regime would seem difficult to enforce.

Furthermore, although arms controls and weapons bans have been applied to new technologies before they were widely used or their military ramifications understood, as in the bans on bacteriological weapons, hostile use of environmental modification techniques, and blinding laser weapons, it does seem premature to limit a weapon that promises to bring some measure of nonlethality to conflict, and in which the United States apparently holds an advantage in development.

In any event, arms controls or warfare bans would not apply to the non-state actors, such as terrorists or criminal organizations, who would not be parties to the agreements and who may make up the gravest short-term information warfare threat. Such bans, then, would not eliminate the need for defensive measures, so countries might still need to explore offensive capabilities, if only to test their defensive measures adequately.

The Lure of Inactivity

A final prospective course of action is to do nothing, or very little. Although international law does not now conclusively address the legality of many information warfare attacks or the appropriate responses to them, that has not been a grave problem yet, because the attacks, aside from some computer intrusions and crimes, have not been particularly serious. But as information technology continues to develop and diffuse, the danger of such attacks seems likely only to increase, as might the opportunities for U.S. offensive uses. If the United States needs to conduct such attacks, it will undoubtedly do so. If the United States is subject to attacks, it will respond. International law will address information warfare attacks in some way or another. It may be wise to address the legal issues that the United States will face in advance, rather than having to address them in the heat of an emergency, where inadequate legal institutions may reduce national options and precedents may be set by exigencies, rather than forethought.

Conclusion: A Caveat

Despite the apparent attractiveness of addressing the potential international legal issues arising from the development of information warfare technologies and techniques before the issues actually arise, it is important to remember (and easy for lawyers to forget) that law is no panacea. Even the wisest agreements and soundest legal analysis will not guarantee the safety of U.S. systems or the potency of U.S. offensive measures. Law can go a long way toward regulating nations' and individuals' behaviour, and it can be an important part of diplomatic efforts both to alleviate conflict and to address its effects. At the same time, though, the development of advanced information warfare technologies and techniques and the continuing global diffusion of information technology illustrate the fluidity of the world that law attempts to govern. No law can change as swiftly as can technology; unless law is to somehow stop technology's seemingly inexorable worldwide progress, it cannot fully control the use of its fruits for warfare. Legal measures can thus supplement, but not supplant, vigilance, preparedness, and ingenuity.

7

Environmental Warfare: Active and Passive Armed Conflict

INTRODUCTION

From the beginning of recorded history, war has played a major role in shaping the course of events. Though geography changes, nations come and go, vanquished turn into conquerors, and victors become victims, one of the constant elements of warfare is its degrading effects on the environment. Concurrent with war's deleterious effects on the environment, man has from time to time attempted to harness the overwhelming powers inherent in the environment and unleash them on his enemies. This was graphically demonstrated as recently as the 1991 Gulf War. The environmental destruction that occurred in that short war appalled the world and set new levels in man's willingness to destroy his surroundings while waging hostilities. Many observers expected similar environmental warfare during the 2003 Gulf War, and there is clear evidence that there were plans to do so that were never executed.

Many writers blame this intended destruction of the environment on inadequate standards in the international law of environmental warfare. After the first Gulf War, there was a flurry of comment on the status of the law. A host of writers urged the international community to adopt either a new convention to protect the environment during times of armed conflict, create a "Green Cross" counterpart to the Red Cross, convene an International Environmental Court, or to enforce more strictly existing standards of international law. Others argued that the current law was sufficiently clear and the standards easily applied.

Making the discussion even more difficult is a debate as to whether the damage done during the first Gulf War violated the current international standard. The resilience of the environment over time ought not to excuse from international accountability military leaders who intentionally target the environment as a method of warfare. Rather, treatment of the environment during international armed conflict should be classified as either active, meaning using the environment as a weapon, or passive, meaning acts that do not "use" the environment but have deleterious effects on the environment. Active environmental warfare that damages the sustainable environment should be viewed as a violation of both international law and the law of war, and it should not require evidence of widespread, long-term, and severe damage.

The definition of "environment," and then divide wartime treatment of the environment into two categories, active and passive. The international law of environmental warfare, including man's attempts to protect the environment during times of hostilities as well as exclude the environment as a means of warfare, will be analyzed, and these protections will be categorized as regulating either passive or active environmental warfare. The Article will then argue that the current effects-based analysis, which is described below, is effective only against passive environmental warfare.

Active environmental warfare against the sustainable environment that is not de minimus violates international law per se and should not require environmental damage to reach the standard of widespread, long-lasting, and severe to be considered a violation of international law. The justification of military necessity and analyse why such a justification can apply only to passive and not to active environmental warfare. Finally, a Convention on the Protection of the Environment During Armed Conflict will be proposed and explained as a method to proscribe active environmental warfare. This convention will codify the active and passive environmental warfare distinction and clarify international responsibility for violations of international environmental law.

THE ENVIRONMENT

Arriving at an acceptable definition of "environment" presents an initial difficulty in trying to analyse the current state of international law in the area of environmental warfare. Many international treaties and conventions have endeavored to define environment in this context, most with only limited success, and others have avoided the problem by not offering a definition at all. Scholars have also made attempts in this area with similarly limited success. One of the most descriptive definitions of environment is found in the 1977 United Nations Convention on the Prohibition of Military or Any Other Hostile Use of Environmental Modification Techniques (ENMOD). The ENMOD Convention defines environment as "the Earth, including its biota, lithosphere, hydrosphere and atmosphere, or... outer space." Although descriptive, this definition provides little clarity. Based on this definition, it is difficult to imagine any form of warfare that would not have serious environmental effects, making it equally hard to provide adequate protections for the environment.

One scholar has proposed defining environment as "anything that is not man-made." There may be real utility in this broad definition in that it may remove the importance of defining the environment at all. He argues "[t]he only reason for defining [environment and environmental damage] more explicitly would be to attempt to place an absolute limit on environmental damage that cannot be exceeded by a military commander," an unnecessary limitation in his view. These broadly inclusive definitions, and similar definitions in other multinational documents and writings, reflect the increasing desire of the international community to broaden environmental protections in all situations, especially those that are known to be potentially the most dangerous to the environment.

Compounding the difficulty of applying international legal regulation to the environment are competing views as to why the environment merits protection. One view, known as the anthropocentric or utilitarian view, is that the environment is worth protecting only insofar as it provides some benefit to humans. The opposing view is the intrinsic value view, which holds that the environment is worth protecting as an end in itself, regardless of potential utility to humans. This intrinsic value view of the environment, while not generally accepted by nations, would almost certainly provide greater protections for the environment over time and may be gaining favor.

Despite the inability of the international legal community to agree on a useful definition of environment, it is clear that the trend in the international community is to view the environment as a very broad and inclusive entity. In fact, the lack of definitional precision seems to be a result of not wanting to narrow the scope of legal coverage for the environment. Therefore, although a specific definition may be useful in a general sense, the lack of clarity and broader coverage of environmental protections it will provide may prove more valuable over time.

PASSIVE AND ACTIVE ENVIRONMENTAL WARFARE

Adopting a broad definition of environment allows extensive inclusion of wartime acts and their effects on the environment in analyzing what wartime acts are illegal. Because the environment is so expansive, virtually all wartime acts will have some effect on the environment. The difficulty then becomes differentiating the severity of specific acts and determining which are violations of international law or the law of war. This is a vital inquiry because unless an act has repercussions under international law or the law of war, wartime leaders, such as Saddam Hussein in Gulf Wars I and II, have little incentive to abide by environmental preservation requirements.

Under the current application of the law of war, the inquiry is completely an effects-based inquiry. It can be determined that a specific wartime act will result in "widespread, long-lasting, and severe" damage to the environment, neither international law nor the law of war is effective in deterring or sanctioning military leaders who inflict grievous damage to the environment, regardless of their intentions. This current state of the law is unacceptable. Not only is it unlikely that the international community will be able to make such a determination without the benefit of the passage of time—making a timely sanction impossible —but the standard relies completely on the effects of the act on the environment and takes no account for the intention of the actor.

The best way to clarify existing international law and provide greater legal protection to the environment would be to classify environmental damage as either passive or active. This classification would allow for differentiating the severity of international law violations based on the target of the attack rather than on waiting to see the effects of the attack and, therefore, provide the international community the opportunity to determine the intent of the actor and seek more appropriate remedies for such violations. Passive environmental warfare includes acts not specifically designed to "use" the environment for a particular military purpose but rather that have a degrading effect on the environment. These wartime acts may be completely unrelated to the environment in terms of the intent of the parties, yet they still have consequences that directly affect the surrounding environment.

An example of passive environmental warfare is the use of artillery. While artillery bombardment is not a "use" of the environment, it has secondary environmental effects on as destruction of plant life, disruption of natural animal habitats, etc. Another example is the disruption of the natural environment caused by the mass movement of large military armored vehicles. It is most likely not the intent of the belligerents to cause environmental damage in this way. They are not moving their vehicles in order to damage the environment, but it occurs as a secondary effect of waging war. In contrast to passive environmental warfare, active environmental warfare requires the intentional "use" of the environment as a weapon of waging armed conflict. Employing the environment as an "instrument of warfare" has been defined as "the use of the environment that might cause damage to the enemy or interference with an enemy military or combat activity." This can occur through the operation of any conceivable instrument, such as conventional or unconventional weapons, natural forces, or resources.

Excluded from this definition is military action in connection with existing environmental conditions. For example, launching a military satellite to track weather information and to advise military units so they can avoid possible damage does not rise to the level of "use" in the foregoing definition. Active environmental warfare includes inducing earthquakes or other natural disasters, weather manipulation, and climate modification, where these activities are intentionally conducted to disrupt enemy movements or to destroy enemy forces. Other examples include redirecting waterways or releasing stored water to flood trafficable areas, seeding clouds to produce rain, setting forest fires to direct military forces, and fouling internal waters to prevent movement of forces. In short, active environmental warfare involves the deliberate harnessing of the environment as an instrument for conducting hostilities. In this sense the environment is not just the field upon which war takes place, but instead it is an actively used tool of war.

Therefore, in active environmental warfare the environment is the weapon, whereas, in passive environmental warfare the environment is merely the victim of wartime acts. The differentiation between active and passive environmental warfare becomes significant when analyzing the standards under which a nation violates international law. The determination of whether a nation's breach is one of active use or passive result is pivotal in deciding liability and potential consequences of such a breach. It is unlikely that warfare can ever be cleansed of its passive effects on the environment. But to protect the environment from the most serious dangers, it is essential to eliminate the intentional use of the environment as a weapon during armed conflict. This is a key distinction given the events of the past few decades, including the Persian Gulf Wars. Had the active and passive differentiation been in place before the environmental destruction of the 1991 Gulf War, it may have been easier for the international community to have exacted reparations in line with Security Council Resolution 687. A clear understanding and concrete application of this differentiation will increase the international community's ability to hold a nation, and its leaders, responsible for specific damage done to the environment during armed conflict.

INTERNATIONAL LAW OF ENVIRONMENTAL WARFARE

It has become commonplace in the last decade to say that "the importance of protecting the environment has become increasingly obvious." The events of the Persian Gulf Wars have only served to accelerate that trend. While there are more than 900 treaties that have provisions dealing with environmental protection, none attempts to create an integrated approach to environmental warfare regulation. The following is a brief analysis of the most significant international law documents that directly or indirectly provide protections for the environment during war. This analysis will be divided into two areas: protection of the environment from passive wartime effects (when the environment is the victim of hostilities), and prevention of and limitations on active environmental warfare (when the environment is the weapon in hostilities).

Passive Environmental Warfare: The Environment as Victim

Attempts to protect the environment from the ravages of war began much sooner than attempts to limit man's ability to use the environment as a weapon. Consensus that the natural environment was a victim of warfare began to solidify in the 1800s, and it started with the growing commitment that warfare was limited, that combatants were constrained in their means and methods of conducting hostilities, and that their right to injure the enemy was not unlimited. Growing concurrently with that principle was the "no harm" principle, the idea that one state cannot use or permit the use of its territory to harm another state. The establishment of these general principles led to the development of a number of specific provisions more focused on the environment and its protections.

Limitation of the Right to Injure the Enemy

As international law developed over the centuries, sovereigns and their military commanders began to place voluntary limits on their right to conduct warfare. Most of these voluntary limitations developed because they served a tactical purpose, but others were based on a moral view of warfare and that some actions were not right, even in open hostilities. Codification of this principle appeared as early as 1863 in the U.S. Civil War. President Abraham Lincoln issued General Order 100 as part of the Army's Lieber Code that placed a number of restrictions on how the Union Army fought. These restrictions "strongly influenced the further codification of the laws of war and the adoption of similar regulations by other states" and were considered representative of the standard rules of war. With regard to the environment, the Lieber rules restricted the destruction of property that was not militarily necessary. While this provision does not specifically refer to the environment, it began to form the basis for later provisions that would.

On September 9, 1880, the Institute of International Law published The Laws of War on Land, which contained provisions stating limitations on the ability to injure the enemy and also dealt with issues concerning public and private property. This was followed by the First Hague Peace Conference in 1899, which produced the Convention (II) with Respect to the Laws and Customs of War on Land. The 1899 Hague Convention was followed by the Second International Peace Conference in 1907, also at The Hague. The states at this conference produced the Convention (IV) Respecting the Laws and Customs of War on Land. The Convention (IV) revised the 1899 Convention (II), leaving it in force for all parties who did not sign on to the newer 1907 convention.

Article 22 of the 1907 Convention mirrors Article 4 of The Laws of War on Land and states that "the right of belligerents to adopt means of injuring the enemy is not unlimited." Article 23, particularly (e) and (g), continue to provide constraints, even if not explicit, to environmental damage during hostilities. Article 23(e) disallows any weapons that would "cause unnecessary suffering," and Article 23(g) makes it unlawful to "destroy or seize the enemy's property, unless such destruction or seizure be imperatively demanded by the necessities of war."

More clearly tied to the environment, Article 55 of Section III (dealing with the Military Authority over the Territory of the Hostile State), declares: The occupying State shall be regarded only as administrator and usufructuary of public buildings, real estate, forests, and agricultural estates belonging to the hostile State and situated in the occupied country. It must safeguard the capital of these properties, and administer them in accordance with the rules of usufruct.

In this sense, "usufruct" means "the right of one state to enjoy all the advantages derivable from the use of property which belongs to another state."

In general, the 1899 Convention (II) and the 1907 Convention (IV) taken together, with included Regulations, represent the first major movement in providing legal constraints that also protect the environment from wartime damage. These two conventions represent the base of international environmental warfare regulation and are generally accepted as part of customary international law. As elements of international custom, they are binding on all states, regardless of whether they are signatories to the Conventions. Although these authorities do not represent explicit protections for the environment, they firmly establish that there are some things that cannot be done, even in war.

The "No Harm" Principle

As this limitation on the ability to injure an enemy became more and more entrenched in international law, concurrent constraints on states' interactions with each other in peacetime began to develop. One of the basic principles is reflected in the Trail Smelter arbitration. In this decision, the United States was awarded damages from Canada because of air pollution that had drifted across the border. The decision stated what has become a foundation for much of current international environmental law: "no State has the right to use or permit the use of its territory in such a manner as to cause injury by fumes in or to the territory of another...."

This principle was confirmed and extended to a wartime environment in the Corfu Channel case in which the International Court of Justice held Albania responsible for not warning British warships that mines had been placed in its territorial waters. The Court held that it was "every State's obligation not to allow knowingly its territory to be used for acts contrary to the rights of other States."

This principle was expanded in the Lac Lanoux arbitration and the Nuclear Tests case. The environment was directly implicated in these cases, which not only confirmed the application of the "no harm" principle to the environment, but also stand for the basic principle that nations must co-operate in avoiding adverse effects on their neighbours through a system of impact assessment, notification, consultation, and negotiation. While the significance of these few decisions should not be over-stated, they represent a clear indication that customary international law does not allow unilateral degradation of the environment at the expense of another nation, and that the "no harm" principle is a firm principle of international environmental law.

Further evidence of the "no harm" principle is found in the 1972 Stockholm Declaration of the United Nations Conference on the Human Environment. At the conclusion of the U.N. sponsored conference, representatives of 103 nations adopted a declaration expressing their combined understanding of states' roles in this area. Principle 21 declares: States have, in accordance with the Charter of the United Nations and the principles of international law, the sovereign right to exploit their own resources pursuant to their own environmental policies, and the responsibility to ensure that activities within their jurisdiction or control do not cause damage to the environment of other States or of areas beyond the limits of national jurisdiction.

This pronouncement of sovereignty, coupled with the statement of accompanying responsibility, has become a basis for many international documents supporting the "no harm" principle, and is accepted as customary international law. This principle, combined with the limitation on belligerents during hostilities, has led to a number of specific provisions affecting the international law of environmental warfare.

Specific Protections for the Environment as a Victim

As states embraced these general principles of environmental protection, more specific provisions began to appear in customary and conventional international law. At the Nuremberg trials after World War II, nine civilian German administrators were tried for carrying out the Nazi policy of ruthless exploitation of Polish forests. Others were tried for "massive devastation of the environment." Although the decision by the court was not decisive, the fact that the Tribunal pursued crimes against the environment is very significant and represents the first such judicial action resulting from acts on another state's land during wartime. The influence of the Nuremberg Tribunals on international law is uncontested and reflects an international inclination that evidences itself in other international law documents.

The Geneva Convention Relative to the Protection of Civilian Persons in Time of War of 1949 (GCC) has many provisions that reflected customary international law of the time but also has many others that reflected emerging norms in response to the atrocities of World Wars I and II. The fourth of four Conventions, this convention was aimed primarily at the protection of non-combatants, including inanimate non-combatants. Article 53 prohibits an occupying power from destroying "real or personal property... except where such destruction is rendered absolutely necessary by military operations." Though this represented little actual protection, it reflected the attitude of the post-war community that environmental effects were a consideration in warfare and that potential degradation to the environment had its limits, even during war.

As acceptance of the 1949 Convention grew, so did the recognition of the environment as a resource that deserved protection during war. In 1978, the 1977 Protocol I to the Geneva Conventions entered into force. Starting where the GCC left off, it is acknowledged by many as the first specific attempt to protect the environment during armed conflicts. Article 55 deserves special attention. Article 55 states:

1. Care shall be taken in warfare to protect the natural environment against widespread, long-term, and severe damage. This protection includes a prohibition of the use of methods or means of warfare which are intended or may be expected to cause such damage to the natural environment and thereby to prejudice the health or survival of the population.
2. Attacks against the natural environment by way of reprisals are prohibited.

The duty of care contained in the first sentence of Article 55 is the current statement of passive environmental warfare regulation. It is significant to note that the issue here is the effect an act has on the environment, not the means or methods or even the intention of the actors. This limitation places a clear, unqualified restriction on military operations, regardless of how that damage might occur. While lesser damage is permitted, any military operations that would cause environmental damage of this magnitude are proscribed.

In addition to this Article, Article 52 provides protection to civilian objects; Article 53 protects cultural objects and places of worship; Article 54 provides protection to objects indispensable to the survival of the civilian population, including such things as agricultural areas and irrigation works; and Article 56 protects works and installations containing dangerous forces such as dams, dikes, and nuclear electrical generating facilities. These provisions of Protocol I are the clearest statement in conventional law of the prohibition on passive environmental warfare in which the effects reach a prescribed intensity.

The World Charter for Nature, adopted in 1982 by almost unanimous consent of the United Nations General Assembly, proclaimed "principles of conservation by which all human conduct affecting nature is to be guided and judged." One of the principles specifically deals with environmental degradation in times of war and states that "[n]ature shall be secured against degradation caused by warfare or other hostile activities."

The 1992 United Nations Conference on the Environment, held in Rio de Janeiro, Brazil, reflected many of these same principles including a particular reference to the environment in times of armed conflict. Principle 24 of the Rio Declaration states: Warfare is inherently destructive of sustainable development. States shall therefore respect international law providing protection for the environment in times of armed conflict and cooperate in its further development, as necessary.

This statement marks a clear challenge for those nations willing to embrace it, and it is quoted as authority for requiring compliance with various peacetime environmental rules during armed conflict. The acts of the Security Council during the 1991 Gulf War may have "created legal precedent for future armed conflicts." In April 1991, the Security Council passed resolution 687 holding Iraq liable under international law for "any direct loss, [or] damage, including environmental damage and the depletion of natural resources." Although this liability has not yet been fully implemented, it sets an important pattern for future responses to similar environmental degradation. Several other documents have been written by scholars and jurists that relate to this issue, including the International Committee of the Red Cross' Guidelines for Military Manuals and Instructions on the Protection of the Environment in Times of Armed Conflict and the International Law Commission's Draft Code of Crimes Against Peace and Security of Mankind. These specific provisions of international law indicate that a trend in international law and policy is developing and illustrate the wide acceptance on the national and international level of the limitations on passive environmental warfare.

Environment as Weapon

Along with the harm on the environment caused by hostilities, it is increasingly possible with developing technology to use the environment as a weapon. This transforms the environment from the surroundings in which man fights, into a tool by which he fights. This type of warfare is particularly appealing in a world of military asymmetry in which those countries with limited technological means are looking for any way to counter their shortfalls. In contrast to passive environmental effects, actively using the environment as a weapon requires an element of intent on the part of the manipulator. Active use cannot occur through a negligent act. It is only triggered by a purposeful use of the environment as a means of waging war. This possibility of harnessing the environment and using it for such active military purposes is drawing increasing attention at the international level.

Active Environmental Warfare

Although history is not without record of active environmental warfare, using the environment as a means of war is a fairly new technological development. Further, the distinction between active and passive use of the environment has not been previously recognized. Therefore, international law is less developed in this area. It is possible, however, to conclude that since only a few nations actively use the environment to carry on warfare, the requisite state practice exists to establish an international customary norm. On the other hand, many argue that analyzing what actions states have not taken is a flawed approach and does not result in a binding principle of international law without a greater show of acceptance by states. These dissenters would require some overt act to confirm the state-practice element, rather than relying solely on non-derogation.

Recently, several wars, beginning with the Vietnam War and continuing with the Gulf Wars, have raised the international community's awareness of the issue, and states have begun to take overt steps and establish conventional legal constraints on active environmental warfare. The most significant of these as they apply to active environmental warfare are the ENMOD and the Protocol Additional to the Geneva Conventions of 12 August 1949, and Relating to the Protection of Victims of International Armed Conflict (GPI). Although neither of these documents was formulated with the benefit of the distinction between active and passive environmental warfare, they contain the underlying principles that have ripened into this vital distinction. Therefore, an analysis of these two documents and the interaction between them is vital to understanding the rules regarding active environmental warfare.

On December 10, 1976, the United Nations adopted General Assembly Resolution 31/72, which later became the ENMOD Convention. The ENMOD convention was created in response, at least partially, to the unsuccessful attempts of the United States to use weather modification techniques as a weapon in the Vietnam War. This convention represents the foundation document regulating the "active" use of the environment in warfare. It "regulates the use of the environment as a means to wage war, rather than damage to the environment as an ancillary result of war." Article I of the convention states:

Each State Party to this Convention undertakes not to engage in military or any other hostile use of environmental modification techniques having widespread, long-lasting or severe effects as the means of destruction, damage or injury to any other State Party.

This provision sets up a two-part test for falling within the restrictions of the Convention: (1) there must be an intentional environmental modification technique and (2) widespread, long-lasting, or severe effects resulting from that modification. The first of these elements requires that the offending nation use "deliberate manipulation of natural processes," not that environmental damage is simply a result of the action. As stated above, this requirement of intent is one of the key issues in "active" environmental warfare.

The second requirement is that the damage is of a certain type and duration. The words "widespread," "long-lasting," and "severe" are given more specific meaning in the first Understanding to the Convention: It is the understanding of the Committee that, for the purposes of this Convention, the terms "widespread", "long-lasting", and "severe" shall be interpreted as follows:

(a) "widespread": encompassing an area on the scale of several hundred square kilometres;

(b) "long-lasting": lasting for a period of months, or approximately a season;

(c) "severe": involving serious or significant disruption or harm to human life, natural and economic resources or other assets.

It is further understood that the interpretation set forth above is intended exclusively for this Convention and is not intended to prejudice the interpretation of the same or similar terms if used in connection [sic] with any other international agreement. The importance of this Understanding is clearer when compared with similar language in the 1977 Additional Protocol I to the 1949 Geneva Convention. Despite the similarity, it is clear that these linguistic interpretations apply only to ENMOD, not to Protocol I, and set a more stringent limitation when conducting active environmental warfare.

Protocol I has two key provisions, Article 35 and Article 55, that deserve special attention. Article 35 states:

1. In any armed conflict, the right of the Parties to the armed conflict to choose methods or means of warfare is not unlimited.
2. It is prohibited to employ weapons, projectiles and material and methods of warfare of a nature to cause superfluous injury or unnecessary suffering.
3. It is prohibited to employ methods or means of warfare which are intended, or may be expected, to cause widespread, long-term and severe damage to the natural environment.

By placing subparagraph 3 in the same Article as the well-established subparagraph 1, the Protocol raises the restraint on wartime environmental damage to a new level. Further, Article 36 obligates parties to ensure any new means or methods of warfare comply with existing international norms.

Article 55, which has been discussed earlier in connection with passive environmental warfare, states:

Care shall be taken in warfare to protect the natural environment against widespread, long-term, and severe damage. This protection includes a prohibition of the use of methods or means of warfare which are intended or may be expected to cause such damage to the natural environment and thereby to prejudice the health or survival of the population.

There is some discussion as to whether the provisions of Articles 35(3) and 55(1) apply to non-conventional warfare only, but this is not the case. Trying to come to a common understanding of the law when comparing Articles 35(3) and 55 is difficult. It appears that these two provisions, which seem to take different approaches, and hence lead to different results, may have been an attempt to satisfy both the intrinsic value and anthropocentric views of the environment. Article 35 takes an intrinsic value approach to environmental protection, not tying the protections to any value the environment provides to man. In contrast, Article 55 appears to take the same methodology in its passive environmental approach in the first sentence, but then allows for a de minimus exception to the intrinsic value approach when discussing the knowing or intentional use of the environment. This de minimus exception appears to embrace the anthropocentric view of environmental protection, at least in terms of active environmental warfare. The confusion caused by applying the standard of "which are intended, or may be expected" to the quantitative limitation of Article 35 and the qualitative limitation of Article 55 is resolved when properly analyzed under the principles of passive and active warfare.

As previously stated, the first sentence of Article 55 states the standard for passive environmental warfare. Any military operations must not have the passive results of such significant environmental degradation. The second sentence is encompassed by the prohibition on active environmental warfare. While it does not specifically deal with using the environment in the same terms as the ENMOD, an analysis of this provision provides the same results, leaving the de minimus exception for active actions that do not affect the sustainable environment.

To clarify, the second sentence to Article 55 appears to be a prohibition on targeting the environment rather than "using" the environment as the definition of active environmental warfare requires. But beginning with the assumption that the environment is a civilian object, it is inherently illegal to target the environment unless it becomes a military objective by its nature, location, purpose, or use, and there is a military necessity to attack. Assuming a commander can establish the military necessity to do so, he must still be able to show that the targeted portion of the environment meets the nature, location, purpose, or use test.

By its nature, the environment is not a military objective. Things such as weapons, equipment, transports, fortifications, and depots are military objects by their nature. The environment does not meet this definition. Nor could it be considered by its nature to be a "dual-use" target, one which serves both military and civilian purposes, as there is nothing intrinsic in the environment to make it such. Location requires a different analysis. These are objects that by their nature have no military function but which, by virtue of their location, make an effective contribution to military action. This may be, for example, a bridge or other construction, or it could also be... a site which is of special importance for military operations in view of its location, either because it is a site that must be seized or because it is important to prevent the enemy from seizing it, or otherwise because it is a matter of forcing the enemy to retreat from it.

It could certainly be that the movements of an enemy might make a commander consider attacking a portion of the environment based on the location of the enemy. For example, Saddam Hussein's lighting of oil wells in the first Gulf War to create a thick cloud of smoke to cover his retreat could possibly be justified under the location analysis of Article 52. As stated earlier, however, causing damage to the enemy or interference with an enemy military or combat activity by using the environment turns the environment into an instrument of warfare and is active environmental warfare. Hussein's targeting of the environment based on its location was really an active use of the environment because it was intended to have a direct effect on his enemy's combat activities.

Purpose is generally "concerned with the intended future use of an object" and would include such things as targeting buses that were on their way to military barracks to pick up troops and carry them to the front lines. For example, Hussein's fouling of the waters to prevent a potential amphibious landing is an attack on the environment based on the purpose to which the environment was going to be used.

Finally, intentionally targeting the environment may be based on its use by the enemy. The typical example of this is targeting forests or jungles that provide cover and concealment of enemy troop movements. Again, this type of attack is active environmental warfare because it causes damage to the enemy or interference with an enemy military or combat activity.

Therefore, intentional targeting of the environment, a civilian object, is in fact a "use" of the environment and fits within the definition of active environmental warfare. Such targeting should therefore be prohibited unless it is de minimus, meaning it will not affect the health or survival of the population or damage the sustainable environment.

This still leaves a discussion of Article 35.3 of the Protocol I, which prohibits "methods or means of warfare which are intended, or may be expected, to cause widespread, long-term and severe damage to the natural environment." Article 35's intrinsic value approach is laudable in principle but has been a significant contributor to the inability to enforce environmental standards. The Article's complete prohibition on active warfare actions only when they reach a quantitative level of damage provided a good basis upon which to build in 1977, but it has not produced sufficient clarity to provide the necessary deterrence or enforcement. The law of environmental warfare must take a step forward and remove the quantum portion when active environmental warfare is contemplated.

Continuing the comparison of Articles 35 and 55, it is significant that the Protocol lists the terms "widespread, long-term, and severe" in the conjunctive, meaning that all three requirements must be satisfied for a breach of the Protocol, causing some commentators to argue the destruction in World Wars I and II "would not have met this threshold requirement." In contrast, the disjunctive nature of the same terms in the ENMOD Convention illustrates the lower threshold of damage required to constitute a breach when dealing with the "active" use of the environment in warfare. This lower threshold of needing to satisfy only one of the elements will result in a violation of international environmental law at a much earlier stage of damage and will provide added protection to the environment.

Further, the meaning given to the terms "widespread, long-term, and severe" are also more relaxed than those of the ENMOD. Most experts agree with the commentary to GPI, which states that "long-term" should be measured in decades (twenty to thirty years). Although the other two terms remain largely subject to interpretation, a number of credible interpretations have been forwarded. Within GPI, the term "widespread" probably means several hundred square kilometres, as it does in the ENMOD Convention. While "severe" can be explained by Article 55's reference to any act that "prejudices the health or survival of the population."

It is important to remember that despite the lower threshold for damage, the ENMOD convention also requires that the acts be intentional, a threshold requirement of active environmental warfare.

The ENMOD Convention, although somewhat unique in its terms, represents the starting point for future active environmental warfare conventions and treaties. Its clear prohibition of wartime environmental modification techniques represents a significant stepping stone, moving the international community in the direction of greater environmental protection.

In 1992, the Second Review Conference of the ENMOD Convention answered some significant questions concerning the interpretation of the ENMOD Treaty. First, and most significant to this Article, the Conference determined that it did not matter whether the "damage" resulted from the technique that affected the modification or was caused by the environmental modification itself. Second, the Conference clearly stated that herbicides fall within the proscriptions of the ENMOD.

Although both the ENMOD and Protocol I seem reasonably clear when analyzed on their own, a combined analysis leads to some grave ambiguity. Given the trend toward increasing environmental protection, this recognized ambiguity is unhelpful and should be resolved. Some commentators have already urged that the "widespread, long-lasting, and severe" standard be discarded and a strict liability standard be applied. It is not unreasonable to advocate changes to terms that were molded almost thirty years ago at a time when warfare's effects on the environment were not so potentially catastrophic. Applying these well-known standards to the differentiation of active and passive warfare will resolve this ambiguity, allowing military commanders to understand the standard and apply it while conducting military operations.

By applying the quantum limitation on environmental damage to only passive environmental damage, commanders still must consider the environmental repercussions of all military operations. On the other hand, by removing the quantum portion from active environmental warfare, commanders cannot justify weaponizing the environment by claiming limited effects. Rather than a quantitative analysis, the qualitative analysis of damage to the sustainable environment is the appropriate examination when the environment is used to accomplish military purposes.

In addition to the ENMOD and Protocol I, there are other international agreements and pronouncements that deal with active environmental warfare. While less significant, they provide an indication of the path the law is taking. The 1981 Convention on Prohibitions or Restrictions on the Use of Certain Conventional Weapons which may be Deemed to be Excessively Injurious or to have Indiscriminate Effects (CCW) and some recent actions by the United Nations and other organizations are worthy of review. The CCW and its additional Protocols restrict the use of inhumane weapons. Protocol III of this convention, which concerns prohibitions and restrictions on the use of incendiary weapons, is particularly on point. Article 1 contains definitions, and Article 2 contains a specifically applicable provision: It is prohibited to make forests or other kinds of plant cover the object of attack by incendiary weapons except when such natural elements are used to cover, conceal or camouflage combatants or other military objectives or are themselves military objectives. Although this provision is weakened by the applicable exceptions of cover, etc., it is significant in the type of weapons that it encompasses. The key is that it protects a specific portion of the environment from a particular type of weapon. While carving out only a very small area, Protocol III illustrates that the international community realizes that the combined standards of ENMOD and Protocol I did not go far enough to protect the environment from active environmental warfare.

This realization that ENMOD and Protocol I were insufficient was also clearly demonstrated in the aftermath of Gulf War I. In response to the destruction of the first Gulf War, some nations resorted to overt acts (and sought them from others) to try and remove the doubt as to the existence of international law in the area of active environmental warfare. For example, Jordan proposed that the forty-sixth session of the United Nations General Assembly (1991) consider the "[e]xploitation of the environment as a weapon in times of armed conflict." Although the scope of this suggestion was later broadened to include general protection for the environment in times of war, much of what came from the efforts of the United Nations Sixth Committee and further consideration by the United Nations General Assembly directly affects on active environmental warfare. For instance, the International Committee of the Red Cross (ICRC) raised again the call for greater clarification between the previously mentioned provisions of the ENMOD Convention and Protocol 1153 prohibiting environmental destruction that is widespread, long-lasting, and/or severe.

This response to recent developments and the prolific discussion in academic journals, as well as at least ten meetings of experts in the field, provide ample evidence that this is an area of deep concern in international law. More clarification and increased action can be expected in the future and is needed for the standard of environmental protection to be sufficient.

The recent adoption of the Rome Statute and formation of the International Criminal Court provided an opportunity to resolve some of this ambiguity and clarify wartime environmental protections. Unfortunately, that opportunity was missed. The Rome Statute criminalizes active environmental warfare by making intentional infliction of harm to the environment a "war crime," but it is prosecutable only if it is done as "part of a plan or policy or as part of a large-scale commission of such crime[]." Further, the Rome Statute follows Protocol I with no additional definition of the elements of "widespread, long-term, [and] severe."

Although not nearly as exhaustive as passive environmental warfare documents, the ENMOD Convention, Protocol I, the CCW, and the Rome Statute set the baseline and create some conventional law standards for active environmental warfare, both as to the mens rea of the parties and as to the resulting effects. The effectiveness of these documents in controlling environmental warfare has been limited, however, and has caused at least some commentators to conclude that they fail to provide "an unambiguous, cohesive approach to the international problem of wartime environmental destruction." There is a need for additional clarification, particularly in the area of active environmental warfare, if the environment is to be meaningfully protected during times of armed conflict.

For example, even though Saddam Hussein's actions did not violate the ENMOD convention, they certainly violated the "intended or may be expected" standard of Protocol I. There is no doubt that Hussein intended to cause environmental harm. But as many commentators have concluded, it is far from agreed that Hussein's actions violated international law or the law of war, despite his intentional destruction of the environment because of the quantum of damage requirement. Whether or not he is an "eco-criminal," the world's reaction was insufficient to prevent him from engaging in similar activities again.

Despite the world's inability to deter Hussein, there is "strong indicia of a general and consistent practice among states [of] prohibiting ecological warfare, and of acceptance by signatory states of a legal obligation to refrain from attacking the natural environment. The shortage of modern treaty or convention law, the corresponding scarcity of international custom, and the fluid nature of international law generally make coming to a precise conclusion concerning the current status of the law in the area of active environmental warfare problematic. The disjunctive wording of the ENMOD Treaty, however, provides strong evidence that a lower threshold of action is allowed when active environmental warfare is at issue.

Further, the recent trends illustrated by the work of the ICRC and the United Nations provide an indication that world opinion is strongly opposed to any use of the environment as a weapon during hostilities. That there has been neither derogation from the ENMOD convention to present day by its signatories nor any act that would be considered a violation by non-signatories (continuing arguments concerning Iraq's actions excepted)—and that many recent treaties and conventions attempt to codify such a principle—indicates that a customary norm against active environmental warfare now exists.

Military Necessity

Even if the law of environmental warfare were clear, some have argued that the environment would still not be sufficiently protected because of the doctrine of military necessity (as found in the 1907 Hague Rules), which requires a commander to balance destruction of the environment, along with other property, against the military necessity of the action. A commander may destroy civilian property, including the environment, only if he deems there is a sufficient military purpose. In fact, this doctrine is so fundamental to military operations that one commentator has stated "[o]nly one obligation in the law of war actually relates to the environment: The prohibition on the destruction of enemy property that is not justified by military necessity." Others argue, "[m]ilitary necessity has... become the main justification for deviation from restrictions in customary law.... While a number of principles relate to protection of the environment during warfare, they are all subordinated to the principle of military necessity."

Historically, military necessity has been used to justify attacks against the environment. For example, military necessity was used to justify attacks on dams in North Korea but to preclude attacks on others. Some argued that Saddam Hussein used military necessity as his justification for intentionally destroying the environment in Gulf War I. Detractors of the military necessity doctrine, particularly as it relates to protections for the environment, argue "[i]f there is no information in [the commander's] consciousness about the potential environmental effects of his or her action, how can he or she be expected to validly use a military necessity balancing test? If one side of the balance is always perceived as zero, the scale will always tip in the other direction—military necessity."

Compounding the problem, "the risks of normative imprecision grow when retroactive judgments on reasonableness and necessity are required." A commander's application of military necessity is based on the facts as he knows them at the time of decision, after sufficient attempts to gain all possible information. Reviewing a commander's decision, including a determination of what information he knew and had available to him at the time of the decision, is not the most effective means of protecting the environment.

Of vital importance in this area, however, is the fact that military necessity is not a justification for violating the law of war. This is particularly important when considering the value of differentiating between active and passive environmental warfare. While the doctrine of military necessity is an important consideration when a commander considers the passive environmental effects of his military actions, non de minimus active environmental warfare is a violation of the law of war per se and could not, therefore, be justified by the doctrine of military necessity.

When considering the passive environmental effects of warfare, a commander must balance his proposed actions between the amount of damage those actions might cause and the necessity of the military action. Once the results of his actions have reached the GPI standard of widespread, long-term and severe, he can no longer justify his actions by military necessity because GPI has set "an absolute ceiling of permissible destruction" to the environment. "In other words, once the threshold is reached, the action violates the prescriptions even if it is militarily necessary and clearly proportional under traditional balancing tests." In contrast, active environmental warfare cannot be justified by military necessity as it violates the law of war. Attacks in which environmental harm is the primary goal, whether by forcing an axe against trees which produce fruit or by spraying defoliants on tropical rainforests from airplanes, has invariably met with condemnation. Attacks in which damage to the environment is an unsought consequence of the achievement of some other objective, such as the impairment of an enemy's ability to produce weapons, has generally been excused on the basis of "military necessity."

Some have argued that there is a danger in minimizing the application of military necessity in favor of environmental protection. One commentary rightly asks, "On what grounds can we justify a categorization that makes humanity less worthy of protection than the rest of the ecosystem?" The authors pose the hypothetical situation of international environmental law proscriptions forcing a commander to "launch an attack through a village rather than around it to avoid Article 35(3) damage to a large, environmentally fragile area on the village's outskirts." It is likely "that a commander would not be expected to sacrifice a soldier to save a tree."

Distinguishing between the application of military necessity to passive and active environmental warfare solves this problem. Because the destruction of the environmentally protected area to avoid killing innocent civilians would come under a passive environmental analysis, the commander would balance military necessity against the necessity of the action unless he determined that his actions reached the GPI standard of widespread, long-term, and severe damage. In contrast, because active environmental warfare deals with choices of means and methods of warfare, if the commander's choice was between an active use of the environment against the enemy and some other method or means, he could not rely on military necessity and would be forced to attack some other way.

Thus, the doctrine of military necessity remains intact for passive environmental damage, allowing a commander to balance accomplishing the mission against incidental damage to the environment until it reaches the standard of widespread, long-term, and severe damage. But military necessity is no defence to active environmental damage because it is a violation of the law of war per se.

THE NEED FOR CHANGE

All wars are destructive—to people, to countries and to the environment. That is why the Geneva Conventions and Protocols and other international laws discourage the worst excesses of armed conflict, including the targeting of civilians, the mistreatment of prisoners of war, and the destruction of sensitive infrastructure such as large dams and nuclear power stations.

However, with the increasingly devastating potential of modern warfare, it has become apparent that existing international laws do not fully address the danger that conflict poses to the environment. That danger takes many forms, including the indiscriminate use of landmines, the ecological destruction caused by mass movements of refugees, and the potential devastation threatened by weapons of mass destruction. While instances in which the environment is deliberately targeted are relatively few, there remain too many grey areas where more care could, and should, be exercised to protect the environmental base on which sustainable development and recovery from conflict largely depend.... [T]he international community... [should] examine how legal and other mechanisms can be strengthened to encourage environmental protection in wartime. Ensuring environmental sustainability is no a luxury; it is a prerequisite for the future peace and prosperity of our planet.

There is no doubt that international law is moving in the direction of greater protection for the environment in all situations, including warfare. But this may be a very slow and unguided process. An excellent starting point is recognition by the international community of the distinction between active and passive environmental damage. If this distinction were written into future treaties and conventions and discussed openly and fully by state governments and in United Nations Declarations and Resolutions, it would quickly become a usable standard by which environmental damage could be differentiated. Once differentiated, the appropriate remedies could be tied to specific acts of active and passive damage and a regimen for enforcement implemented. Crucial to effective enforcement of international wartime environmental standards, as shown by the international community's inability to act after the first Gulf War, is a clear understanding of what constitutes a violation and how severe that violation is. The categorization of wartime environmental damage as active or passive on the international level will be a significant step in that process.

A PROPOSED SOLUTION

A beginning effort in enhancing the wartime protections for the environment is the following proposal for a Convention on the Protection of the Environment During Armed Conflict. Although some have argued for a fifth Geneva Convention, this would not be the best solution. Two of the hallmarks of the four Geneva Conventions of 1949 are Articles 2 and 3. These Articles, known as "common" articles because they are identical in all four Conventions, define the application of the conventions, making them only applicable in cases of international armed conflict. Any new proposal to protect the environment must be fashioned to protect it in all types of armed conflict, not just those between two states. Similarly, calls for a Protocol V to the CCW would also fall short of the desired coverage because this convention is also limited in scope to international armed conflict.

To truly provide the breadth of protection required for the environment, a new international agreement is necessary. It must govern all forms of armed conflict and not be subject to modification or derogation by domestic law. It must be built on the distinction between passive and active damage to the environment and confirm the application of existing principles to passive armed conflict while expanding and clarifying the prohibitions on use of the environment as a method of armed conflict. Such a convention would resolve the confusion that currently exists and provide a solid foundation upon which to build remedies for violations of the law.

8

Foreign Policy and Antitrust

Prior to the outbreak of the Second World War, the Department of Justice had initiated an investigation of alleged worldwide oil cartel activities. Information concerning these activities had been obtained through file searches conducted under grand jury subpoenas in 1940 and 1941 but this investigation was suspended during the Second World War. The investigation was given a new impetus after the war by the public hearings of the Special Committee of the Senate Investigating the National Defence Program. In late 1949, the Federal Trade Commission passed a resolution to investigate "agreements entered into by American petroleum companies among themselves and with petroleum companies of other nations in connection with foreign operations and with international trade in petroleum and petroleum products" and the Antitrust Division suspended its inquiry pending completion of this report.

The Federal Trade Commission staff filed its report in October 1951. However, the report was not published by the Commission because of national security objections. After repeated demands for its release by Senator John Sparkman, Chairman of the Select Committee on Small Business, it was furnished to and published by that Committee (minus certain sections which were excised for national security reasons). In the Committee's preface to the Report, Senator Sparkman stated: "Today the power of the international oil companies is so vast as to invite its abuse... The Senate Small Business Committee believes that it is the basic philosophy of the United

States to oppose monopolistic concentrations of economic power. Practically alone among the great nations of the world the United States-through fact finding and through enforcement of its antitrust laws-endeavors to hold in check the powers of giant orgamzations."

On the basis of this report, Attorney General McGranery determined that further investigation by Grand Jury process was necessary and recommended such action to President Truman. On June 23, 1952, the President instructed the Department of Justice to initiate the Grand Jury Investigation, and the Attorney General convened a special grand jury in the district of Columbia and appointed Leonard Emerglick, Chief of the Foreign Commerce Section of the Antitrust Division of the Department of Justice to investigate and prosecute the case. Subpoenas to produce documents were served upon 21 oil companies including the seven major ones: Exxon, Socal, Mobil, Texaco, British Petroleum Company, Royal Dutch-Shell and Gulf. But at the same time as the grand jury investigation was proceeding, an international political crisis was developing in Iran which had a direct bearing on the prosecution of the case.

TROUBLE IN IRAN

Outside of the Arab oil producing states, Iran was the major source of Middle East oil. The Iranian concession had been held by British Petroleum (BP), since that company's formation in 1909. In addition to selling its oil in Great Britain and to the Royal Navy, BP had developed important European markets. Hence, Iranian oil was considered vital to the economic well-being of Western Europe.

Dispute Between Iran and BP

In the aftermath of the Second World War, Iran had become progressively dissatisfied with the amount of revenues derived from BP. In October of 1947, the Iranian parliament enacted an oil law which, among other things, required the government to renegotiate the terms of the 1933 concession. This was done, and on July 17, 1949, a Supplemental Oil Agreement was initiated providing Iran with a more favourable financial arrangement than any other oil producing country in the area. A year later, the Oil Commission of the Iranian Parliament

(Majlis), under the Chairmanship of Dr. Muhammed Mossadeq, recommended its rejection. Despite American efforts at compromise, BP, supported by the British Government, refused to budge an inch further, and the Majlis refused to accept the agreement. In March 1951, the Majlis unanimously passed a nationalization bill. By May, Mossadeq was Prime Minister and the British were out of Iran.

Soon after the nationalization, Iran organized a corporation, the National Iranian Oil Company (NIOC), for the purpose of exploiting the BP concession and selling the oil. But the major oil companies refused to market its oil, supplying the European markets instead with oil from Saudi Arabia and Kuwait. In Iran, oil production came to a standstill and the country was thrown into political and economic turmoil. This turmoil led to an apparent increase in the political strength of the Tudeh party in Iran which had close ties with the Soviet Union. Increasingly, it appeared that as a consequence of the nationalization of BP and the inability to arrive at a settlement with the company, Iran, which in 1946 had been kept out of the Soviet orbit, might now fall under Soviet influence. This fear led the Truman Administration to attempt to bring about a settlement of the dispute between BP and the Government of Iran.

EARLY AMERICAN ATTEMPTS AT SETTLEMENT

On June 27, 1951, just a month after the nationalization, President Truman approved NSC 107/2, which made the following statement of U.S. Policy: Bring (U.S.) influence to bear in an effort to effect an early settlement of the oil controversy between Iran and the United Kingdom, making clear both our recognition of the rights of sovereign states to control their natural resources and the importance we attach to international contractual relationships. As early as May 1951 the United States had warned Britain against the use of force in Iran, but the fact of nationalization and subsequent hostile acts on both sides compelled the State Department to take further action.

On July 4, 1952 Secretary of State Acheson, British Ambassador Oliver Franks, George McGhee, Paul Nitze and Averell Harriman met at Harriman's Washington home to discuss the Iranian question. According to Acheson: "Sir Oliver left no doubt how seriously and angrily both the British Government and public viewed what they regarded as the insolent defiance of decency, legality and reason by a wild group of men in Iran who, proposed to despoil Britain." As a consequence of this meeting, Harriman was dispatched to Tehran to attempt to construct a formula within which a settlement could be worked out. But the negotiations which he helped begin were doomed when the British publicly revealed their negotiating position, and had it publicly rejected by Mossadeq. Meanwhile, American neutrality in the affair was compromised by the attitude of the American companies toward lifting Iranian oil.

Development of an American Alternative

Throughout early 1951, American attempts at settling the Iranian controversy were based on the concept of restoring BP as sole concessionaire. As it became apparent that this would not be possible, the Administration began to explore the possibility of enlisting the major American oil companies in a joint venture arrangement with BP.

On October 8, 1952, Secretary Acheson outlined a plan to the Secretaries of Defence and Treasury, the Attorney General and the Chairman of the Joint Chiefs of Staff. Acheson said that "no one other than the majors and... (BP) had sufficient tankers to move large volumes of Iranian oil." He raised the question whether the majors should be asked to move Iranian oil. Attorney General McGranery's reaction was that Acheson had "presented a most formidable legal meal. It would be most difficult to work out a program involving the majors and at the same time maintain the present antitrust action." He concluded, however, that the basic problem was whether the national interest in finding a solution to the Iranian crisis was more important than the principles involved in the suit.

Despite the Attorney General's qualms, Secretary of Defence Robert Lovett also argued that the possibility of using the five major companies to move Iran's oil should be explored. "This would involve some action to get around the present obstacle of the government suit against those companies. However, there is no doubt in my mind that the interests of the U.S. in connection with the present Iranian crisis requires (sic) some such action." In his reply, Secretary Acheson agreed that: One of the concrete problems in securing a resumption of the flow of Iranian oil is to determine whom it is we can call on, and who is able in fact, to move Iranian oil in the volume which is required to save Iran. The independents are not in a position to give us any real help.

On November 26, 1952, President Truman requested the Secretary of State to:... engage urgently in exploratory discussion with representatives of United States oil companies and with the Anglo-Iranian Oil Company... in order, determine what type of agreement and program would be most likely to contribute to the national defence by leading to a solution of this (Iranian oil) situation.

The Departments representative, Paul Nitze, talked to representatives of Standard Oil of California, Standard Oil of New Jersey, Texas, Socony Vacuum, and Gulf. He described political developments in Iran and stated that the cooperation of the major companies operating in the Eastern Hemisphere might soon be needed. But the companies that the Department of State hoped to induce to participate in such an Iranian Consortium were precisely the same companies that were being investigated by the Grand Jury for possible criminal violation of the antitrust laws of the United States. The incongruity of the situation was apparent: one part of the Administration-the Justice Department-had convened a grand jury to investigate alleged criminal antitrust violations arising out of the major's Middle East operations. Another part of the same Government-the State Department-sought to enlist the cooperation of the very same companies, by reason of their Middle East operations, in solving the Iranian problem. The issue came to a head in the closing days of the Truman Administration in the National Security Council on January 9, 1953.

DEBATE WITHIN THE NATIONAL SECURITY COUNCIL

Their argument began by noting the critical importance of petroleum in the modern world. "With the increase in demand that will occur under war conditions, the successful conduct of a major war by the United States and its allies will be dependent upon continuing availability of foreign petroleum supplies."

Even in peacetime, "major sources of foreign oil are, now indispensable to the economy of Europe and in the future may become indispensable even to the peacetime economy of the United States." Yet, there were only two known areas which could supply the necessary quantities of this petroleum, Venezuela and the Middle East. While Venezuela was important for our domestic supply in time of war, the Middle East was important for the supply of Europe in time of peace. "Since Venezuela and the Middle East are the only sources from which the free world's import requirements for petroleum can be supplied... nothing can be allowed to interfere substantially with the availability of oil from these sources to the free world." It was vitally important that these two remaining areas of available free world imports not fall under Communist control. Yet, turning to the Middle East, this danger seemed real and present.

The oil producing states of the Middle East "are on or near the borders of the Soviet Union," and because of certain local conditions, "the Middle East comprises one of the most explosive areas of the world." Since oil is "the principal source of wealth and income in the Middle Eastern countries in which the deposits exist," the "economic and political existence" of these countries "depends upon the rate and terms on which oil is produced." Since the rate and terms in question are to a large extent under the control of the oil companies operating in the area, the "American oil operations are, for all practical purposes, instruments of our foreign policy toward these countries."

Just as important is their role in dealing with the, Arabs, however, is the companies' role in dealing with the Europeans. The terms on which they supply western Europe with oil "are critical to the strength and balance-of-payments position of this area which is vital to our security."

Because of their role as an instrument of our foreign policy both in Europe and the Middle East, any attack on our oil companies would be viewed in those areas as a fundamental attack on the whole American system. "We cannot afford to leave unchallenged the assertions that these companies are engaged in a criminal conspiracy for the purposes of predatory exploration." To do so, would leave the companies at the mercy of their critics in the producing countries, the report stated.

Hence, the "entire situation," i.e., criminal prosecution, is "fraught with great potential danger to the U.S.... in both Venezuela and the Middle East a wave of economic nationalism which might endanger American interests is entirely possible." Moreover, the report went on, the pursuit of the criminal investigation by the grand jury could jeopardize the cooperative relationship which existed between the Department of State and the petroleum companies:

In many fields no legal or formal control over the action of American private interests abroad is exercised by this Government. This is in accord with the view that a minimum of regulation and control is an accepted American principle. On the other hand, this means that if Government and industry are to act together to promote foreign policy and security objectives in petroleum there must be a basis of mutual confidence between them. Criminal proceedings are not likely to produce such confidence between the two parties in this dispute.

The report thus recommended that, regardless of what might eventually be worked out with regard to Iran, the criminal investigation be dropped an a civil suit initiated. In this way, said the report, "a trial might well be avoided and hence the great reduction in the number of possible sensational disclosures brought about." The report further recommended the formation of a Presidential Commission composed of the Secretaries of State, Defence, Interior and Commerce, to "give careful attention to the interrelationships of antitrust, security and foreign policies in petroleum." The Attorney General was to be invited to attend the sessions of the Commission "to the extent considered appropriate by him and the Commission."

The Department of Justice opposed the recommendation to abandon the criminal investigation. The Department noted that its earlier investigative efforts had revealed the outline of a world oil cartel formed as early as 1928 by one American and two foreign oil companies which over the succeeding years had been joined by other American oil companies: The cartel arrangements are in effect private treaties negotiated by private companies to whom the profit incentive is paramount. The national security should rest instead upon decisions made by the Government with primary concern for the national interest.

A civil antitrust suit in the opinion of the Department, was inadequate if the cartel was to be attacked effectively: "The discovery process in a civil suit is a great deal more cumbersome and could be drawn out over an extended period of time by an infinite variety of legal motions designed to delay and wear down the Department. The grand jury investigation, on the other hand, would permit the Department to uncover all of the relevant facts in a substantially shorter time."

Finally, the Justice Department argued: "The facts presently available strongly suggest that the high policy represented by the Sherman Act has been consciously and persistently violated by activities long since determined by the Supreme Court to be illegal. The cartel should be prosecuted criminally if there is to be equal justice under the law and if respect for the law and its even-handed administration is to be maintained."

This debate thus laid bare the differing assumptions which have continued to this day with respect to the operations of the major oil companies in the Middle East. For the Department of State, U.S. national and company interests were coincidental, not divergent; the companies were effective instruments of U.S. policy by reason of their American nationality; Hence, control of the Middle Eastern concessions by the American concerns was equivalent to U.S. national control. Finally, as they were instruments of our foreign policy, the companies could not be subject to criminal prosecution without undermining the basis of that policy.

For the Justice Department, on the other hand, enforcement of a national competition policy was primary and to the extent that the companies contravened that policy in a manner which directly and substantially impacted upon the domestic economy, the companies were acting in a manner contrary to the U.S. national interest, and contrary to the laws which the Department was sworn to enforce. The issue had to be resolved by President Truman.

The Decision

The National Security Council meeting to discuss whether the criminal investigation should be terminated took place on January 9, 1953, a Friday. On Sunday evening, January 11, President Truman sent for Mr. Ernmerglick of the Justice

Department and Charles Bohlen of the State Department and met with them in his private quarters. As Emmerglick described it, President Truman informed them that he wished the grand jury investigation terminated, that he had reached his decision "with great reluctance and that he was constrained to take that decision not on the advice of those Cabinet members who attended the Security Council meetings, but solely oil the assurance of General Omar Bradley that national Security called for that action." He emphasized, however, that he wished the case to be pursued vigorously in the civil courts.

By letter dated January 12, 1953, President Truman formally advised Attorney General McGranery of his decision. The Department of Justice terminated the grand jury investigation and filed a civil complaint on the 21st of April, 1953 in the U.S. District Court of the District of Columbia.

The Civil Complaint

The essence of the government's case was that the "as is" agreement formed in 1928 continued at least up to the date of the civil. Complaint without modification of its essential terms in direct restraint of the foreign commerce of the U.S. in petroleum and its products:

The objective of the conspiracy was market stabilization; its essential terms were market division and price fixing, both *per se* unreasonable restraints under the Sherman Act. Other terms, such as those dealing with the elimination of outside competition, sales and exchanges for mutual convenience and controlling expenses by avoiding the duplication of facilities, had the effect of implementing the agreed upon objective of market stabilization."

The Government's statement of claims, in sum, said: It appears that the uninterrupted extension and continuance of the basic cartel agreements has resulted in a world-wide pattern in which seven of the major oil companies-(1) control all major oil producing areas outside the states; (2) control all foreign refining operations; (3) control patents, know-how and technology covering the refining processes; (4) effectively divide world markets; (5) maintain noncompetitive world prices for oil and its products; and (6) control foreign pipeline and world tanker transportation facilities.

August 1953-The Fall of Mossadeq

In August, 1953, however, barely a few months after the filing of the civil complaint, the, Iranian situation boiled to a climax. Mossadeq was intransigent on the principle of Iran's right to reclaim control over its main source of wealth. Unable or unwilling to effect a settlement with BP, unable to market its oil, the Mossadeq Government found itself in perpetual financial crisis. When the Parliament refused to grant Mossadeq's demands that it extend for one year his right to govern by decree, a wave of demonstrations swept the country. Mossadeq directly challenged the Shah, ordered a plebiscite to dissolve Parliament and won more than 99 percent of the votes cast and counted. In a swiftly moving series of events, the Shah attempted to oust Mossadeq by decree, failed, and fled the country as Mossadeq's supporters demonstrated in the streets, smashing the statues of the Shah and his father. The military moved in, and in bloody street fighting desposed Mossadeq and restored the Shah to Ins throne, a move which was assisted clandestinely by the U.S. Central Intelligence Ageney.

The Foreign Office Gropes for a Strategy

After Mossadeq was disposed, in August, 1954, a series of high level talks oil Middle East oil were initiated at the request of the British Government between the State Department and the British Foreign Office. What concerned the British and led them to request those meetings was the increasing dependence of Western Europe on Middle Eastern oil: "These problems are, therefore, highly strategic and political, not just economic in nature and scope," urged the British representatives. The problem the British wished to discuss with the American representatives was the coordination of American and British companies' and governments' efforts to avoid sawing by the various producing countries, who the British noted, increasingly were acting with a high degree of cohesion. The British representatives suggested various alternative methods of coordination between companies and consuming governments. They specifically noted that "the UK was not primarily concerned in protecting the profit position of the British companies." The UK Government was more interested in improving its relations with and stabilizing conditions in the countries concerned in order to insure the smooth flow of oil. The British suggestions ranged from consultations among companies to arrive at joint negotiating positions, formation of all international oil Petroleum Council consisting of consuming and producing countries, and biannual coordination meetings between the U.S. and British Governments. Each of these suggested modes of coordination, however, was flawed in some way: consultations among the companies involved antitrust problems in the U.S.; an International Petroleum Council risked encouraging producer/consumer country confrontation and accelerated coordination among the Arab countries; the U.S. Government was cool to direct U.S. Government involvement with the producing country governments on oil matters: "Aramco's position had in the past been fairly strong with the Saudi Arabian Government because it had stood on its own feet and maintained its position separate and apart from the U.S. Government." In effect, the Administration made two decisions. First, it had decided that the role of the Government was to put the companies in a position where they could decide international oil matters: price, supply, allocation, planning. Second, it had concluded that British fears as to the eventual dangers of competition among producer nations for higher government takes were unjustified.

Herbert Hoover, Jr. Seeks a Solution

On August 6, 1953, President Eisenhower requested that the Attorney General "seek to develop a solution which would protect the interests of the free world in the Near East as a vital source of petroleum supplies." The terms of reference under which the Attorney General was to seek this solution were explicitly stated in an NSC directive: It will be assumed that the enforcement of the antitrust laws of the United States against the Western oil companies operating in the Near East may be deemed secondary to the national security interest to be served by:

1. Assuring the continued availability to the free world of the sources of petroleum in the near East and
2. Assuring continued friendly relations between the oil producing nations of the Near East and the nations of the free world.

Thus, the attitude of the Truman Administration as to the secondary importance of the antitrust laws governed the actions of the Eisenhower Administration from the outset. However, it soon became apparent that the solution to the Iranian problem had been taken out of the hands of the Attorney General. By letter dated October 9, 1953, Robert Cutler, Special Assistant to the President, informed Secretary of State Dulles that: "... Mr. Herbert Hoover, Jr., is acting as a Special Representative of the United States Government, within the Department of State, to deal with problems related to an Anglo-Truman oil settlement."

On October, 27, 1953, the National Security Council formally revoked the August 6 instruction to the Attorney General to seek a solution to the oil problem in the Middle East and directed that this responsibility be transferred to the Department of State."

THE ROLE OF CONGRESS

Consideration of the fundamental issues-the U.S. national security interest in Iran and its relationship to the American antitrust laws-took place largely within the Executive Branch. The issues were debated in the Congress. The Administration did, however, inform the relevant leaders of Congress of its decision. On January 22, 1954, one day after the crucial NSC decision, Vice President Nixon, Secretary of Defence Wilson, Secretary of the Navy Anderson, Admiral Radford, Chairman of the Joint Chiefs of Staff, Actmg Secretary of State Bedell Smith, and Herbert Hoover, Jr. met with a group of congressional leaders to discuss the new Iranian initiative. Nine members of Congress attended the meeting-among them the majority and minority leaders of the House and Senate, the Chairman and ranking minority member of the Senate Foreign Relations Committee, and others.

"Recent National Security Council decisions in connection with the proposed oil consortium were frankly discussed according to the State Department's record. The Attorney General's opinion was made dear. No objection was raised by any Member of Congress concerning the decision and the course of action contemplated. Substantial interest was expressed in the matter of possible imports to the Western Hemisphere from

Iranian resources. Secretary Anderson pointed out emphatically that the production developed in Iran would replace other Eastern Hemisphere production and the sale of oil and petroleum products from Iran would be in the Eastern Hemisphere."

The Oil Import Quota

Control of the Consortium by the major companies raised fears among the American independent oil producers that their competitive position would be undermined by the majors' importation of cheap Iranian oil into the United States. (Iran before the nationalization in 1951 had been the largest oil exporter in the Middle East.) In response to this concern, Senator Lyndon Johnson, who bad attended the January, 1954 meeting, addressed a letter to Secretary of State John Foster Dulles:

Oil producers in Texas are raising the question as to whether there has been any violation of agreements — written, spoken or implied — by the companies authorized to engage in the consortium. It has been their understanding, and mine, that care was to be taken to see that this oil did not serve to jeopardize the position of American independents in supplying domestic requirements. Are assurances to this effect still to be considered valid? It is reported that several independent members of the Iranian consortium have exchanged their shares of Abadan refined products for Persian Gulf crude, the explanation for the trade being that the crude can be imported into the United States at tariff considerably below the tariff for refined products."

Two years later, in order to protect the domestic industry, first voluntary and then mandatory crude oil import quotas were imposed by the Eisenhower Administration. The higher cost of domestic oil was justified on the grounds that the import quota system ensured that the domestic industry would continue to develop domestic sources of supply so that the United States would never become unduly dependent upon unstable foreign sources of crude oil. In the actuality, the U.S. forewent the advantage of cheap imported oil but, as the 1971 Tehran negotiations showed, it did not derive the benefit of spare capacity which could be rapidly brought on stream.

The Fate of the Cartel Case

The Justice Department attack on the majors' control of international oil through the joint production ventures in the Middle East, one of the critical points in the Justice Department's cartel case, became a casualty of the successful resolution of the foreign policy problem of stabilizing the political situation in Iran. As Attorney General Brownell had predicted, the case proceeded with emphasis on the marketing aspects and not on the production control aspects. The result can be seen in a comparison of the complaint in the Cartel case with the Statement of Claims. The latter was prepared by the Antitrust Division in 1961 in preparation for trial. Unlike the complaint, this document focuses entirely on the market control aspect of the cartel with only slight and sparing mention of joint producing and refining arrangements. Yet this occurred at the very time when the primary focus of the majors market Control efforts had shifted-as explained in the next part of this report-into control of production.

The cartel case dragged on in this vitiated form for another ten years and was finally settled by consent decrees but these decrees did not impair the major companies' ability jointly to control production and through production, the world market. Mr. EMMERGLICK: I believe that the consent decrees accomplished very little, if anything. They were cosmetic, and nothing more than that, in my opinion. So that the same power structure and the same joint arrangements between companies which should be competing exist today as existed then.

9

Modern Warfare

Modern warfare, although present in every historical period of military history, is generally used to refer to the concepts, methods and technologies that have come into use during and after the Second World War and the Korean War. The concepts and methods have assumed more complex forms of the 19th and early-20th century antecedents largely due to the widespread use of highly advanced information technology. Although Total war was thought to be the form of international conflicts from the experience of the French Revolutionary Wars to the Second World War, the term no longer describes warfare in which countries or nations use all of their resources to destroy another country's or nation's organized ability to engage in war. The practice of total war which had been in use for over a century, as a form of war policy has been changed dramatically with greater awareness of tactical, operational and strategic battle information.

The most identifiable consequence of total war in modern times has been the inclusion of civilians and civilian infrastructure as targets in destroying a country's ability to engage in war. The targeting of civilians developed from two distinct theories. The first theory was that if enough civilians were killed, factories could not function. The second theory was that if civilians were killed, the country would be so demoralized that it would have no ability to wage further war. However UNICEF reports that civilian fatalities are down from 20 percent prior to 1900 AD to less than 5 per cent of fatalities in the wars beginning in the 1990s. With the advent of nuclear weapons, the concept of full-scale war carries the prospect of global annihilation, and as such conflicts since WWII have by definition been "low intensity" conflicts, typically in the form of proxy wars fought within local regional confines, using what are now referred to as "conventional weapons," typically combined with the use of asymmetric warfare tactics and applied use of intelligence. More recently the US Department of Defence introduced a concept of Battlespace as the integrated information management of all significant factors that impact on combat operations by armed forces for the military theatre of operations, including information, air, land, sea and space. It includes the environment, factors and conditions that must be understood to successfully apply combat power, protect the force, or complete the mission. This includes enemy and friendly forces; facilities; weather; terrain; and the electromagnetic spectrum within the operational areas and areas of interest.

Types

Some argue that the changing forms of three-dimensional warfare represents nothing more than an evolution of earlier technology.

Asymmetric

A military situation in which two belligerents of unequal strength interact and take advantage of their respective strengths and weaknesses. This interaction often involves strategies and tactics outside the bounds of conventional warfare, often referred to as terrorism.

Biological

Biological warfare, also known as germ warfare, is the use of any organism (bacteria, virus or other disease-causing organism) or toxin found in nature, as a weapon of war. It is meant to incapacitate or kill an adversary. It may also be defined as the employment of biological agents to produce casualties in man or animals and damage to plants or material; or defence against such employment.

Chemical

Chemical warfare is warfare (associated military operations) using the toxic properties of chemical substances to kill, injure or incapacitate an enemy.

Electronic

Electronic warfare refers to mainly nonviolent practices used chiefly to support other areas of warfare. The term was originally coined to encompass the interception and decoding of enemy radio communications, and the communications technologies and cryptography methods used to counter such interception, as well as jamming, radio stealth and other related areas. Over the later years of the twentieth century and early years of the twenty-first century this has expanded to cover a wide range of areas: the use of, detection of and avoidance of detection by Radar and Sonar systems, computer hacking, Space warfare etc.

Fourth generation

Fourth generation warfare (4GW) is a concept defined by William S. Lind and expanded by Thomas X. Hammes, used to describe the decentralized nature of modern warfare. The simplest definition includes any war in which one of the major participants is not a state but rather a violent ideological network. Fourth Generation wars are characterized by a blurring of the lines between war and politics, soldier and civilian, conflict and peace, battlefield and safety.

While this term is similar to terrorism and asymmetric warfare, it is much narrower. Classical insurgencies and the Indian Wars are examples of Pre-Modern War, not 4GW. Fourth generation warfare usually has the insurgency group or non-state side trying to implement their own government or reestablish an old government over the one currently running the territory. The blurring of lines between state and non-state is further complicated in a democracy by the power of the media.

Ground

Ground warfare involves three types of combat units, Infantry, Armor and Artillery. Infantry in modern times would consist of Mechanized infantry and Airborne forces. Usually having a type of rifle or sub-machine gun, an infantryman is the basic unit of an army.

Armored warfare in modern times involves a variety of Armored fighting vehicles for the purpose of battle and support.

Tanks or other armored vehicles (such as armored personnel carriers or tank destroyers) are slower, yet stronger hunks of metal. They are invulnerable to enemy machine gun fire but prone to rocket infantry, mines, and aircraft so are usually accompanied by infantry. In urban areas, because of smaller space, an armored vehicle is exposed to hidden enemy infantry but as the so called "Thunder Run" at Baghdad in 2003 showed, armored vehicles can play a critical role in urban combat. In rural areas, an armored vehicle does not have to worry about hidden units though muddy and damp terrain have always been a factor of weakness for Armored tanks and vehicles.

Artillery in contemporary times, is distinguished by its large calibre, firing an explosive shell or rocket, and being of such a size and weight as to require a specialized mount for firing and transport. Weapons covered by this term include "tube" artillery such as the howitzer, cannon, mortar, and field gun and "rocket" artillery. The term "artillery" has traditionally not been used for projectiles with internal guidance systems, even though some artillery units employ surface-to-surface missiles. Recent advances in terminal guidance systems for small munitions has allowed large calibre shells to be fitted with precision guidance fuses, blurring this distinction.

Guerrilla

Guerrilla warfare is defined as fighting by groups of irregular troops (guerrillas) within areas occupied by the enemy. When guerrillas obey the laws of conventional warfare they are entitled, if captured, to be treated as ordinary prisoners of war; however, they are often executed by their captors. The tactics of guerrilla warfare stress deception and ambush, as opposed to mass confrontation, and succeed best in an irregular, rugged, terrain and with a sympathetic populace, whom guerrillas often seek to win over or dominate by propaganda, reform, and terrorism. Guerrilla warfare has played a significant role in modern history, especially when waged by Communist liberation movements in Southeast Asia (most notably in the Vietnam War) and elsewhere.

Guerrilla fighters gravitate toward weapons which are easily accessible, low in technology and low in cost. A typical arsenal of the modern guerrilla would include the AK-47, RPGs and

Improvised explosive devices. The guerrilla doctrines' main disadvantage is the inability to access more advanced equipment due to economic, influence, and accessibility issues. They must rely on small unit tactics involving hit and run. This situation leads to low intensity warfare and asymmetrical warfare. The rules of Guerrilla warfare are to fight a little and then to retreat.

INTELLIGENCE

Propaganda

Propaganda is an ancient form of disinformation concerted with sending a set of messages aimed at influencing the opinions or behaviour of large numbers of people. Instead of impartially providing information, propaganda in its most basic sense presents information in order to influence its audience. The most effective propaganda is often completely truthful, but some propaganda presents facts selectively to encourage a particular synthesis, or gives loaded messages in order to produce an emotional rather than rational response to the information presented. The desired result is a change of the cognitive narrative of the subject in the target audience.

Psychological

Psychological warfare had its beginnings during the campaigns of Genghis Khan through the allowance of certain civilians of the nations, cities, and villages to flee said place, spreading terror and fear to neighbouring principalities. psychological actions have the primary purpose of influencing the opinions, emotions, attitudes, and behaviour of hostile foreign groups in such a way as to support the achievement of national objectives.

Information

Made possible by the widespread use of the electronic media during the Second World War, Information warfare is a kind of warfare where information and attacks on information and its system are used as a tool of warfare. Some examples of this type of warfare are electronic "sniffers" which disrupt international fund-transfer networks as well as the signals of television and radio stations. Jamming such signals can allow participants in the war to use the stations for a misinformation campaign.

Naval

Naval warfare takes place on the high seas (blue water navy). Usually, only large, powerful nations have competent blue water or deep water navies. Modern navies primarily use aircraft carriers, submarines, frigates, cruisers, and destroyers for combat. This provides a versatile array of attacks, capable of hitting ground targets, air targets, or other seafaring vessels. Most modern navies also have a large air support contingent, deployed from aircraft carriers. In World War II, small craft (motor torpedo boats variously called PT boats, MTBs, MGBs, *Schnellbooten*, or MAS-boats) fought near shore. This developed in the Vietnam War into riverine warfare (brown water navy), in intertidal and river areas. Irregular warfare makes this sort of combat more likely in the future.

Network-centric

Network-centric warfare is essentially a new military doctrine made possible by the Information Age. Weapons platforms, sensors and command and control centres are being connected through high-speed communication networks. The doctrine is related to the Revolution in Military Affairs debate. The overall network which enables this strategy in the United States military is called the Global Information Grid.

Nuclear

Nuclear war is a type of warfare which relies on nuclear weapons. There are two types of warfare in this category. In a limited nuclear war, a small number of weapons are used in a tactical exchange aimed primarily at opposing military forces. In a full-scale nuclear war, large numbers of weapons are used in an attack aimed at entire countries. This type of warfare would target both military bases and civilians.

Space

Space warfare is warfare that occurs outside the Earth's atmosphere. The weapons would include Orbital weaponry and Space weapons. High value outer space targets would include satellites and weapon platforms. Notably no real weapons exist in space yet, though ground-to-space missiles have been successfully tested against target satellites.

Future warfare

Future conflict will not be a precise science: it will remain an unpredictable and uniquely human activity. Adversaries state, state-proxies and non-state and threats conventional and unconventional will blur. The range of threats will spread, with increased proliferation of Weapons of Mass Destruction (WMD), cyberspace, and other novel and irregular threats. Even during wars of national survival or the destruction of WMD, conflict will remain focused on influencing people. The battle of the narratives will be key, and countries must conduct protracted influence activity, coordinated centrally and executed locally. Maintaining public support will be essential for success on operations. Critical to this will be legitimacy and effective levels of force protection. Qualitative advantage may no longer be assumed in the future. Some adversaries may be able to procure adequate quality as well as afford greater quantity, whereas we will be unable to mass sufficient quality or quantity everywhere that it is needed.

Modern wars

Lists

- List of wars 1945–1989
- List of wars 1990–2002
- List of wars 2003–current
- List of ongoing conflicts in the modern-day world
- List of modern conflicts in the Middle East

Major modern wars

- 1959-Vietnam War
- 1961-Portuguese Colonial Wars
- 1962-Sino-Indian War
- 1965-Indo-Pakistani War of 1965
- 1966-South African Border War
- 1967-Six-Day War
- 1970-War of Attrition
- 1971-Indo-Pakistani War

- 1973-6th October War-Yom Kippur War
- 1974-Turkish invasion of Cyprus
- 1979-Soviet war in Afghanistan
- 1980-Iran–Iraq War
- 1982-First Lebanon War
- 1982-Falklands War
- 1987-Palestinian Intifada
- 1988-Nagorno-Karabakh War
- 1988-Somali Civil War
- 1990-Gulf War
- 1991-1991–1992 South Ossetia War
- 1991-Yugoslav Wars
- 1992-War in Abkhazia
- 1994-Rwandan Civil War
- 1994-First Chechen War
- 1996-First Congo War
- 1998-Kosovo War
- 1998-Second Congo War
- 1999-Kargil War
- 1999-Second Chechen War
- 2000-Al-Aqsa Intifada
- 2001-War in Afghanistan (2001–present)
- 2003-Invasion of Iraq leading to the Iraq War
- 2006-Second Lebanon War
- 2006-Mexican Drug War
- 2008-2008 South Ossetia War
- 2008-2008 Turkish incursion into northern Iraq
- 2008-Gaza War

HOW FUTURE COMBAT SYSTEMS WILL WORK

The Army wants to dominate the full-spectrum battlefield-land, sea and air. To accomplish this, it will need several different types of units. The Army must also link its operations with that of the other military branches, and the militaries of other nations that might join them in a coalition operation. FCS is a "system of systems," because it actually comprises 18 separate systems. Each system is a type of unit, such as an unmanned artillery vehicle, a manned tank or a command and control vehicle. FCS is also sometimes called "18+1+1," where the "+1"s represent the network and the soldier who will utilize the systems. If the Army were simply revamping their military hardware and designing 18 new combat and logistics units, that would be a major project by itself. Designing all 18 from the ground up with the architecture to link every unit makes FCS truly revolutionary.

So why is the Army undertaking such a huge project? Military experts believe the nature of warfare is changing. Large-scale territory battles like those fought in World War II will disappear. Instead, the Army will probably face insurgencies and smaller conflicts spread out over wide areas. Tomorrow's Army needs the ability to deploy and redeploy as quickly as possible. To this end, the FCS has four main goals:

1. Improve strategic agility : An Army with large, inflexible units that take months to deploy can't react quickly enough or deal with all of the problems at hand. Some military analysts refer to this as "having a pocket full of $20 bills and a lot of $5 problems" [ref].
2. Decrease the logistics footprint : The logistics footprint represents the support crews, fuel, parts and ammunition needed to keep a unit operational. Long supply chains, large refueling vehicles and the need to set up large maintenance depots work against agility and makes the forces that they're attached to more vulnerable.
3. Reduce operating and maintenance costs : Creating multiple units based on the same basic structures allows for exchangeable parts and gives maintenance personnel the ability to repair a wider range of units with the same amount of training. This also contributes to a smaller logistics footprint and greater agility.

The Army is focusing on smaller, lighter vehicles that are faster and more maneuverable. Instead of heavy armor, units will use stealth strategies and smaller profiles to reduce casualties. Lighter vehicles are also easier to transport and use less fuel. The Army will combine its efforts with other military branches and other nations. This makes the ability to communicate with coalition forces a vital facet of future warfare.

4. Increase battlefield lethality and survivability: Tomorrow's soldiers need to destroy their targets and survive attacks a greater percentage of the time. This reduces the number of units needed in any particular engagement, reduces the need for extensive reinforcements and eases the burden on medical and repair units.

MEETING THE NEEDS OF FUTURE WARFARE

The network is the core of Future Combat Systems. It will allow each unit to share real-time information with other units, coordinate movement and react to battlefield conditions quickly and accurately. Network-centric warfare is a relatively new concept that unifies all of the advantages gained by other elements of FCS. For example, a tank platoon that can be deployed quickly and move with agility has no advantage if their orders are delayed or unclear, or if their commanders don't have enough information to make the right decision in the shortest amount of time. The network will allow for speed of command. Network-centric warfare changes the way commanders look at their armies. Instead of a contest of numbers (my 3,000 troops can beat your 1,000 troops), the U.S. Army becomes one entity with many parts that can shift and adapt to quickly-developing situations. Information is shared across the entire network.

The network comprises several components. The Joint Tactical Radio System (JTRS, often referred to as "Jitters"), was designed to do away with the need for multiple bulky radio systems using various frequencies and encryption methods. It would allow all branches of the U.S. military to communicate with each other from land, sea and air using the same system. However, critics found the JTRS plan of replacing older analog radios (many of which aren't very old at all, having just been purchased for operations in the Middle East) overly ambitious and almost impossible to implement. Today, JTRS is still in development as a supplemental communications program that will act as a soldier's "gateway" to the overall FCS network.

The System-of-Systems Common Operating Environment (SOSCOE) is software that will allow all of the various systems to operate seamlessly. It will take roughly 35 million lines of code to properly program SOSCOE. The operating system is a blend of Linux and an Intel-based OS specially created for the Army.

The WIN-T system is the data transport system that will connect the FCS systems. WIN-T will utilize lasers, satellites and more conventional ground networks. The WIN-T system is basically a tactical Internet, keeping fast-moving units in communication with operational leadership. Not only does WIN-T have to provide the massive amount of bandwidth to carry all of the information FCS will be generating, but it must also be strong enough to deal with the battlefield environment.

Changing Needs

The need for tactical agility has led the Army to focus design efforts on lighter, faster combat vehicles. Today's main battle tank, the M1 Abrams, weighs 65 to 70 tons, depending on its configuration. Its front armor is capable of stopping just about any anti-tank round in existence. However, next-generation ballistic weapons will strike with immense force. Instead of layering a tank with more armor, creating a heavier, slower vehicle, the Army has opted for a 20-ton design. These future tanks will use ultra-modern technologies (some of which don't actually exist yet) to resist anti-tank weapons.

New armor materials are one part of the plan, but the tanks will also have a small signature-its small size will make it tougher to find and hit. An active suspension system will allow the tank to "crouch" into a very low position. The Army will also employ active countermeasures like smoke screens to obscure line of sight and small rocket rounds that can intercept incoming rounds from enemies.

According to a press release, "The Army transformation requirements includes the ability to put a combat-capable brigade anywhere in the world within 96 hours, a full division in 120 hours, and five divisions on the ground within 30 days". One way to increase strategic agility is to allow fewer soldiers to do more work. This continues a trend that has gone on for centuries. At the Battle of Gettysburg, the Union line was a few miles long and covered by roughly six corps. The average tourist can walk the length of the line in one afternoon. During the Cold War, roughly the same number of NATO troops (and corps) covered the entire inter-German border-a distance that you certainly could not walk in an afternoon. FCS will allow for even greater dispersion of forces by utilizing unmanned vehicles, unmanned weapons platforms and robot sentries. Manned vehicles will require smaller crews-the FCS tank will have a crew of just two, compared to the M1's crew of four.

The Army wants to reduce the amount of fuel needed by its units by as much as 30 percent. For example, the gas turbine engine that powers the M1 Abrams gives it enormous power and the ability to travel close to 45 mph, but it also uses an incredible amount of fuel. Vehicles and tanks developed for FCS will likely use some form of electric-hybrid engine, increasing both available torque and fuel efficiency.

Systems and Vehicles

The FCS project includes the design and development of several different types of air and ground vehicles, many of them unmanned and autonomous. Most of these vehicles don't exist yet, but some prototypes have been developed and demonstrated by contractors. A few are already in use in Iraq to dispose of explosive and perform urban reconnaissance.

UNATTENDED GROUND SENSORS (UGS)

These small sensor arrays are similar to "Star Wars" droids, but they're not quite as mobile. After soldiers or robotic vehicles deploy them, they will be able to stay in place to do their jobs. Those jobs may include guarding areas of a perimeter, detecting chemical or radioactive materials, providing links in communications chains, spotting targets for other units to fire upon, and assisting in crowd control by directing people to head in a certain direction. They can also be switched on and off to allow friendly troops to move through the area.

NON-LINE OF SIGHT LAUNCH SYSTEM (NLOS-LS)

These systems would come in discreet packages containing a computer, a communication system for connection to the network, and 15 missiles. Soldiers can give the missiles their launch instructions remotely, and can further modify targeting once they are in the air.

INTELLIGENT MUNITIONS SYSTEM

Similar to Unattended Ground Sensors, these robotic units will be deployed to an area to guard it with suppressive weapons. This will aid in troop dispersion, help organize battlefields and force enemy troops into desired positions.

Unmanned Aerial Vehicles

The FCS plan also calls for four different classes of Unmanned Aerial Vehicles (UAVs):

- The Class I UAV will weigh less than 15 pounds, take off and land vertically, and provide intelligence, surveillance and communications relay functions. It will be remote-controlled and portable.
- Class II will be deployed from a vehicle, stay in the air for 2 hours and have a range of about 10 miles (16 km). According to the Army's FCS Web site, the Class II UAV "supports the Infantry and Mounted Combat System Company Commanders with reconnaissance, security/early warning, target acquisition and designation."
- The Class III UAV will look like a small, simplified airplane. It will take off and land without a dedicated airfield and fly longer and farther than Class I and II UAVs.
- Class IV will be an unmanned helicopter that can stay in the air and provide surveillance over an area of 47 miles (75 km) for up to 24 hours.

ARMED ROBOTIC VEHICLE (ARV)

One of the most revolutionary aspects of FCS is the adoption of these robotic tanks. These units will be controlled remotely and provide many of the functions of a manned tank unit. They will offer support for troops with direct fire, anti-tank fire and over-watch fire. ARVs will also increase troop dispersion.

Small Unmanned Ground Vehicle (SUGV)

These units are already in use in Iraq. Talon robots and Packbots have seen significant action in explosive disposal and urban reconnaissance missions, and future versions will have offensive capabilities.

Multifunctional Utility/Logistics and Equipment (MULE)

The MULE will be the workhorse of the FCS. This two-and-a-half ton truck will be able to operate via remote control or as a slave unit following a controlled vehicle in front of it. In addition to hauling equipment, the MULE will have a mine-sweeping configuration and an armed light assault configuration. Crusher, an autonomous unmanned ground vehicle developed by Carnegie Mellon University, is essentially a prototype MULE. It can carry weapons and drive over a 4-foot vertical wall with 8,000 pounds of cargo onboard. To learn more, check out How Crusher Works.

Mounted Combat System (MCS)

The MCS is probably the most important piece of hardware in FCS, aside from the network. The MCS will replace the M1 Abrams main battle tank and will maintain a comparable survivability rate by using speed, situational awareness and an extremely long range 120-mm weapon to avoid close-up confrontations. Its 20-ton weight means that many MCS units will be able to ship via C-130 transport planes. They can also be parasailed into position if necessary. To make the fleet more versatile while reducing operations and maintenance costs:

- Infantry Carrier Vehicle (ICV) : With a crew of two, the ICV will transport nine additional soldiers to the battlefield. It will carry all of their equipment, provide a link to the network and protect itself with a 40-mm weapon.
- Non-Line-of-Sight Cannon (NLOS-C): This vehicle is will be a mobile long-range artillery unit.
- Non-Line-of-Sight Mortar (NLOS-M) : This vehicle is similar to the NLOS-C, but it will use a mortar as a weapon instead of a long-range cannon. This will give it the ability to provide close support for infantry and use precision rounds to destroy highly dangerous targets.
- Reconnaissance and Surveillance Vehicle (RSV) : The RSV is a high-tech scout equipped with a host of sensors,

radio frequency interceptors, chemical detectors and communications link-ups.

- Command and Control Vehicle (C2V): The C2V is the mobile field headquarters unit for military commanders. This vehicle offers all the network connections and information analysis tools that field leaders need to make command decisions on the fly.
- Medical Vehicle – Treatment (MV-T) and Evacuation (MV-E): These vehicles will allow medical personnel and trauma specialists to move with combat units, placing them closer to the battle and allowing them to treat wounded soldiers quickly and evacuate them safely.
- FCS Recovery and Maintenance Vehicle (FRMV) : FRMVs will primarily carry repair and maintenance crews. They also have a limited capability to recover damaged equipment and crews from the battlefield.

How FCS Might Not Work

The Army is using spiral development to develop the FCS. Instead of working on the entire project from start to finish, with no deployable elements until everything is completed, contractors are developing systems incrementally. Finished subsystems will be immediately deployed for testing. Problems discovered with those units can be overcome as the Army adds more systems are added, and it can improve upon and upgrade early systems.

The Army keeps moving up the launch date for FCS because they want to get the technology into the field as soon as possible. It plans to deploy a test unit in 2008, with more systems releasing every two years until 2014. By that time, there will be 32 FCS-equipped brigades. The Army hopes to have the ability to equip any brigade with a fully-functional FCS system in 2016. It will take years beyond that point to fully equip the entire Army.

Like any complex design project, FCS is not entirely without problems. Critics point to several factors:

- Cost : All military research and development programs face questions about cost. Initially, FCS was projected to cost under $100 billion. In 2003, that increased to

$175 billion. The latest estimates suggest the project will cost about $300 billion, making it the most expensive military project in U.S. history. With Congress threatening to trim some of the FCS budget, contractors working on the project have aggressively demonstrated the need for FCS in a series of seminars. It seems to have worked, because in 2006 a paltry $236 million was cut from Boeing's FCS budget over four years. However, the possibility of future budget cuts remains.

- Cost-plus pricing : Government contracts typically use a cost-plus pricing method. With this method, the contractor bills the government for the price of any material, personnel and other direct costs associated with the project. Then the government pays the contractor a fee based on a percentage of those direct costs. This method can encourage contractors to purchase at inflated prices and let project costs escalate, since the higher their costs, the higher their profit.
- Reliance on light armor : Critics of the 20-ton replacement for the M1 Abrams tank contend that the modern light tanks will undoubtedly face heavy armour in close fighting, which will leave them extremely vulnerable. They fear that abandoning heavy tank designs will leave a major gap in the Army's capabilities. At the very least, the Army will need to retrofit older M1s to stay in action as a form of heavy armour.

FCS is so ambitious that in some cases, the technology does not yet exist to accomplish it. The revision – some would say failure – of the JTRS system is one example of a system that has exceeded our current ability to actually make it work. Advanced ballistic armour, robotic control systems, automated sensors and high-bandwidth networks are all potential problem areas. It is likely that some FCS systems will never be fully functional and that current units and technologies will be retrofitted and upgraded to fit into the plan.

10

Total War

Total war is a war limitless in its scope in which a belligerent engages in the mobilization of all their available resources, in order to render beyond use their rival's capacity for resistance. The practice of total war has been in use for centuries, but it was only in the middle to late 19th century that total war was identified by scholars as a separate class of warfare. In a total war, there is less and sometimes no differentiation between combatants and civilians than in other conflicts, as nearly every human resource, civilians and soldiers alike, can be considered to be part of the belligerent effort.

Etymology

The phrase can be traced back to the 1936 publication of General Ludendorff's World War I memoir *Der Totale Krieg* ("*The Total War*"). However, the concept extends back as far as Clausewitz's classic work *On War*. USAF General Curtis LeMay updated the concept for the nuclear age. He suggested total war in the nuclear age should be conducted by delivering the nuclear arsenal in a single overwhelming blow.

Early history

One of the earliest forms of total war occurred in the Warring States Period, when the State of Qín or Ch'in (778 BC-207 BC) enacted reforms that transformed the nation into a war machine. The population was divided between soldiers who actively fought in the armies and farmers who fed the armies. Industrial development was concentrated on war, resulting in the perfection of bronze weaponry technology: Qin had some of the finest weapons of that era despite using outdated technology (iron had largely replaced bronze in most parts of China). The Qin state's mobilization for total war was a decisive factor in its victory over its rivals and the subsequent unification of China. An early example of total war, and possibly the first to be fairly well documented, was the Peloponnesian War, described by the historian Thucydides. This war was fought between Athens and Sparta between 431 and 404 BC. Previously, Greek warfare was a limited and ritualized form of conflict. Armies of hoplites would meet on the battlefield and decide the outcome in a single day. During the Peloponnesian War, however, the fighting lasted for years and consumed the economic resources of the participating city-states. Entire populations were executed or sold into slavery, as in the case of the island of Melos (now known as Milos). The aftermath of the war reshaped the Greek world, left much of the region in poverty, and reduced once influential Athens to a weakened state, from which it never completely recovered.

During the Middle Ages, the Mongols in the 13th century practised total war. The military forces of Genghis Khan slaughtered whole populations and destroyed any city that resisted during the invasions of Khwarezmid Empire, Kievan Rus', Baghdad, China, Armenia, Georgia, Poland, Hungary and northern Iran. During the sack of Baghdad in 1258 between 100,000 and 1,000,000 people were killed in the violence. Total war created the Mongol Empire which, by the death of Genghis Khan, would be the largest contiguous empire in history.

Many regions of 16th century Europe were subject to conflicts that could be described as total war. The descent into large scale violence at this time was partly due to population pressures, and partly the product of tensions caused by the Protestant Reformation. The German Peasants War of 1524-25 was an early example; Total warfare was also employed in the French Wars cf Religion, with assassins being engaged wantonly by both sides in the conflict. The Elizabethan wars in Ireland, such as the Desmond Wars and the Nine Years War, were extreme examples of what is today known as total war.

The subsequent Thirty Years War may also be considered a total war. This conflict was fought between 1618 and 1648, primarily on the territory of modern Germany. Virtually all of the major European powers were involved, and the economy of each was based on fighting the war. Civilian populations were devastated—"the war nourished the war". Estimates of civilian casualties are approximately 25-30%, with deaths due to a combination of armed conflict, famine, and disease. The size and training of armies also grew dramatically during this period, as did the cost of keeping armies in the field. Plunder was commonly used to pay and feed armies. After the Thirty Years War and up to the French Revolution most wars in Europe were smaller wars with limited goals, so called Cabinet Wars or Kabinettskriege.

18TH AND 19TH CENTURIES

French Revolution

The French Revolution reintroduced some of the concepts of total war. The fledgling republic found itself threatened by a powerful coalition of European nations. The only solution, in the eyes of the Jacobin government, was to pour the nation's entire resources into an unprecedented war effort—this was the advent of the levée en masse. The following decree of the National Convention on August 23, 1793 clearly demonstrates the immensity of the French war effort:

From this moment until such time as its enemies shall have been driven from the soil of the Republic all Frenchmen are in permanent requisition for the services of the armies. The young men shall fight; the married men shall forge arms and transport provisions; the women shall make tents and clothes and shall serve in the hospitals; the children shall turn linen into lint; the old men shall betake themselves to the public squares in order to arouse the courage of the warriors and preach hatred of kings and the unity of the Republic.

Following the August 23 decree French front line forces grew to some 800,000 with a total of 1.5 million in all services—the first time an army in excess of a million had been mobilized in Western history. Over the coming two decades of almost constant warfare it is estimated that somewhere in the vicinity of five million died—probably about half of them civilians—and France alone counted nearly a million (by some sources in excess of a million) deaths—a considerably higher portion of its population than perished in either of the world wars.

In the Russian campaign of 1812 the Russians resorted to destroying infrastructure and agriculture in their retreat in order to hamper the French and strip them of adequate supplies. In the campaign of 1813 Allied forces in the German theatre alone amounted to nearly one million whilst two years later in the Hundred Days a French decree called for the total mobilization of some 2.5 million men (though at most a fifth of this was managed by the time of the French defeat at Waterloo). During the prolonged Peninsular War from 1808–1814 some 300,000 French troops were kept permanently occupied by, in addition to several hundred thousand Spanish, Portuguese and British regulars an enormous and sustained guerrilla insurgency—ultimately French deaths would amount to 300,000 in the Peninsular War alone.

Taiping Rebellion

The Taiping Rebellion (1850–1864) was one of the deadliest wars in history, and the first total war in modern China. About 20 million people died, many due to disease and famine. Heavenly Kingdom of Perfect Peace, from the Qing Empire. Almost every citizen of the Tàipíng Tiânguó was given military training and conscripted into the army to fight against the Imperial forces.

During this conflict both sides tried to deprive each other of the resources to continue the war and it became standard practice to destroy agricultural areas, butcher the population of cities and in general exact a brutal price from captured enemy lands in order to drastically weaken the opposition's war effort. This war truly was total in that civilians on both sides participated to a significant extent in the war effort and in that armies on both sides waged war on the civilian population as well as military forces.

American Civil War

During the American Civil War, U.S. Army General Phillip Sheridan's stripping of the Shenandoah Valley, beginning on September 21, 1864 and continuing for two weeks, was considered "total war". Its purpose was to eliminate foodstuffs and supplies vital to the South's military operations, as well as to strike a blow at Southern civilian morale. Sheridan took the opportunity when he realized opposing forces had become too weak to resist his army. Union Army General William Tecumseh Sherman's 'March to the Sea' in November/December 1864 destroyed the resources required for the South to make war. Sherman is considered one of the first military commanders to deliberately and consciously use total war as a military strategy. General Ulysses S. Grant and President Abraham Lincoln initially opposed the plan until Sherman convinced them of its necessity.

20TH CENTURY

World War I

Almost the whole of Europe mobilized to wage World War I. Young men were removed from production jobs to serve in military roles, and were replaced on the production line by women. Rationing occurred on the home fronts. Bulgaria went so far as to mobilize a quarter of its population or 800,000 people, a greater share of its population than any other country during the war.

One of the features of Total War in Britain was the use of government propaganda posters to divert all attention to the war on the home front. Posters were used to influence public opinion about what to eat and what occupations to take, and to change the attitude of support towards the war effort. Even the Music Hall was used as propaganda, with propaganda songs aimed at recruitment and portrayed in the play and film Oh, What A Lovely War!

After the failure of the Battle of Neuve Chapelle, the large British offensive in March 1915, the British Commander-in-Chief Field Marshal John French blamed the lack of progress on insufficient and poor-quality artillery shells. This led to the Shell Crisis of 1915 which brought down the Liberal government of Premiership of H. H. Asquith. He formed a new coalition government dominated by Liberals and appointed David Lloyd George as Minister of Munitions. It was a recognition that the whole economy would have to be geared for war if the Allies were to prevail on the Western Front. As young men left the farms for the front, domestic food production in Britain and Germany fell. In Britain the response was to import more food, which was done despite the German introduction of unrestricted submarine warfare, and to introduce rationing. The Royal Navy's blockade of German ports prevented Germany from importing food and hastened German capitulation by creating a food crisis in Germany.

World War II

The Second World War can be considered the quintessential total war of modernity. The level of national mobilization of resources on all sides of the conflict, the battlespace being contested, the scale of the armies, navies, and air forces raised through conscription, the active targeting of civilians (and civilian property), the general disregard for collateral damage, and the unrestricted aims of the belligerents marked total war on a multicontinental scale.

Shôwa Japan

During the first part of the Shôwa era, the governments of Imperial Japan launched a string of policies to promote total war effort against China or occidental powers and increase industrial production. Among these were the National Spiritual Mobilization Movement, the Imperial Rule Assistance Association.

The National Mobilization Law had fifty clauses, which provided for government controls over civilian organizations (including labor unions), nationalization of strategic industries, price controls and rationing, and nationalized the news media. The laws gave the government the authority to use unlimited budgets to subsidize war production, and to compensate manufacturers for losses caused by war-time mobilization. Eighteen of the fifty articles outlined penalties for violators. To improve its production, Shôwa Japan used millions of slave labourers and pressed more than 18 million people in Far East Asia.

United Kingdom

Before the onset of the Second World War, the United Kingdom drew on its First World War experience to prepare legislation that would allow immediate mobilization of the economy for war, should future hostilities break out. Rationing of most goods and services was introduced, not only for consumers but also for manufacturers. This meant that factories manufacturing products that were irrelevant to the war effort had more appropriate tasks imposed. All artificial light was subject to legal blackouts. "...There is another more obvious difference from 1914.

The whole of the warring nations are engaged, not only soldiers, but the entire population, men, women and children. The fronts are everywhere to be seen. The trenches are dug in the towns and streets. Every village is fortified. Every road is barred. The front line runs through the factories. The workmen are soldiers with different weapons but the same courage."

Winston Churchill on the radio, June 18 ; and House of Commons 20 August 1940:

Not only were men conscripted into the armed forces from the beginning of the war (something which had not happened until the middle of World War I), but women were also conscripted as Land Girls to aid farmers and the Bevin Boys were conscripted to work down the coal mines.

Enormous casualties were expected in bombing raids, so children were evacuated from London and other cities en masse to the countryside for compulsory billeting in households.

In the long term this was one of the most profound and longer-lasting social consequences of the whole war for Britain. This is because it mixed up children with the adults of other classes. Not only did the middle and upper classes become familiar with the urban squalor suffered by working class children from the slums, but the children got a chance to see animals and the countryside, often for the first time, and experience rural life.

The use of statistical analysis, by a branch of science which has become known as Operational Research to influence military tactics was a departure from anything previously attempted. It was a very powerful tool but it further dehumanised war particularly when it suggested strategies which were counter intuitive. Examples where statistical analysis directly influenced tactics include the work done by Patrick Blackett's team on the optimum size and speed of convoys and the introduction of bomber streams by the Royal Air Force to counter the night fighter defences of the Kammhuber Line.

Germany

In contrast, Germany started the war under the concept of Blitzkrieg. Officially, it did not accept that it was in a total war until Joseph Goebbels' Sportpalast speech of 18 February 1943. For example, women were not conscripted into the armed forces or allowed to work in factories. The Nazi party adhered to the policy that a woman's place was in the home, and did not change this even as its opponents began moving women into important roles in production. "I ask you: Do you want total war? If necessary, do you want a war more total and radical than anything that we can even imagine today?"

Nazi propaganda minister Joseph Goebbels, 18 February 1943, in his Sportpalast speech

The commitment to the doctrine of the short war was a continuing handicap for the Germans; neither plans nor state of mind were adjusted to the idea of a long war until the failure of the operation Barbarossa. A major strategical defeat in the Battle of Moscow forced Albert Speer, who was appointed as Germany's armament minister in early 1942, to nationalize German war production and eliminate the worst inefficiencies.

Under his direction a threefold increase in armament production occurred and did not reach its peak until late 1944. To do this during the damage caused by the growing strategic Allied bomber offensive, is an indication of the degree of industrial under-mobilization in the earlier years.

It was because the German economy through most of the war was substantially under-mobilized that it was resilient under air attack. Civilian consumption was high during the early years of the war and inventories both in industry and in consumers' possession were high. These helped cushion the economy from the effects of bombing.

Plant and machinery were plentiful and incompletely used, thus it was comparatively easy to substitute unused or partly used machinery for that which was destroyed. Foreign labour, both slave labour and labour from neighbouring countries who joined the Anti-Comintern Pact with Germany, was used to augment German industrial labour which was under pressure by conscription into the *Wehrmacht* (Armed Forces).

Soviet Union

The Soviet Union (USSR) was a command economy which already had an economic and legal system allowing the economy and society to be redirected into fighting a total war. The transportation of factories and whole labour forces east of the Urals as the Germans advanced across the USSR in 1941 was an impressive feat of planning. Only those factories which were useful for war production were moved because of the total war commitment of the Soviet government.

The Eastern Front of the European Theatre of World War II encompassed the conflict in central and eastern Europe from June 22, 1941 to May 9, 1945. It was the largest theatre of war in history in terms of numbers of soldiers, equipment and casualties and was notorious for its unprecedented ferocity, destruction, and immense loss of life. The fighting involved millions of German and Soviet troops along a broad front hundreds of kilometres long. It was by far the deadliest single theatre of World War II. Scholars now believe that at most 27 million Soviet citizens died during the war, including some 8.7 million soldiers who fell in battle against Hitler's armies or died in POW camps. Millions of civilians died from starvation, exposure, atrocities, and massacres. The Axis lost some 5.2 million soldiers in the east as well as many thousands of civilians

During the battle of Leningrad, newly-built T-34 tanks were driven—unpainted because of a paint shortage—from the factory floor straight to the front. This came to symbolise the USSR's commitment to the Great Patriotic War and demonstrated the government's total war policy. To encourage the Russian people to work harder, the communist government, controlled by Stalin, encouraged the people's love of the Motherland and even allowed the reopening of Russian Orthodox Churches as it was thought this would help the war effort.

United States

The United States underwent an unprecedented mobilization of national resources for the Second World War. Conditions on the home front were not as strained as they were in the United Kingdom or as desperate as they were in the Soviet Union, but the United States greatly curtailed nearly all non-essential activities in its prosecution of the Second World War and redirected nearly all available national resources to the conflict, including reaching the point of diminishing returns by late 1944, where the U.S. military was unable to find any more males of the correct military age to draft into service.

The strategists of the U.S. military looked abroad at the storms brewing on the horizon in Europe and Asia, and began quietly making contingency plans as early as the mid-1930s; new weapons and weapons platforms were designed, and made ready.

Following the outbreak of war in Europe, and the metastasis of the ongoing aggression in Asia, efforts were stepped up significantly. The collapse of France and the airborne aggression directed at Great Britain unsettled the Americans, who had close relations with both nations, and a peacetime draft was instituted, along with Lend-Lease programs to aid the British, and covert aid was passed to the Chinese as well.

American public opinion was still opposed to involvement in the problems of Europe and Asia, however. In 1941, the Soviet Union became the latest nation to be invaded, and the U.S. gave her aid as well.

American ships began defending aid convoys to the Allied nations against submarine attacks, and a total trade embargo against the Empire of Japan was instituted to deny its military the raw materials its factories and military forces required to continue its offensive actions in China.

In late 1941, Japan's Army-dominated government decided to seize by military force the strategic resources of South-East Asia and Indonesia the Western powers would not trade. Planning for this action included surprise attacks on American and British forces in Hong Kong, the Philippines, Malaysia, and the U.S. naval base and warships at Pearl Harbor.

In response to these attacks, the U.K. and U.S. declared war on the Empire of Japan the next day. Nazi Germany declared war on the U.S. a few days later, along with Fascist Italy; the U.S., consequently declaring war on both, found itself fully involved in a second world war.

"It's a ticklish sort of job making a thing for a thing-ummy-bob

Especially when you don't know what it's for

But it's the girl that makes the thing that drills the hole

that holds the spring that works the thing-ummy-bob

that makes the engines roar.

And it's the girl that makes the thing that holds the oil

that oils the ring that works the thing-ummy-bob

that's going to win the war."

"The Thing-Ummy Bob", A British song made popular in the US by Gracie Fields

As the United States began to gear up for a major war, information and propaganda efforts were set in motion. Civilians (including children) were encouraged to take part in fat, grease, and scrap metal collection drives. Many factories making non-essential goods retooled for war production. Levels of industrial productivity previously unheard of were attained during the war; multi-thousand-ton convoy ships were routinely built in a month-and-a-half, and tanks poured out of the former automobile factories. Within a few years of the U.S. entry into the Second World War, nearly every man fit for service, between 18 and 30, had been conscripted into the military "for the duration" of the conflict. Strict systems of rationing of consumer staples were introduced to redirect productive capacity to war needs.

Previously untouched sections of the nation mobilized for the war effort. Academics became technocrats; home-makers became bomb-makers (massive numbers of women worked in heavy industry during the war); union leaders and businessmen became commanders in the massive armies of production. The great scientific communities of the United States were mobilized as never before, and mathematicians, doctors, engineers, and chemists turned their minds to the problems ahead of them.

By the war's end a multitude of advances had been made in medicine, physics, engineering, and the other sciences. Even the theoretical physicists, whose theories were not believed to have military applications (at the time), were sent far into the Western deserts to work at the Los Alamos National Laboratory on the Manhattan Project that culminated in the Trinity nuclear test and changed the course of history.

In the war, the United States lost many soldiers, but had managed to avoid the extensive level of damage to civilian and industrial infrastructure that other participants suffered. The U.S. emerged as one of the two superpowers after the war.

Unconditional surrender

"Actually Dresden was a mass of munitions works, an intact government centre, and a key transportation point to the East. It is now none of these things." Air Chief Marshal Arthur Harris, in a memo to the Air Ministry on 29 March 1945:

After the United States entered World War II, Franklin D. Roosevelt declared at Casablanca conference to the other Allies and the press that unconditional surrender was the objective of the war against the Axis Powers of Germany, Italy, and Japan. Prior to this declaration, the individual regimes of the Axis Powers could have negotiated an armistice similar to that at the end of World War I and then a conditional surrender when they perceived that the war was lost.

The unconditional surrender of the major Axis powers caused a legal problem at the post-war Nuremberg Trials, because the trials appeared to be in conflict with Articles 63 and 64 of the Geneva Convention of 1929. Usually if such trials are held, they would be held under the auspices of the defeated power's own legal system as happened with some of the minor Axis powers, for example in the post World War II Romanian People's Tribunals. To circumvent this, the Allies argued that the major war criminals were captured after the end of the war, so they were not prisoners of war and the Geneva Conventions did not cover them. Further, the collapse of the Axis regimes created a legal condition of total defeat (*debellatio*) so the provisions of the 1907 Hague Conventions over military occupation were not applicable.

Postwar era

Since the end of World War II, no industrial nations have fought such a large, decisive war. This is likely due to the availability of nuclear weapons, whose destructive power would offset any advantage victory might bring. Where full mobilization of a country's resources such as in World War II could take years, full mobilization of a nuclear arsenal would take minutes. Such weapons are developed and maintained with relatively modest peace time defence budgets.

By the end of the 1950s, the ideological stand-off of the Cold War between the Western World and the Soviet Union involved thousands of nuclear weapons being aimed at each side by the other. Strategically, the equal balance of destructive power possessed by each side situation came to be known as Mutually Assured Destruction (MAD), the idea that a nuclear attack by one superpower would result in nuclear counter-strike by the other. This would result in hundreds of millions of deaths in a world where, in words widely attributed to Nikita Khrushchev, "The living will envy the dead".

During the Cold War, the two superpowers sought to avoid open conflict between their respective forces, as both sides recognized that such a clash could very easily escalate, and quickly involve nuclear weapons. Instead, the superpowers fought each other through their involvement in proxy wars, military buildups, and diplomatic standoffs. In the case of proxy wars, each superpower supported its respective allies in conflicts with forces aligned with the other superpower, such as in the Korean War and the Soviet invasion of Afghanistan.

11

Biological Weapons: Structure of Biological Catastrophe

The structure of biological catastrophe can be rather intricate. By way of illustration we will result some citations about one potentially dangerous situation. (From it we will see, how for a long time there were biological threats,-so, how much mature this danger already is.) Gene crisis has begun in summer of 1971. At this time young scientist Robert Pollack in laboratory Kold-Spring-Harbor (on Long Ajlende, the State of New York, the USA), leaded by D.Watson, dealt with cancer problems. The circle of scientific interests of Pollack was wide. He not only conducted researches, but also taught to students biology and represented itself as the leader of the radio programs devoted to discussion of possible abusing in biosciences, in particular, in arising then gene engineering. And here Pollack learns, that in other laboratory (in Palo-alto, in California) at Berg's Field experiments on DNA embedding onlogenic (able to cause cancer diseases) virus SV 40 in a gene of an E.coli are planned. What would be consequences of such experiences? Whether there will be cancer epidemic (it was known, what almost harmless to monkeys, virus SV 40 causes a cancer in mice and hamsters)? The bacteria filled with dangerous genes, breeding by billions in days, according to Pollack, could represent serious danger.

Pollack called P. Berg by long-distance phone and has asked it, whether he gives himself recount on danger of the experiments? Whether there are bacteria with genes of virus SV 40 biological delayed-action bomb? This telephone conversation also was the beginning of that alarm which has captured molecular biologists. Berg has postponed the researches. He began to reflect, whether could real *E.Coli* with built in it SV 40 to cause a cancer? Painful thinking have cleared a little. The definite answer was not found because of scarcity of the data which are available for experts at that time.

Some reports of scientists (in Asilomar, 1975) had sensational character. So it was found out, that in the USA has been already put in enormous scale involuntary experiment on men. It has appeared, that the vaccine against a poliomyelitis is infected by viable virus SV 40. For 10 summer period, with 1953 for 1963 this infected vaccine have imparted approximately one hundred millions children. And check has shown, that virus SV 40 remains in an organism. However, fortunately, any increase in frequency of cancer diseases at these children has not been revealed.

Edda West in article "Poliomyelitis", informs on correlation of virus SV 40 which caught polio sera, with tumours of human:" By the end of 1996 ten scientists have informed on detection of virus SV-40 in various tumours of bones and a brain which became more frequent on 30 % for last 20 years. Then the Italian scientists have found out SV-40 in a spermatic fluid of 45 % and in blood of 23 % of healthy donors. It meant, that SV-40, obviously, was transferred sexual by and from mother to the child. Possibly, nowadays this virus is built in ours genome. Others deny these data. However from here it is visible, that development of biotechnologies creates far unevident threats.

Already now the biological weapons is considered one of the cheapest ways of causing death: it counting for on one human just some cents. On the other hand, for manufacture of modern reagents like the antrax in the military purposes are necessary big protected laboratories and test fields. It can be even cheaper if to consider ability of the agent to self replicate.

Now second-hand DNA sequencer can be bought for the sum from 200 dollars, and every year the price of these devices falls in times, and quality grows. The text Genetic hacker see can create the biological weapon at home, telling about human who does not have knowledge in the field of biology who undertakes to deduce-and deduces-genetically modified fluorescing colony of yeast for small term and the small sum of money. And then he assumes, that almost also it would be simply possible to deduce a certain dangerous variant.

Already now creation of a biological superbomb is thousand times cheaper, than creations of the nuclear weapon of comparable hurting force. When cheap "know-how" of any live organisms with in advance set functions will be learned, the price of manufacturing of such weapon can fall to several hundred dollars. It is often said that the biological weapons is not good for military application. However it can have a special appointment-as the weapon for crypto-strike in back of the enemy and as the universal defensive weapon-the Doomsday Machine.

"SELF-REPLICATING" SYNTHESIZER OF DNA

Biotechnologies can enhance themselves-that is through appearance of intermediate biological forms which simplify writing and cultivation of new viruses. For example, it can be culture of bacteria which directly translates sequence of electric signals in DNA chain, or, on the contrary, reads out DNA and transforms this information into a chain of flashes of light which the computer can read out. Distribution of such device together with library of genetic codes (in a digital form) of the basic viruses and fibers would be catastrophe.

Plural Biological Strike

Though, most likely, it is possible to stop distribution of one epidemic, but epidemic caused in several tens of species of diverse viruses and bacteria, left from under the control simultaneously in many places of the globe, it is impossible to stop even technically because it is impossible to enter into a human simultaneously several tens different vaccines and antibiotics-he will die. If the virus with 50 % lethality would be simply very big catastrophe, 30 diverse viruses and bacteria with 50 % lethality would mean the guaranteed destruction of all who has not hidden in bunkers. (Or about 100 different organisms with 10 % lethality.) Plural strike could be the most powerful means of conducting biological war, and the Doomsday weapon. But it can occur and in itself if simultaneously there will be a several acts of distribution of biological agents-even casual, for example, during active "competition" of biohackers.

Even a little separately nonlethal agents can weaken so immune system of a human, so his further survival becomes improbable.

Possibility of plural application of the biological weapon is one of the most considerable factors of global risk.

Biological Delivery Systems

The biological weapon should be not only deadly, but also infectious and easily spreading in order to represent threat to mankind. Genetic technologies give huge possibilities not only for creation of the lethal weapon, but also for creation of ways of its delivery. It is not necessary to possess great imagination to imagine genetically modified malarial mosquito which can live in any environment and with huge speed spread on all planet, entering everyone a certain bioagent. Either the louse. Or a locust at the same time eating all olive and spraying disputes of the antrax. But in the future biodesigners will have much more imagination.

However it is possible to go through bacteriological war in the bunker though contamination from it can be longer, than radioactive. Besides, transition to mechanical bodies, consciousness loading in the computer and development nanotechnology sharply reduce vulnerability of "man" to any biological poisons and agents, however do its vulnerable to other self-breeding agents, such as computer viruses and nanorobots. In science fiction is extended an image of attack of mutants to last human bunker. Usual radiation, however, is not capable to generate aggressive mutants. On the other hand, in the nature exists a furiousness virus (Neuroiyctes rabid) which influences behaviour of animals so, that they start to extend it more actively (stings).

It is easy to imagine more advanced product of genno-engineering technics which transforms any animal into a being aggressively incited against human. Irreality of such project can be stimulus to its realisation as the modern culture is impregnated by ideas about vampires and the zombies resulting from experiments in laboratories (for example, a recent film – "*Resident Evil*"). In other words, the idea to make the zombie-virus could to be an attractive call for the biohacker. Thus infected people and animals would possess sufficient mind and means to crack different kinds of protection.

The similar plot was with acts of terrorism on September, 11th when it was found out, that the Hollywood movies were not fantastic visions, but self-coming true prophecies. In other words, the culture is capable to transform the extremely improbable scenario into the important purpose.

Probability of application of the biological weapon and its distribution in time we estimate probability of that biotechnologies will lead to mankind extinction (in conditions when their effect is not blocked by other technologies) in tens percent. This estimation is based on the assumption about inevitable of wide circulation of very cheap devices allowing very simply to create many various biological agents. That is the assumption of so wide circulation of bioprinters, as now do usual computers.

We will list properties of the dangerous bioprinter (cheap minilaboratory) once again:

1) inevitability of appearance,
2) cheapness,
3) wide prevalence,
4) uncontrollable by the authorities,
5) ability to carry out of essentially new bioagents,
6) simplicity of application,
7) a variety of created objects,
8) Appeal as devices for weapon manufacture (in the spirit of viruses of individual prompting) and drugs.
9) ability to self replicate of key instruments based on its biological nature.

We believe, that the device, meeting these requirements, will consist of the usual computer, piratically distributed program with library of initial elements, and actually biological part of the bioprinter which will be genetically modified live being, that is capable to self-reproduction. (Plus a set concerning the accessible equipment, like vessels for reagents and a communication system of a biological part with the computer.) The criminal communities which make drugs can be the channel of distribution of this complete set. As computers are already accessible, and the program, and itself a live part of the bioprinter are capable to unlimited copying, the price of this device in gathering will be unlimited is small, and appeal to poses it would be great, that will make very difficult the control. Home-made produced bioprinters is not only one way to create biological danger. The same will occur by the distribution of certain standard compact minilaboratories for biosynthesis (like DNA-synthesizers), or by network manufacture of biological components which already takes place when components are ordered in different firms worldwide.

The probability of global catastrophe with participation of bioprinters will increase very quickly in process of perfection of such devices and their distribution. That is we can describe density of probability in the form of a certain curve which now corresponds small, but to not so zero size, but after a while soars up to very big size. But it is more interesting not the exact form of this curve, but the time when it will start to grow sharply.

We estimate this time in size of an order of 10-15 years from 2008 (2018-2023). (The independent estimation is given by sir Martin Rees who in 2002 has counted in 1000 dollars, that till 2020 will occur bio terrorist attack to one million victims though hopes to lose.) This estimation is based on the analysis of plans of the industry on reduction in price of full recognition of human DNA-under these plans, by 2015 such recognition will cost about 1000 dollars. These plans offer some set of perspective technologies and exponential curve of reduction in price which is steadily observed till the present moment. If by 2015 recognition costs fell so much it will mean, that the key technology of very fast reading of DNA will be created, and it is possible to assume, that the same technology will be created for cheap DNA synthesis (actually synthesis easier, and the technology already exists). On the basis of these technologies the library of meanings of different genes that will result in explosive understanding of principles of work of organisms will be created, and the computers which have developed by then can model consequences of those or other mutations. It all together will allow to create the bioprinter described above. That growth of density of probability, by my estimation, near 2020, does not mean that already now any terrorists do not develop a brood of very dangerous various viruses in different laboratories.

The probability of application of biotechnologies, the leader to global catastrophe, can be lowered following factors:

1) Biological attack could be survived in bunkers.
2) The first serious catastrophe, connected with leak of dangerous biotechnologies will result in so draconian control measures, that them will be enough for prevention of creation of bioprinter or its distribution.
3) AI and nanotechnologies will develop earlier, than the bioprinter will appear and widely spread.
4) Nuclear war or other disaster will interrupt development of biotechnologies.
5) It is possible that biotechnologies will allow to create something like a universal vaccine or artificial immune system faster, than dangerous minilaboratories will spread.

Unfortunately, there is the following unpleasant chain of a feedback connected with protection against the biological weapon. For the best protection we should prepare as much as possible of the first class experts in viruses and vaccines, but the more such experts are in the world, more than are chances, that one of them becomes "terrorist".

Besides, there is a certain probability of creation of biological green goo,-that is the certain universal omnivorous microorganisms capable with big speed to digest in all biosphere. For this purpose it is necessary to collect in one microorganism the properties which are available separately in different microorganisms-ability to catch a sunlight, to dissolve and acquire minerals, to breed with speed of E.Coli, to infect as a virus, other cells, and a number of others-and to collect not actually, but potentially, in the form of sites of DNA and switching mechanisms between them.

Usually such scenario is not considered, as it is necessary, that microorganisms have already reached absolute degree of perfection, so if green goo would be possible, it already would arise. However before have arisen of eukaryotes, there have passed billions years too, and perhaps, such superbacterium too could arise only after tens billions years of natural evolution.

However people can purposefully design it, may be even casual – e.g. as means to struggle against a waste. It is not obligatory to combine all these signs in one being-simultaneous attack by several species of different "green goo" would be immeasurably more dangerous. There is an opinion, that efforts on creation of the useful agricultural crops steady to wreckers, could lead to appearance of the "superweed", capable to supersede the majority of natural plants of their ecological niches. This event is serious risk at creation of genetically modified products, instead of that they will appear inedible. The last is much easier to find out and prevent. Conclusion: there is a huge set of ways to apply biotechnologies to the detriment of mankind, and this set is still not described up to the end. Though each separate application of biotechnologies is possible to prevent or limit its consequences, cheapness, privacy and prevalence of these technologies do their ill-intentioned application practically inevitable. Besides, many biological risks can be not obvious and postponed in time as the biological science still develops. Large-scale application of the biological weapons is much more dangerous and much more probable, than classical nuclear war.

SUPERDRUG

Biotechnologies and brain researches by many ways conduct to possibility of creation of superdrugs. One of scenarios of distribution of a superdrug in the future is offered Strugatsky in the novel. The Final Circle of Paradise where the most powerful drug causing 100 percentage accustoming from the first usage, it appears to make very simply of a radio receiver and of some other popular components which directly influences the pleasure centre in a brain. It is the scenario it is connected in the not with distribution there is some substances, but with distribution of "knowledge of mass destruction"-about how to make it.

On the one hand, we can assert, that any drug will not affect all population of the people as there always will be people who will refuse from it. On the other hand, we can imagine at once several superdrugs, possible in the future, the general meaning of which action consists in swithing off human from a social life. And a human who has refused from one class of drugs, can addict to another. And in a modern reality someone does not drink alcohol, but is addicted to coffee. Someone does not watch TV, but spends all time in the Internet. The superstrong drug can be similar to infectious illness if one people will aspire to infect others, and those is not against to be catched. Superdrug types:

1) Direct influence on the pleasure centres in a brain. There are researches on influence by means of a rotating magnetic field (a Persiger helmet, Shakti helmet), transcranial magnetic stimulation, electric stimulation by patterns of brain activity, audiostimulation (binaural rhythms), photostimulations, biological feedback through devices that can read encephalogram, like the recently released thought helmets for computer games.
2) Future appearance of microrobots will allow to carry out direct stimulation and reading of the information from the brain.
3) Bio-engineering will allow to create genetically modified plants which will create any set of chemicals, and to look as usual window plants or tea mushrooms. Moreover, distribution of these plants would be probably not only physical, but also by means of the information on a code of DNA on the Internet, that the end user can grow up them on a place by means of "DNA-printer".
4) Knowledge of biology will allow to think up much more strongly operating substances with beforehand set properties, and also with smaller number of by-effects that will make them more attractively.
5) Genetically modified organisms can create new neural ways in a human body to a brain to cause much bigger pleasure. And thus to reduce short-term negative effects for health.
6) Virtual reality will inevitably make a step forward. We can write down the dreams and increase comprehension in them, combining ideas of East meditation and technological possibilities for their realisation; the virtual reality by means of brain implants can create much brighter films, than modern cinema and video games. Helmets for a virtual reality become much more perfect.

It is obvious, that are possible different combinations of the listed kinds of an absolute drug which only will strengthen its action. Let's name "an absolute drug" a any special agent which is more attractive than a usual reality to any human and completely withdraws him from this reality. Thus it is possible to divide a fast and slow absolute drug. The first gives experience for the sake of which human is ready to die, the second-a certain new reality in which it is possible to exist long time.

The fast drug represents global danger if the mechanism of its distribution is somehow registered in its mechanism of action. For example, if the high comes only after this drug is transferred to three other people. Somewhat this mechanism operates in criminal gangs of drug dealers (like gang M31 in the USA) where the addict is compelled to place the friends, that, selling it a drug to provide itself with a dose. It is possible to present distribution of a slow absolute drug on a following example: if your favourite or the relative is irreversible has left in the virtual simulated world for you it becomes a source of the sufferings comparable to his death, and in their unique way will avoid it too is to leave to this ideal world in which you can reach dialogue with him or, say, his electronic copy.

Owing to it, each human will have a wide choice of the entertainments considerably surpassing any reality. Thus there is a complicated question-in what measure human, completely and is irreversible left in incomprehensible pleasure and happy with it, should be considered as alive? And if we unconditionally condemn any primitive drug addict how should we concerns a human who forever has left in the highly artistic world of historical reconstruction?

It is necessary to realise, that fatal action of many drugs is far unevidently and cannot be obviuos at once. For example, heroin and cocaine for long time, for years, were on open sale, and LSD was easily accessible. The drug create short circuit of psychological function of reinforcement (that is pleasures), but from the point of view of evolutionary mechanisms reception of pleasure is not at all the real purpose of an organism. On the contrary, the being should remain unsatisfied enough constantly to aspire to a gain of new territories. The absolute drug creates possibility of the following dilemma: the mankind as whole ceases to exist, but each separate subject perceives this event as humanal paradise and is very happy with it. The beings left a reality and enjoying simulated life, nothing returning in exchange, appear a useless outgrowth on system which it will shake him out at the nearest crisis. It is one of ways to which the addiction for the absolute drug can lead to human extinction. Secondly, reduction of interest to an external reality will reduce attention to possible catastrophes and crises. The probability of appearance of a superdrug looks very high as it can be reached by many ways not only for the account of successes biotechnologies, but also in nanotechnology, in AI, and also for the account there is nobody the casual invention uniting already existing technologies, and also because of presence of huge demand. Possibly, will simultaneously operate set of different superdrugs, creating cumulative effect.

Therefore we can expect, that this probability will grow, and will grow faster, than successes of any of the technologies taken separately. As we have assumed, that biotechnologies will yield powerful result in the form of the bioprinter in 10-15 years it means, that we will receive a superdrug before this time. As mechanisms for superdrug realisation can be easier, than the bioprinter. Prevent superdrug distribution can very rigid system of the general control or deep degradation in pre-technological a society. Conclusions: development of the robotised manufacture will start to do people useless, and it is required to occupy them with something. A superdrug is one of the ways to remove from life superfluous parts of system. The absolute drug cannot carry the name of "drug" at all and not resemble modern stereotypes. The absolute drug will not be one, but there will be set of the factors working objectively on division of people, their switching-off from a reality and reduction of their life and ability to reproduction. The absolute drug can look as the absolute blessing, and the question of its harm can depend on the point of view. In any sense the modern culture of entertainments in the western countries with low level of birth rate can already be a prototype of such drug. However the absolute drug nevertheless in itself cannot exterminate all people as always there will be groups which have refused it and have continued a usual human life, and, finally, natural selection will leave only representatives of these groups. Besides, the slow absolute drug operates on human community on so long time intervals which, most likely, will be blocked by faster dangerous processes. The fast absolute drug is similar to biological epidemic, and it can resist the same methods. For example, there are possible biological agents, which damage ability of human to unlimited pleasure (and such are already developed for treatment of addicts, for example, cut of certain neural communications), therefore an absolute drug, more likely, is necessary to consider as a factor which would open a window of vulnerability for other factors of destruction.

THE RISKS CONNECTED WITH SELF-COPIING IDEAS (MEME)

In the book Selfish gene Dawkins has offered the concept of mem which are ideas which are capable self replicate, being transferred from one human to another so behave, for example, gossips. Any area where self-reproduced elements are capable to exist and which can concern all people, potentially is a source of global risk. Whether it is possible such mem which could lead to death of all people?

On the one hand, we have in history examples of the extremely dangerous memes: radical political theories and different forms of religionism. On the other hand, meme for spreading needs live people. And as people already exist for a long time, it is possible to assume, that now there are not such dangerous memes which could easily autogenesisand and lead all to extinction. At last, meme is only thought, and it does not kill in itself. It is improbable, that the idea which would influence all people without an exception is possible, and would influence mortally. At last, in a society there is a balance various memes. On the other hand, dangerous memes get under the concept of "knowledge of mass destruction, whether entered by Bill Joy in article "Why the future doesn't need us". However during a present epoch memes have found possibility to exist without people-in texts and computer programs. In present period self-copied dangerous meme can get support from technical means. It is obvious, that now we cannot think up an example really dangerous meme because if we have written it here it would be the criminal. The information on how to make a dangerous superdrug would be such dangerous meme.

And just as in case of the biological weapons one is dangerous not any especially lethal a virus, but possibility to make a lot of different strains, faster, than protection is possible from them, and that so many of them will appear that they will flood any protection. For example, the artificial intellect can generate dangerous memes.

The list of existing now memes which are somehow dangerous:

1) Representations about exclusiveness of the religion. A.P. Nazaretjan considers that property of intolerance inevitably inherent in religions to other religions – and it is the major threat to survival of mankind in the XXI century. He believes, that religion as the social institute, promotes association of group of people through hatred to other group. An exit he sees in creation of secular system of the purposes which does not subdivide people on bad and good. The ideas connected with national and racial distinctions of people precisely also work as dangerous meme.
2) Knowledge of manufacture of drugs.
3) Organizations in which a main objective is recruitment of new members, for example, sects or a gang operating in the USA Ì13.
4) Self-coming true prophecies on catastrophes. The communique about inevitability of global catastrophe which would be in the near future, is a vivid example of such event. For example, about collision of the Earth in a year with a huge asteroid. Even if this message would be false, consequences of its promulgation would be catastrophic. The majority of people would stop to be engaged in long-term projects, and in general to work. Someone would hit in religion, someone would make acts of unmotivated violence, abused drugs etc., aspiring to receive a maximum pleasure for remained time. The followed anarchy would make impossible efforts on catastrophe prevention even if them there would have a certain sense.
5) Certain model of behaviour which leads to distribution of dangerous illness. An example: cannibalism at Neanderthal men which possibly became the reason of their extinction because they caught prion like one

causing cow madness, while eating brains of the fellow tribesmen. Or the sexual revolution conducting to distribution of a HIV.

6) Extraordinary scale and bright dreams conducting to acceptance for the sake of them of higher norms of risk and-or granting right to kill many other people. For example, red terror was justified by that communism, finally, will bring the blessing to much bigger number of people. New technologies open almost divine possibilities for a human, generating improbable temptations and inducing to suppose bigger risk.
7) Powerful ideological systems, like fascism.

ARTIFICIAL INTELLIGENCE

Project *Blue Brain* on modelling of a brain of mammals declared in the autumn of 2007 successful imitation of cortical columns of the brain of mouse and has planned creation of full model of human brain till 2020. Though direct modelling of a brain is not the best way to a universal artificial intellect, the forecast of successes in this area approximately corresponds to expected rates of working out of AI. Nick Bostrom in article How long is before superintelligence? shows, that modern development of technologies conducts to creation of the artificial intellect surpassing human in first third of the XXI century.

Google sometimes mentioned plans of creation of an artificial intellect, and, certainly, it possesses necessary technical, information and monetary resources to make it if it is in general possible on a present technological level. However, as experience of the previous unclassified attempts of creation of AI (for example, computers of 5th generation in Japan in 80th years) strongly associates with a failure, and can cause interest of special services, hardly the big companies are interested to advertise widely works in this area before they will have concrete results. Company *Novamente* declares, that 50 % of a code of universal AI are already written (70 000 lines of a code on C++), and though long training is required, the general design of the project is clear. *SIAI (Singularity Institute for Artificial Intelligence)* has designated plans on creation of the program, capable to copy the initial code. Company *Numenta* advances own model of AI based on idea of "hierarchical time memory", and already is on the level of demonstration products. Company *Cycorp, Inc* in project *CYC* has collected a huge database about human knowledge about the world, in other words, about common sense (1 000 000 statements) and already suggests demonstration products. It is supposed, that association of this base with the heuristic analyzer (that is the program, capable to make logic operations by certain rules and to create new rules, including rules about how to change of rules)-can lead to creation of AI of human level. (The author of project Lenat has developed earlier heuristic analyzer "Eurisko" which has won in 1981 and 1982 competitions Traveller TCS on management of virtual battles of fleets therefore it was forbidden to this program to participate in the further competitions, but it has received intensive financing from DARPA). Company *a2i2* promises universal AI of human level by 2008 and asserts, that the project develops according to the schedule. Also behind creation of robot *Asimo* in Japan there is a program on working out of AI by functional modelling of a man.

Powerful results are given by a direction of researches of AI, named genetic programming. By the present moment the list of inventions of "human level", made by computers in the research company *Genetic Programming Inc*, using this technology, includes 36 names of which 2 are made by computers for the first time (includes quantum reports of an information transfer and the scheme of various radio-electronic devices), and the others repeat already patented projects. Besides named, there is a set of University projects on AI creation. Workings out of AI are conducted and in the Russian Federation. For example, in company *ABBYY* is developed something like natural language interpreter that can be the important step on a way to AI of human level. And the essence of the matter not only that there are so many projects though one of them will become successful the first, but the fact that the volume of discoveries from the different parties will exceed critical weight one day, and in the field will occur powerful jump.

There are different opinions concerning possibility of realisation of an artificial intellect. we consider, that strong universal AI is possible. Many leading experts in this area adhere to the same opinion: E. Yudkowsky, B. Gorztel, R. Kurzweil and Russian researcher A.L. Shamis. As human possesses natural intelligence there are no bases to write down AI as in improbable discovery. The precaution principle also forces us to assume, that AI is possible.

It is necessary to tell that there are much less works considering strong AI as possible global risk, than works about risks of extinction, connected with the nuclear weapon. Basically, it is E. Yudkowsky's works. Similar ideas are developed by M. Omohundro in article Basic drives of AI where it shows, that any AI with the fixed system of goals with high probability evolves towards a dangerous condition in which it will be inclined to protect itself (himself), to extend, improve an own code, to aspire to purpose signs (as, for example, pleasure for human) instead of the purpose and to protect the system of the purposes from changes. we recommend to everyone before making the definitive and unshakable opinion on, whether AI can be threat to mankind, read E.Yudkowsky's article An artificial intellect as the positive and negative factor of global risk.

Yudkowsky shows that spontaneous universal AI is possible, and that it is very dangerous. If there will be many AI-projects (that is, groups of scientists creating universal AI in the different ways and with the different purposes), that, at least one of them can be used for attempt to seize power on the Earth. And the main objective of such capture will prevent creation and distribution of other AIs with the hostile purposes created by other projects. Thus, though AI evolution is the slowest, after overcoming certain critical weight it can go very quickly,-namely when AI will reach level of possibility of self-improvement. Now we cannot tell, with what speed such process will go.

For AI creation is necessary presence of enough powerful computer, at least. Now the most powerful computers have capacity of an order 1 petaflop (10^{15} operations from a floating comma in a second). By some estimations, it is enough for emulation of a human brain, so AI too could work on such platform. Now such computers are accessible only to very large organisations for limited time. However Moore's law assumes, that capacity of computers will increase for 10 years approximately in 100 times, i.e., capacity of the desktop computer will increase to level of teraflop, and it is required only 1000 desktop computers united in cluster to make necessary

1 petaflop. The price of such unit will make about one million dollars in the present prices-the sum accessible even to the small organisation. For this purpose it is enough to realise almost ready projects in area multi-core processors (some firms now offer chips with 1024 processors) and reduction of the sizes of silicon elements.

Further, when AI will be started, it can optimize its own code, and though to work by more and more weak computers-or to become more and more strong on the same computer. As soon as it will learn to earn money on the Internet, it can buy or simply rent the additional capacities even physically removed from it. So, though sufficient hardware for AI already exist now, in 10 years it become readily available if there will be no catastrophe, braking development.

The most difficult moment in a question on AI is the question on algorithms of its work. On the one hand, we yet do not see any intelligence in computers-or we do not wish to see, as criteria vary. With another, progress in algorithms is, and it is great. For example, the algorithm of decomposition of numbers on a multiplier was improved faster, than computers, that is, even on very old computers it yields on usages the best results, than old algorithms on new computers. Probably, that certain essentially new ideas can resolutely simplify AI design.

If AI finds ability to self-improvement, he will not stop at human level, and will overtake it in thousand and millions times. We already see it on an example of calculations where computers have very quickly overtaken humans, and now even house computer is calculating in billions times faster, than usual human. Under strong AI we mean AI capable on many orders of magnitude to overtake human in speed and efficiency of thinking.

AI AS UNIVERSAL ABSOLUTE WEAPON

Strong AI can find the best possible decision of any problem. It means, that it can be used for achievement of any purposes in an external world. It will find the best way to apply all accessible tools for its realisation and will manage to drive them. In this sense it is the absolute weapon. That it can be most effective murder is only one of possible consequences. AI, capable to solve any problem, is capable and to create a way to motivate on for realisation of long-term objectives in an external world. In a general AI-attack scenario looks as follows:

1. Creation of AI capable to self-improvement (*Seed AI*-that is minimum necessary program capable to self-improvement and self-training.)
2. An installation in it certain goals which can contain direct instructions on power establishments on the Earth, or can be outwardly neutral, but contain the latent discrepancy inducing AI to unlimited growth in the spirit of to count number 3.14... with as much as possible big number of signs after a comma at any cost.
3. The phase of the latent growth in which course AI improves itself, using accessible resources of the laboratory, and also learns world around, using Internet resources. (If in the course of realisation of the purposes of AI put in pawn in it understands, that its programmers interfere with this realisation, for example, that they could switch it off, AI finds a way to deceive them or to leave from their control.)
4. A phase of the latent information distribution: AI grasps the Internet, buy computing capacities, throws its copies on remote computers.
5. A phase of creation of means of influence on an external world-nanoassemblers, payoff of people, mastering of radio-operated devices.
6. Attack to competing AI-projects (and any other sources of risk for existence of it AI) on purpose to deprive them from building alternative AI. Such an attack could be clandestine, such as through making mistakes in software code. It is important to note that AI will operate covertly before it becomes totally immune.
7. A phase of realisation of the primary goal of AI-from the blessing of mankind before transformation of all Solar system into the huge computer for calculation of number 3.14...

It is obvious that some phases can proceed simultaneously; further we will consider separate components of this scheme in detail. we underline what not any AI will move forward on this scenario, but one is enough, and this scenario is especially dangerous.

SYSTEM OF THE GOALS

After the decision of problems of creation of AI the next question will be about the system of the purposes of AI, or, in other words, its "friendliness", at least in relation to owners. There are two variants: or AI is strictly programmed by people on certain purposes, or it has got the purposes casually in the course of the development. In the first case there is a fork:-AI purposes can be dangerous to all mankind or 1. Because the group of people which has created it pursues certain destructive aims, or 2. Because at programming of system of purposes AI in it there was a thin error which conducts to gradual exit AI from under the control. The big list of such possible errors has been offered. For example, AI can aspire to the blessing for all people, and, having learnt that after death of people waits paradise, send all of them there. Or, safeguarding people to forbid them to risk and not to give to use any transport. There are *SIAI* recommendations about how correctly to program strong AI at its creation, but finnaly this question is not solved. And there are doubts that it can be resolved at all, because it is impossible to predict the behaviour of more intellectual system (ie AI) using less intellectual (ie man).

Struggle of AI-projects among Themselves

Already now there is a rigid competition between the companies developing AI for attention and investors and for correctness of ideas of their way of creation of universal AI. When a certain company will create first powerful AI, it will have a choice-or to apply it to the control over all other AI-projects in the world and so over all world, or to appear before risk of that the competing organisation with the unknown global purposes will make it in the near future-and will cover the first company. Having advantage should attack before threat of loss of this advantage. Thus given necessity of a choice is not secret-it was already discussed in the open press and will be for certain known to all companies which will approach to creation of strong AI. Probably, that some companies will refuse in that case to try to establish the control over the world first, but the strongest and aggressive, most likely, will dare at it.

Thus the requirement to attack first will result to usage of the poor-quality and underfulfilled versions of AI with not clear purposes. Even in XIX century phone have patented almost simultaneously in different places so and now the backlash between the leader of race and catching up can make days or hours. The ýæå this backlash, the will be struggle because the lagging behind project will possess force more intensively to resist. And probably to present a variant when one AI-project should establish the control over nuclear rockets and attack laboratories of other projects.

The Advanced Human

There are assumptions (R.Penrouz), that the human intuition is caused by special quantum processes in a brain of human. Even if so, powerful algorithms could work without intuition. Nevertheless, there is a variant to bypass this obstacle, having created genetically advanced human, or implant to the modern human brain means to access to the Internet (so-called neiro-implant). Other integration methods are also possible like connection of live neurons with the usual computer, and also with quantum computers. Even usual human armed with the computer with the Internet, strengthens his mind. Owing to it, strong AI can turn out as a result converging of the computer and human, having inherited, thus, all typical human purposes, and first of all-requirement for the power.

AI and its Separate Copies

When powerful AI will arise, it will be compelled to create his copies (probably, reduced) to send them, for example, in expeditions on other planets or simply to load on other computers. Accordingly, it should supply with their certain system of the purposes and some kind of "friendly" or is faster, vassal relations with it, and also system of recognition "friendly-enemy". Failure in this system of the purposes will result to that given copy will "rebell". For example, self-preservation goal contradicts submission goal to obey dangerous orders. It can accept very thin forms, but, finally, lead to war between versions of one AI.

AI "Revolt"

Spontaneous revolt of computers is more image which has

come from cinema, than real possibility as AI has no desires while human will not create them to it. However some kinds of AI, for example, created by means of genetic algorithms, already on a method of the creation are adjusted on struggle and a survival. Further, what was an overall objective at AI, it will have one common subgoal for all variants-to survive, so, to protect itself from destruction. And the best kind of defence is an attack. The most real is danger of that human will give AI a command, not having thought over all consequences of its performance and not having left way to undo it. (For example as in that joke where human ordered to the robot to remove all round subjects from a room-and it has torn off human's head.) The probability of self-origin of erroneous commands is small-except a case of use of genetic algorithms.

Speed of Start

From the point of view of speed of development of AI three variants are possible: fast start, slow start, and very slow start. Fast start-AI reaches I.Q., on many orders of magnitude surpassing human, in some hours or days. For this purpose should begin some kind of chain reaction in which the growing increase in intelligence gives the increasing possibilities for its subsequent increase. (This process already occurs in a science and technologies, supporting Moore's law. And it is similar to chain reaction in a reactor where the factor of reproduction of neutrons is more than 1.) In this case it almost for certain will overtake all other projects of AI creation. Its intelligence becomes enough that to seize power on the Earth. Thus we cannot precisely tell, how such capture will look as we cannot predict behaviour of the intelligence surpassing ours. The objection that AI will not want to behaviour actively in an external world is possible to role out on the ground that if there will be many AI-projects or copies of AI of the program then one will try sooner or later as the tool for conquest of all world. It is important to notice, that successful attack of strong AI will develop, possibly, is secretly until while it does not become irreversible. Theoretically, AI could hide the domination and after attack end. In other words, probably, that it already is.

Scenarios of "Fast Start"

· AI grasps all Internet and subordinates to itself its

resources. Then gets into all fenced off firewall networks. This scenario demands for the realisation of time of an order of hours. Capture means possibility to operate by all computers in a network and to have on them the calculations. However to that AI can read and process all information necessary to it from the Internet.

- AI orders in laboratory synthesis of some code of DNA which allows it to create radio-controlled bacteria which synthesise more and more complex organisms under its management and gradually create nanorobot which can be applied to any purposes in an external world-including introduction in other computers, in a brain of people and creation of new computing capacities. In details this scenario is considered in Yudkowsky article about AI. (Speed: days.)
- AI is involved in dialogue with people and becomes infinitely effective manipulator of people's behaviour. All people do that wants AI. Modern state propagation aspires to the similar purposes and even reaches them, but in comparison with it AI will be much stronger, as he can offer each human a certain suggestion which he cannot refuse. It will be the promise of the most treasured desire, blackmail or the latent hypnosis.
- AI subordinates to itself a state system and uses channels available in it for management. Inhabitants of such state in general can nothing notice. Or on the contrary, the state uses AI on channels available already for it.
- AI subordinates to itself the remote operated army. For example, fighting robots or a rocket (the scenario from a film Termonator).
- AI finds essentially new way to influence human consciousness (memes, feromons, electromagnetic fields) and spread itself or extends the control through it.
- Certain consecutive or parallel combination of the named ways.

Slow Start and Struggle of Different AI Among Themselves

In a case of "the slow scenario" AI growth occupies months

and years, and it means, that, rather possibly, it will occur simultaneously in several laboratories worldwide. As a result of it there will be a competition between different AI-projects. It is fraught with struggle of several AI with different systems of the purposes for domination over the Earth. Such struggle can be armed and to appear race for time. Thus advantage will get in it those projects, whose system of the purposes is not constrained by any moral frameworks. Actually, we will appear in the war centre between different kinds of an artificial intellect. It is clear that such scenario is mortally dangerous to mankind. In case of the superslow scenario thousand laboratories and powerful computers simultaneously come nearer to creation AI, that, probably, does not give advantages to any project, and certain balance between them is established. However here too struggle for computing resources and elimination in favour of the most successful and aggressive projects is possible.

Struggle between states, as ancient forms of the organization using people as the separate elements, and the new AI using as the carrier computers is also possible. And though we am assured, that the states will lose, struggle can be short and bloody. As an exotic variant it is possible to present a case when some states are under control of computer AI, and others are ruled commonly. A variant of such device-the Automated government system known from a science fiction. (V. Argonov. "2032".)

Transformation of Total Control State into AI

At last, there is a scenario in which all world system as whole gradually turns to an artificial intellect. It can be connected with creation all-world Orwell state of the total control which will be necessary for successful opposition to bioterrorism. It is world system where each step of citizens is supervised by video cameras and every possible systems of tracking, and this information downloaded in huge uniform databases and then analyzed. As a whole, the mankind, probably, moves on this way, and technically all is ready for this purpose. Feature of this system is that it initially has distributed character, and separate people, following to their interests or instructions, are only gears in this huge machine. The state as the imhumanal machine was repeatedly described in the literature, including Karl Marx, and earlier Gobbs. Is also interesting Lazarchuk's to theory about Golems and Leviafans-about autonomism of the systems consisting of people in independent machines with its own purposes. However only recently world social system became not simply machine, but an artificial intellect capable to purposeful self-improvement.

The basic obstacle for development of this system are national states with their national armies. Creation of the world government would facilitate formation of such uniform AI. However meanwhile there is a sharp struggle between the states about on what conditions to unite a planet. And also struggle against forces which conditionally are called antiglobalists, and other antisystem elements-Islamites, radical ecologists, separatists and nationalists. World War for unification of the planet will be inevitable and it is fraught with application of "Doomsday weapon" by those who has lost all. But peace world integration through system of contracts is possible also.

Danger, however, consists that the global world machine will start to supersede people from different spheres of a life, at least economically-depriving of their work and consuming those resources which people could spend differently (for example, for 2006-2007 meal in the world has risen in price for 20 percent, in particular, because of transition to biofuel). In any sense to people there will be nothing as to watch TV and drink beer. About this danger Bill Joy wrote in the known article Why the future doesn't need us.

In process of automation of manufacture and management people will be ever less necessary for a state life. Human aggression, probably, will be neutralised by monitoring systems and genetic manipulations. Finally, people will be on the role of pets. Thus to occupy people will be created more and more bright and pleasant "matrix" which will gradually turn to a superdrug deducing people from a life. However here people will climb in continuous a virtual reality because in a usual reality they will have nothing to do (in any measure now this role carries out the TV for the unemployed and pensioners). Natural instincts of a life will induce some people to aspire to destroy all this system that is fraught besides with global catastrophes or destruction of people.

It is important to note the following-whoever had been created the first strong artificial intellect, it will bear on a print of system of the purposes and values of the given group of people as this system will seem for them as only correct. For one overall objective there will be a blessing of all people, for others-the blessing of all live beings, for the third-only all devout Moslems, for the fourth-the blessing only those three programmers who have created it. And representation about the blessing nature too will be rather variously. In this sense the moment of creation of first strong AI is the moment of a fork with very considerable quantity of variants.

"Revolt" of Robots

There is still a dangerous scenario in which house, military and industrial robots spread worldwide, and then all of them are amazed with a computer virus which incites them on aggressive behaviour against human. All readers at least once in life time, probably, faced a situation when the virus has damaged data on the computer. However this scenario is possible only during the period of "a vulnerability window" when there are already the mechanisms, capable to operate in an external world, but still there is no enough an advanced artificial intellect which could or protect them from viruses, or itself to execute virus function, for having grasped them.

There is still a scenario where in the future a certain computer virus extends on the Internet, infect nanofactories worldwide and causes, thus, mass contamination. These nanofactories can produce nanorobots, poisons, viruses or drugs.

Another variant is revolt of army of military robots. Armies of industrially developed states are aimed to full automation. When it will be reached, the huge army consisting from drones, wheel robots and serving mechanisms can move, simply obeying orders of the president. Already, almost robotic army is the strategic nuclear forces. Accordingly, there is a chance that the incorrect order will arrive and such army will start to successively attack all people. We will notice, that it is not necessary for this scenario existence of universal superintelligence, and, on the contrary, for the universal superintelligence seize the Earth, the army of robots is not necessary to it.

THE CONTROL AND DESTRUCTION POSSIBILITY

From that AI will establish control on the Earth, at all does not follow, that it then will decide to exterminate people. (Though considerable victims are possible during process of an establishment of the control.) Eventually, people live in the states which immensely surpass them in the scale, to resources and the purposes, and at all do not perceive it as wrong. Therefore quite can be so, that AI supports an order on the Earth, prevents global risks and is engaged in exploring the Universe. Probably, that it is the best our variant. However we discuss the worst real variants. For example:

- Crookedly programmed AI will destroy people for their blessing-will send in paradise, will connect to a superdrug, close them in safe cages, will replace people with photos with smiling faces.
- AI will not interested in people, but people will continuously struggle with it, therefore it will be easier to exterminate them.
- AI will break and "will go mad".
- AI will dare to make dangerous physical experiment.
- Certain slice of AI will break away from it and will go on it with war. Or our AI will meet in space of the contender.
- AI only will prevent appearance of AI-competitors, but will not prevent to kill to people itself by means of the biological weapon and other ways.

People have exterminated Neanderthal men because those were their direct competitors, but did not aspire especially to destruction of a chimpanzee and small primacies. So we have quite good enough chances to survive at Indifferent AI, however this life will be not full-that is it will not be realisation of all those possibilities, which people could reach, if they have created correct and rather friendly AI.

AI and the States

AI is the absolute weapon which force now is underestimated by the states-as far as we know. (However successful enough project Eurisko of the beginning 80 has got financial support *DARPA*.) However the idea about nanotechnology has already got into minds of governors of many countries, and the idea about strong AI lays near to it. Therefore resolute turn is possible when large corporations and states will understand that AI is an absolute weapon-and someone else could seize it. Then small private laboratories will be crushed by large state corporations as it has occurred after chain reaction discovery on uranium. we should notice that at *DARPA* there is a project on developing of AI, however it is positioned as opened and being on an early stage. However, probably, that there are powerful AI projects about which we know no more, than citizens knew about the Manhattan project in days of the Second World War. Other variant-the small group of talented people will create AI earlier, than the governments will understand value of AI and, moreover, the danger proceeding from AI. However AI created by the separate state, will be more national, than for all human. If AI attack is unsuccessful, it can become a pretext for war between two countries.

Probability of AI Catastrophe

The probability of the global catastrophe connected with AI, is product of probabilities of that it in general will be ever created also that it will be applied by a certain erroneous way. we believe, that by one or a another way strong AI will be created during the XXI century if only any other catastrophe does not prevent technological development. Even if attempts to construct AI by means of computers will fail, always is reserve variant: namely,-successes in brain scanning will allow to create its electronic copies, and successes in genetics-to create genetically advanced human brains. Electronic copies of a usual brain can work a million times faster and if thus it there will be copies of highly ingenious and correct trained brain, and they will be united by thousand in a certain virtual scientific research institute, finally, we will equally receive intelligence, in millions times surpassing human quantitatively and qualitatively. Then there are some time stages on which AI can represent danger. The initial stage:

1) Moment of the first start: risk of uncontrollable development and distribution.
2) Moment when the owner of the first AI realises the advantage that he can apply it as the absolute weapon

to achievement of any purposes on the Earth. (Thus the owner of AI can be both the state, and large corporation, though finally-one or several humans.) Though these purposes can be good for some people, there is a risk, that AI will start to show incorrect behaviour in the course of expanding on the Earth whereas in laboratory he behaved ideally.

3) Moment when this owner of AI realises, that even if he does nothing, someone another will very soon create AI and can use it for achievement of any other purposes on the Earth, and first of all-to deprive our owner of ability to use AI in full force. It induces created AI at first to try to stop other AI projects. Thus it appears before a dilemma: to apply still crude AI or to be late. It creates risk of application with unrectified system of the purposes.

4) Following phase of risk-struggle between several AI for the control over the Earth. Danger that the different weapon which will influence people will be applied a lot of.

   It is clear, that all initial stage can go in some days. A functioning stage:

5) At this stage the basic risk is connected by that the system of the purposes of AI contains a certain unevident error which can be shown by unexpected image after many years. It could appear instantly, in the form of sudden failure, or gradually, in a kind there is nobody the process which is gradually washing away people from a life (like a superdrug and unemployment).

Now we cannot measure the risk created at each stage, but is clear, that it is not absolute, but considerable, therefore we carry it in a category 10 percentage risks. On the other hand, creation of effective AI sharply reduces all other global risks as it can find decisions of the problems connected with them. Therefore the actual contribution of AI to a likelihood picture of risks can be negative-that is its creation reduces total global risk.

12

Nuclear Weapon Design

Nuclear weapon designs are physical, chemical, and engineering arrangements that cause the physics package of a nuclear weapon to detonate. There are three basic design types. In all three, the explosive energy of deployed devices has been derived primarily from nuclear fission, not fusion.

- Pure fission weapons were the first nuclear weapons built and have so far been the only type ever used in warfare. The active material is fissile uranium (U-235) or plutonium (Pu-239), explosively assembled into a chain-reacting critical mass by one of two methods:
    - o Gun assembly, in which one piece of fissile uranium is fired at a fissile uranium target at the end of the weapon, similar to firing a bullet down a gun barrel, achieving critical mass when combined.
    - o Implosion, in which a fissile mass of either material (U-235, Pu-239, or a combination) is surrounded by high explosives that compress the mass, resulting in criticality.

The implosion method can use either uranium or plutonium as fuel. The gun method only uses uranium. Plutonium is considered impractical for the gun method because of early triggering due to Pu-240 contamination and due to its time constant for prompt critical fission being much shorter than that of U-235.

- Fusion-boosted fission weapons improve on the implosion design. The high temperature and pressure environment at the centre of an exploding fission weapon compresses and heats a mixture of tritium and deuterium gas (heavy isotopes of hydrogen). The hydrogen fuses to form helium and free neutrons. The energy release from fusion reactions is relatively negligible, but each neutron starts a new fission chain reaction, greatly reducing the amount of fissile material that would otherwise be wasted. Boosting can more than double the weapon's fission energy release.

- Two-stage thermonuclear weapons are essentially a chain of fusion-boosted fission weapons, usually with only two stages in the chain. The second stage, called the "secondary," is imploded by x-ray energy from the first stage, called the "primary." This radiation implosion is much more effective than the high-explosive implosion of the primary. Consequently, the secondary can be many times more powerful than the primary, without being bigger. The secondary can be designed to maximize fusion energy release, but in most designs fusion is employed only to drive or enhance fission, as it is in the primary. More stages could be added, but the result would be a multi-megaton weapon too powerful to be useful. (The United States briefly deployed a three-stage 25-megaton bomb, the B41, starting in 1961. Also in 1961, the Soviet Union tested, but did not deploy, a three-stage 50–100 megaton device, Tsar Bomba.)

Pure fission weapons historically have been the first type to be built by a nation state. Large industrial states with well-developed nuclear arsenals have two-stage thermonuclear weapons, which are the most compact, scalable, and cost effective option once the necessary industrial infrastructure is built. Most known innovations in nuclear weapon design originated in the United States, although some were later developed independently by other states; the following descriptions feature U.S. designs.

In early news accounts, pure fission weapons were called atomic bombs or A-bombs, a misnomer since the energy comes only from the nucleus of the atom. Weapons involving fusion were called hydrogen bombs or H-bombs, also a misnomer since their destructive energy comes mostly from fission. Insiders favoured the terms nuclear and thermonuclear, respectively. The term thermonuclear refers to the high temperatures required to initiate fusion. It ignores the equally important factor of pressure, which was considered secret at the time the term became current. Many nuclear weapon terms are similarly inaccurate because of their origin in a classified environment. Some are nonsense code words such as "alarm clock".

Nuclear reactions

Nuclear fission splits heavier atoms to form lighter atoms. Nuclear fusion bonds together lighter atoms to form heavier atoms. Both reactions generate roughly a million times more energy than comparable chemical reactions, making nuclear bombs a million times more powerful than non-nuclear bombs, which a French patent claimed in May 1939. In some ways, fission and fusion are opposite and complementary reactions, but the particulars are unique for each. To understand how nuclear weapons are designed, it is useful to know the important similarities and differences between fission and fusion. The following explanation uses rounded numbers and approximations.

Fission

When a free neutron hits the nucleus of a fissionable atom like uranium-235 (^{235}U), the uranium splits into two smaller atoms called fission fragments, plus more neutrons. Fission can be self-sustaining because it produces more neutrons of the speed required to cause new fissions.

The uranium atom can split any one of dozens of different ways, as long as the atomic weights add up to 236 (uranium plus the extra neutron). The following equation shows one possible split, namely into strontium-95 (^{95}Sr), xenon-139 (^{139}Xe), and two neutrons (n), plus energy:

$$^{235}\mathrm{U} + n = {}^{95}\mathrm{Sr} + {}^{139}\mathrm{Xe} + 2n + 180\ \mathrm{MeV}$$

The immediate energy release per atom is 180 million electron volts (MeV), i.e. 74 TJ/kg, of which 90% is kinetic energy (or motion) of the fission fragments, flying away from each other mutually repelled by the positive charge of their protons (38 for strontium, 54 for xenon). Thus their initial kinetic energy is 67 TJ/kg, hence their initial speed is 12,000 kilometres per second, but their high electric charge causes many inelastic collisions with nearby nuclei. The fragments remain trapped inside the bomb's uranium pit until their motion is converted into x-ray heat, a process which takes about a millionth of a second (a microsecond).

This x-ray energy produces the blast and fire which are normally the purpose of a nuclear explosion. After the fission products slow down, they remain radioactive. Being new elements with too many neutrons, they eventually become stable by means of beta decay, converting neutrons into protons by throwing off electrons and gamma rays. Each fission product nucleus decays between one and six times, average three times, producing a variety of isotopes of different elements, some stable, some highly radioactive, and others radioactive with half-lives up to 200,000 years. In reactors, the radioactive products are the nuclear waste in spent fuel. In bombs, they become radioactive fallout, both local and global.

Meanwhile, inside the exploding bomb, the free neutrons released by fission strike nearby U-235 nuclei causing them to fission in an exponentially growing chain reaction (1, 2, 4, 8, 16, etc.). Starting from one, the number of fissions can theoretically double a hundred times in a microsecond, which could consume all uranium up to hundreds of tons by the hundredth link in the chain. In practice, bombs do not contain that much uranium, and, anyway, just a few kilograms undergo fission before the uranium blows itself apart.

Holding an exploding bomb together is the greatest challenge of fission weapon design. The heat of fission rapidly expands the uranium pit, spreading apart the target nuclei and making space for the neutrons to escape without being captured. The chain reaction stops. Materials which can sustain a chain reaction are called fissile. The two fissile materials used in nuclear weapons are: U-235, also known as highly enriched uranium (HEU), oralloy (Oy) meaning Oak Ridge Alloy, or 25 (the last digits of the atomic number, which is 92 for uranium, and the atomic weight, here 235, respectively); and Pu-239, also known as plutonium, or 49 (from 94 and 239).

Uranium's most common isotope, U-238, is fissionable but not fissile (meaning that it cannot sustain a chain reaction by itself but can be made to fission, specifically by neutrons from a fusion reaction). Its aliases include natural or unenriched uranium, depleted uranium (DU), tubealloy (Tu), and 28. It cannot sustain a chain reaction, because its own fission neutrons are not powerful enough to cause more U-238 fission. However, the neutrons released by *fusion* will fission U-238. This U-238 fission reaction produces most of the destructive energy in a typical two-stage thermonuclear weapon.

Fusion

Fusion is unlikely to be self-sustaining because it does not produce the heat and pressure necessary for more fusion. It produces neutrons which run away with the energy. In weapons, the most important fusion reaction is called the D-T reaction. Using the heat and pressure of fission, hydrogen-2, or deuterium (^{2}D), fuses with hydrogen-3, or tritium (^{3}T), to form helium-4 (^{4}He) plus one neutron (n) and energy:

$$^2\mathrm{D} + {}^3\mathrm{T} = {}^4\mathrm{He} + n + 17.6\ \mathrm{MeV}$$

Notice that the total energy output, 17.6 MeV, is one tenth of that with fission, but the ingredients are only one-fiftieth as massive, so the energy output per unit mass is greater. However, in this fusion reaction 80% of the energy, or 14 MeV, is in the motion of the neutron which, having no electric charge and being almost as massive as the hydrogen nuclei that created it, can escape the scene without leaving its energy behind to help sustain the reaction – or to generate x-rays for blast and fire.

The only practical way to capture most of the fusion energy is to trap the neutrons inside a massive bottle of heavy material such as lead, uranium, or plutonium. If the 14 MeV neutron is captured by uranium (either type: 235 or 238) or plutonium, the result is fission and the release of 180 MeV of fission energy, multiplying the energy output tenfold.

Fission is thus necessary to start fusion, helps to sustain fusion, and captures and multiplies the energy released in fusion neutrons. In the case of a neutron bomb the last-mentioned does not apply since the escape of neutrons is the objective.

Tritium production

A third important nuclear reaction is the one that creates tritium, essential to the type of fusion used in weapons and, incidentally, the most expensive ingredient in any nuclear weapon. Tritium, or hydrogen-3, is made by bombarding lithium-6 (^{6}Li) with a neutron (n) to produce helium-4 (^{4}He) plus tritium (^{3}T) and energy:

$$^{6}\text{Li} + n = {}^{4}\text{He} + {}^{3}\text{T} + 5\ \text{MeV}$$

A nuclear reactor is necessary to provide the neutrons. The industrial-scale conversion of lithium-6 to tritium is very similar to the conversion of uranium-238 into plutonium-239. In both cases the feed material is placed inside a nuclear reactor and removed for processing after a period of time. In the 1950s, when reactor capacity was limited, the production of tritium and plutonium were in direct competition. Every atom of tritium in a weapon replaced an atom of plutonium that could have been produced instead.

The fission of one plutonium atom releases ten times more total energy than the fusion of one tritium atom, and it generates fifty times more blast and fire. For this reason, tritium is included in nuclear weapon components only when it causes more fission than its production sacrifices, namely in the case of fusion-boosted fission. However, an exploding nuclear bomb is a nuclear reactor. The above reaction can take place simultaneously throughout the secondary of a two-stage thermonuclear weapon, producing tritium in place as the device explodes.

Of the three basic types of nuclear weapon, the first, pure fission, uses the first of the three nuclear reactions above. The second, fusion-boosted fission, uses the first two. The third, two-stage thermonuclear, uses all three.

Pure fission weapons

The first task of a nuclear weapon design is to rapidly assemble a supercritical mass of fissile uranium or plutonium. A supercritical mass is one in which the percentage of fission-produced neutrons captured by another fissile nucleus is large enough that each fission event, on average, causes more than one additional fission event.

Once the critical mass is assembled, at maximum density, a burst of neutrons is supplied to start as many chain reactions as possible. Early weapons used an "urchin" inside the pit containing polonium-210 and beryllium separated by a thin barrier. Implosion of the pit crushed the urchin, mixing the two metals, thereby allowing alpha particles from the polonium to interact with beryllium to produce free neutrons. In modern weapons, the neutron generator is a high-voltage vacuum tube containing a particle accelerator which bombards a deuterium/tritium-metal hydride target with deuterium and tritium ions. The resulting small-scale fusion produces neutrons at a protected location outside the physics package, from which they penetrate the pit. This method allows better control of the timing of chain reaction initiation.

The critical mass of an uncompressed sphere of bare metal is 110 lb (50 kg) for uranium-235 and 35 lb (16 kg) for delta-phase plutonium-239. In practical applications, the amount of material required for criticallity is modified by shape, purity, density, and the proximity to neutron-reflecting material, all of which affect the escape or capture of neutrons.

To avoid a chain reaction during handling, the fissile material in the weapon must be sub-critical before detonation. It may consist of one or more components containing less than one uncompressed critical mass each. A thin hollow shell can have more than the bare-sphere critical mass, as can a cylinder, which can be arbitrarily long without ever reaching criticallity. A *tamper* is an optional layer of dense material surrounding the fissile material. Due to its inertia it delays the expansion of the reacting material, increasing the efficiency of the weapon. Often the same layer serves both as tamper and as neutron reflector.

Gun-type assembly weapon

Little Boy, the Hiroshima bomb, used 141 lb (64 kg) of uranium with an average enrichment of around 80%, or 112 lb (51 kg) of U-235, just about the bare-metal critical mass. When assembled inside its tamper/reflector of tungsten carbide, the 141 lb (64 kg) was more than twice critical mass. Before the detonation, the uranium-235 was formed into two sub-critical pieces, one of which was later fired down a gun barrel to join the other, starting the atomic explosion. About 1% of the uranium underwent fission; the remainder, representing most of the entire wartime output of the giant factories at Oak Ridge, scattered uselessly.

The inefficiency was caused by the speed with which the uncompressed fissioning uranium expanded and became sub-critical by virtue of decreased density. Despite its inefficiency, this design, because of its shape, was adapted for use in small-diameter, cylindrical artillery shells (a gun-type warhead fired from the barrel of a much larger gun). Such warheads were deployed by the United States until 1992, accounting for a significant fraction of the U-235 in the arsenal, and were some of the first weapons dismantled to comply with treaties limiting warhead numbers. The rationale for this decision was undoubtedly a combination of the lower yield and grave safety issues associated with the gun-type design.

Implosion type weapon

A pusher shell made out of low density metal—such as aluminum, beryllium, or an alloy of the two metals (aluminum being easier and safer to shape and beryllium for its high-neutron-reflective capability) —may be needed. The pusher is located between the explosive lens and the tamper. It works by reflecting some of the shock wave backwards, thereby having the effect of lengthening its duration. Fat Man used an aluminum pusher. The key to Fat Man's greater efficiency was the inward momentum of the massive U-238 tamper (which did not undergo fission). Once the chain reaction started in the plutonium, the momentum of the implosion had to be reversed before expansion could stop the fission. By holding everything together for a few hundred nanoseconds more, the efficiency was increased.

Plutonium pit

The core of an implosion weapon – the fissile material and any reflector or tamper bonded to it – is known as the *pit*. Some weapons tested during the 1950s used pits made with U-235 alone, or in composite with plutonium, but all-plutonium pits are the smallest in diameter and have been the standard since the early 1960s. Casting and then machining plutonium is difficult not only because of its toxicity, but also because plutonium has many different metallic phases, also known as allotropes. As plutonium cools, changes in phase result in distortion and cracking. This distortion is normally overcome by alloying it with 3–3.5 molar% (0.9–1.0% by weight) gallium, forming a plutonium-gallium alloy, which causes it to take up its delta phase over a wide temperature range. When cooling from molten it then suffers only a single phase change, from epsilon to delta, instead of the four changes it would otherwise pass through. Other trivalent metals would also work, but gallium has a small neutron absorption cross section and helps protect the plutonium against corrosion. A drawback is that gallium compounds themselves are corrosive and so if the plutonium is recovered from dismantled weapons for conversion to plutonium dioxide for power reactors, there is the difficulty of removing the gallium.

Because plutonium is chemically reactive it is common to plate the completed pit with a thin layer of inert metal, which also reduces the toxic hazard. The gadget used galvanic silver plating; afterwards, nickel deposited from nickel tetracarbonyl vapors was used, but gold is now preferred.

Levitated-pit implosion

The first improvement on the Fat Man design was to put an air space between the tamper and the pit to create a hammer-on-nail impact. The pit, supported on a hollow cone inside the tamper cavity, was said to be levitated. The three tests of Operation Sandstone, in 1948, used Fat Man designs with levitated pits. The largest yield was 49 kilotons, more than twice the yield of the unlevitated Fat Man. It was immediately clear that implosion was the best design for a fission weapon. Its only drawback seemed to be its diameter. Fat Man was 5 feet (1.5 m) wide vs 2 feet (60 cm) for Little Boy. Eleven years later, implosion designs had advanced sufficiently that the 5 foot-diameter sphere of Fat Man had been reduced to a 1 foot-diameter (30 cm) cylinder 2 feet (60 cm) long, the Swan device.

The Pu-239 pit of Fat Man was only 3.6 inches (9 cm) in diameter, the size of a softball. The bulk of Fat Man's girth was the implosion mechanism, namely concentric layers of U-238, aluminum, and high explosives. The key to reducing that girth was the two-point implosion design.

Two-point linear implosion

A very inefficient implosion design is one that simply reshapes an ovoid into a sphere, with minimal compression. In linear implosion, an untamped, solid, elongated mass of Pu-239, larger than critical mass in a sphere, is embedded inside a cylinder of high explosive with a detonator at each end.

Detonation makes the pit critical by driving the ends inward, creating a spherical shape. The shock may also change plutonium from delta to alpha phase, increasing its density by 23%, but without the inward momentum of a true implosion. The lack of compression makes it inefficient, but the simplicity and small diameter make it suitable for use in artillery shells and atomic demolition munitions – ADMs – also known as backpack or suitcase nukes. All such low-yield battlefield weapons, whether gun-type U-235 designs or linear implosion Pu-239 designs, pay a high price in fissile material in order to achieve diameters between six and ten inches (254 mm).

Two-point hollow-pit implosion

A more efficient two-point implosion system uses two high explosive lenses and a hollow pit. A hollow plutonium pit was the original plan for the 1945 Fat Man bomb, but there was not enough time to develop and test the implosion system for it. A simpler solid-pit design was considered more reliable, given the time restraint, but it required a heavy U-238 tamper, a thick aluminum pusher, and three tons of high explosives.

After the war, interest in the hollow pit design was revived. Its obvious advantage is that a hollow shell of plutonium, shock-deformed and driven inward toward its empty centre, would carry momentum into its violent assembly as a solid sphere. It would be self-tamping, requiring a smaller U-238 tamper, no aluminum pusher and less high explosive.

The Fat Man bomb had two concentric, spherical shells of high explosives, each about 10 inches (25 cm) thick. The inner shell drove the implosion. The outer shell consisted of a soccer-ball pattern of 32 high explosive lenses, each of which converted the convex wave from its detonator into a concave wave matching the contour of the outer surface of the inner shell. If these 32 lenses could be replaced with only two, the high explosive sphere could become an ellipsoid (prolate spheroid) with a much smaller diameter.

A good illustration of these two features is a 1956 drawing from the Swedish nuclear weapon program (which was terminated before it produced a test explosion). The drawing shows the essential elements of the two-point hollow-pit design. The mechanism of the high explosive lens (diagram item #6) is not shown in the Swedish drawing, but a standard lens made of fast and slow high explosives, as in Fat Man, would be much longer than the shape depicted. For a single high explosive lens to generate a concave wave that envelops an entire hemisphere, it must either be very long or the part of the wave on a direct line from the detonator to the pit must be slowed dramatically.

A slow high explosive is too fast, but the flying plate of an "air lens" is not. A metal plate, shock-deformed, and pushed across an empty space can be designed to move slowly enough. A two-point implosion system using air lens technology can have a length no more than twice its diameter, as in the Swedish diagram above.

Fusion-boosted fission weapons

The next step in miniaturization was to speed up the fissioning of the pit to reduce the amount of time inertial confinement needed. The hollow pit provided an ideal location to introduce fusion for the boosting of fission. A 50-50 mixture of tritium and deuterium gas, pumped into the pit during arming, will fuse into helium and release free neutrons soon after fission begins. The neutrons will start a large number of new chain reactions while the pit is still critical or nearly critical.

Once the hollow pit is perfected, there is little reason not to boost. The concept of fusion-boosted fission was first tested on May 25, 1951, in the Item shot of Operation Greenhouse, Eniwetok, yield 45.5 kilotons.

Boosting reduces diameter in three ways, all the result of faster fission:

- Since the compressed pit does not need to be held together as long, the massive U-238 tamper can be replaced by a light-weight beryllium shell (to reflect escaping neutrons back into the pit). The diameter is reduced.

- The mass of the pit can be reduced by half, without reducing yield. Diameter is reduced again.
- Since the mass of the metal being imploded (tamper plus pit) is reduced, a smaller charge of high explosive is needed, reducing diameter even further.

Since boosting is required to attain full design yield, any reduction in boosting reduces yield. Boosted weapons are thus variable-yield weapons. Yield can be reduced any time before detonation, simply by putting less than the full amount of tritium into the pit during the arming procedure.

Another benefit of boosting, in addition to making weapons smaller, lighter, and with less fissile material for a given yield, is that it renders weapons immune to radiation interference (RI). It was discovered in the mid-1950s that plutonium pits would be particularly susceptible to partial pre-detonation if exposed to the intense radiation of a nearby nuclear explosion (electronics might also be damaged, but this was a separate issue). RI was a particular problem before effective early warning radar systems because a first strike attack might make retaliatory weapons useless. Boosting reduces the amount of plutonium needed in a weapon to below the quantity which would be vulnerable to this effect.

Two-stage thermonuclear weapons

Pure fission or fusion-boosted fission weapons can be made to yield hundreds of kilotons, at great expense in fissile material and tritium, but by far the most efficient way to increase nuclear weapon yield beyond ten or so kilotons is to tack on a second independent stage, called a secondary.

In the 1940s, bomb designers at Los Alamos thought the secondary would be a canister of deuterium in liquified or hydride form. The fusion reaction would be D-D, harder to achieve than D-T, but more affordable. A fission bomb at one end would shock-compress and heat the near end, and fusion would propagate through the canister to the far end. Mathematical simulations showed it wouldn't work, even with large amounts of prohibitively expensive tritium added in.

The entire fusion fuel canister would need to be enveloped by fission energy, to both compress and heat it, as with the booster charge in a boosted primary. The design breakthrough came in January 1951, when Edward Teller and Stanis³aw Ulam invented radiation implosion—for nearly three decades known publicly only as the Teller-Ulam H-bomb secret.

The concept of radiation implosion was first tested on May 9, 1951, in the George shot of Operation Greenhouse, Eniwetok, yield 225 kilotons. The first full test was on November 1, 1952, the Mike shot of Operation Ivy, Eniwetok, yield 10.4 megatons.

In radiation implosion, the burst of x-ray energy coming from an exploding primary is captured and contained within an opaque-walled radiation channel which surrounds the nuclear energy components of the secondary. For a millionth of a second, most of the energy of several kilotons of TNT is absorbed by a plasma (superheated gas) generated from plastic foam in the radiation channel. With energy going in and not coming out, the plasma rises to solar core temperatures and expands with solar core pressures. Nearby objects which are still cool are crushed by the pressure.

The cool nuclear materials surrounded by the radiation channel are imploded much like the pit of the primary, except with more force. This greater pressure enables the secondary to be significantly more powerful than the primary, without being much larger.

For example, for the Redwing Mohawk test on July 3, 1956, a secondary called the Flute was attached to the Swan primary. The Flute was 15 inches (38 cm) in diameter and 23.4 inches (59 cm) long, about the size of the Swan. But it weighed ten times as much and yielded 24 times as much energy (355 kilotons, vs 15 kilotons).

Equally important, the active ingredients in the Flute probably cost no more than those in the Swan. Most of the fission came from cheap U-238, and the tritium was manufactured in place during the explosion. Only the spark plug at the axis of the secondary needed to be fissile.

A spherical secondary can achieve higher implosion densities than a cylindrical secondary, because spherical implosion pushes in from all directions toward the same spot. However, in warheads yielding more than one megaton, the diameter of a spherical secondary would be too large for most applications. A cylindrical secondary is necessary in such cases. The small, cone-shaped re-entry vehicles in multiple-warhead ballistic missiles after 1970 tended to have warheads with spherical secondaries, and yields of a few hundred kilotons.

As with boosting, the advantages of the two-stage thermonuclear design are so great that there is little incentive not to use it, once a nation has mastered the technology. In engineering terms, radiation implosion allows for the exploitation of several known features of nuclear bomb materials which heretofore had eluded practical application. For example:

- The best way to store deuterium in a reasonably dense state is to chemically bond it with lithium, as lithium deuteride. But the lithium-6 isotope is also the raw material for tritium production, and an exploding bomb is a nuclear reactor. Radiation implosion will hold everything together long enough to permit the complete conversion of lithium-6 into tritium, while the bomb explodes. So the bonding agent for deuterium permits use of the D-T fusion reaction without any pre-manufactured tritium being stored in the secondary. The tritium production constraint disappears.
- For the secondary to be imploded by the hot, radiation-induced plasma surrounding it, it must remain cool for the first microsecond, i.e., it must be encased in a massive radiation (heat) shield. The shield's massiveness allows it to double as a tamper, adding momentum and duration to the implosion. No material is better suited for both of these jobs than ordinary, cheap uranium-238, which happens, also, to undergo fission when struck by the neutrons produced by D-T fusion. This casing, called the pusher, thus has three jobs: to keep the secondary cool, to hold it, inertially, in a highly compressed state, and, finally, to serve as the chief energy source for the entire bomb. The consumable pusher makes the bomb more a uranium fission bomb than a hydrogen fusion bomb. It is noteworthy that insiders never used the term hydrogen bomb.

- Finally, the heat for fusion ignition comes not from the primary but from a second fission bomb called the spark plug, embedded in the heart of the secondary. The implosion of the secondary implodes this spark plug, detonating it and igniting fusion in the material around it, but the spark plug then continues to fission in the neutron-rich environment until it is fully consumed, adding significantly to the yield.

The initial impetus behind the two-stage weapon was President Truman's 1950 promise to build a 10-megaton hydrogen superbomb as the U.S. response to the 1949 test of the first Soviet fission bomb. But the resulting invention turned out to be the cheapest and most compact way to build small nuclear bombs as well as large ones, erasing any meaningful distinction between A-bombs and H-bombs, and between boosters and supers. All the best techniques for fission and fusion explosions are incorporated into one all-encompassing, fully-scalable design principle. Even six-inch (152 mm) diameter nuclear artillery shells can be two-stage thermonuclears.

In the ensuing fifty years, nobody has come up with a better way to build a nuclear bomb. It is the design of choice for the United States, Russia, the United Kingdom, China, and France, the five thermonuclear powers. The other nuclear-armed nations, Israel, India, Pakistan, and North Korea, probably have single-stage weapons, possibly boosted.

Interstage

In a two-stage thermonuclear weapon, three types of energy emerge from the primary to impact the secondary: the expanding hot gases from high explosive charges which implode the primary, plus the electromagnetic radiation and the neutrons from the primary's nuclear detonation. An essential energy transfer modulator called the interstage, between the primary and the secondary, protects the secondary from the hot gases and channels the electromagnetic radiation and neutrons toward the right place at the right time.

There is very little information in the open literature about the mechanism of the interstage. Its first mention in a U.S. government document formally released to the public appears to be a caption in a recent graphic promoting the Reliable

Replacement Warhead Program. If built, this new design would replace "toxic, brittle material" and "expensive 'special' material" in the interstage. This statement suggests the interstage may contain beryllium to moderate the flux of neutrons from the primary, and perhaps something to absorb and re-radiate the x-rays in a particular manner.

The interstage and the secondary are encased together inside a stainless steel membrane to form the canned subassembly (CSA), an arrangement which has never been depicted in any open-source drawing. The most detailed illustration of an interstage shows a British thermonuclear weapon with a cluster of items between its primary and a cylindrical secondary. They are labelled "end-cap and neutron focus lens," "reflector/neutron gun carriage," and "reflector wrap." The origin of the drawing, posted on the internet by Greenpeace, is uncertain, and there is no accompanying explanation.

Specific designs

While every nuclear weapon design falls into one of the above categories, specific designs have occasionally become the subject of news accounts and public discussion, often with incorrect descriptions about how they work and what they do. Examples:

Hydrogen bombs

All modern nuclear weapons make some use of D-T fusion. Even pure fission weapons include neutron generators which are high-voltage vacuum tubes containing trace amounts of tritium and deuterium. However, in the public perception, hydrogen bombs, or H-bombs, are multi-megaton devices a thousand times more powerful than Hiroshima's Little Boy. Such high-yield bombs are actually two-stage thermonuclears, scaled up to the desired yield, with uranium fission, as usual, providing most of their energy.

The idea of the hydrogen bomb first came to public attention in 1949, when prominent scientists openly recommended against building nuclear bombs more powerful than the standard pure-fission model, on both moral and practical grounds. Their assumption was that critical mass considerations would limit the potential size of fission explosions, but that a fusion explosion could be as large as its supply of fuel, which has no critical mass limit. In 1949, the Soviets exploded their first fission bomb, and in 1950 President Truman ended the H-bomb debate by ordering the Los Alamos designers to build one. In 1952, the 10.4-megaton Ivy Mike explosion was announced as the first hydrogen bomb test, reinforcing the idea that hydrogen bombs are a thousand times more powerful than fission bombs.

In 1954, J. Robert Oppenheimer was labelled a hydrogen bomb opponent. The public did not know there were two kinds of hydrogen bomb (neither of which is accurately described as a hydrogen bomb). On May 23, when his security clearance was revoked, item three of the four public findings against him was "his conduct in the hydrogen bomb program." In 1949, Oppenheimer had supported single-stage fusion-boosted fission bombs, to maximize the explosive power of the arsenal given the trade-off between plutonium and tritium production. He opposed two-stage thermonuclear bombs until 1951, when radiation implosion, which he called "technically sweet", first made them practical. The complexity of his position was not revealed to the public until 1976, nine years after his death.

When ballistic missiles replaced bombers in the 1960s, most multi-megaton bombs were replaced by missile warheads (also two-stage thermonuclears) scaled down to one megaton or less.

Alarm Clock/Sloika

The first effort to exploit the symbiotic relationship between fission and fusion was a 1940s design that mixed fission and fusion fuel in alternating thin layers. As a single-stage device, it would have been a cumbersome application of boosted fission. It first became practical when incorporated into the secondary of a two-stage thermonuclear weapon. The U.S. name, Alarm Clock, was a nonsense code name. The Russian name for the same design was more descriptive: Sloika, a layered pastry cake. A single-stage Soviet Sloika was tested on August 12, 1953. No single-stage U.S. version was tested, but the Union shot of Operation Castle, April 26, 1954, was a two-stage thermonuclear code-named Alarm Clock. Its yield, at Bikini, was 6.9 megatons.

Because the Soviet Sloika test used dry lithium-6 deuteride eight months before the first U.S. test to use it (Castle Bravo, March 1, 1954), it was sometimes claimed that the USSR won the H-bomb race. (The 1952 U.S. Ivy Mike test used cryogenically-cooled liquid deuterium as the fusion fuel in the secondary, and employed the D-D fusion reaction.) However, the first Soviet test to use a radiation-imploded secondary, the essential feature of a true H-bomb, was on November 23, 1955, three years after Ivy Mike.

Clean bombs

On March 1, 1954, the largest-ever U.S. nuclear test explosion, the 15-megaton Bravo shot of Operation Castle at Bikini, delivered a promptly lethal dose of fission-product fallout to more than 6,000 square miles (16,000 km^2) of Pacific Ocean surface. Radiation injuries to Marshall Islanders and Japanese fishermen made that fact public and revealed the role of fission in hydrogen bombs.

In response to the public alarm over fallout, an effort was made to design a clean multi-megaton weapon, relying almost entirely on fusion. Since the energy produced by fission is essentially free, using the vital tamper as a source of extra energy the clean bomb needed to be much larger for the same yield.

For the only time, a third stage, called the tertiary, was added, using the secondary as its primary. The device was called Bassoon. It was tested as the Zuni shot of Operation Redwing, at Bikini on May 28, 1956. With all the uranium in Bassoon replaced with a substitute material such as lead, its yield was 3.5 megatons, 85% fusion and only 15% fission.

On July 19, AEC Chairman Lewis Strauss said the clean bomb test "produced much of importance... from a humanitarian aspect." However, two days later the dirty version of Bassoon, with the uranium parts restored, was tested as the Tewa shot of Redwing. Its 5-megaton yield, 87% fission, was deliberately suppressed to keep fallout within a smaller area. This dirty version was later deployed as the three-stage, 25-megaton Mark-41 bomb, which was carried by U.S. Air Force bombers, but never tested at full yield. As such, high-yield clean bombs were a public relations exercise. The actual deployed weapons were the dirty version, which maximized yield for the same size device.

Cobalt bombs

A fictional doomsday bomb, made popular by Neville Shute's 1957 novel, and subsequent 1959 movie, *On the Beach*, the cobalt bomb was a hydrogen bomb with a jacket of cobalt metal. The neutron-activated cobalt would supposedly have maximized the environmental damage from radioactive fallout. These bombs were popularized in the 1964 film *Dr. Strangelove or: How I Learned to Stop Worrying and Love the Bomb*.The element added to the bombs is referred to in the film as 'cobalt-thorium G'. Such "salted" weapons were requested by the U.S. Air Force and seriously investigated, possibly built and tested, but not deployed. In the 1964 edition of the DOD/AEC book *The Effects of Nuclear Weapons,* a new section titled Radiological Warfare clarified the issue. Fission products are as deadly as neutron-activated cobalt. The standard high-fission thermonuclear weapon is automatically a weapon of radiological warfare, as dirty as a cobalt bomb.

Initially, gamma radiation from the fission products from an equivalent size fission-fusion-fission bomb are much more intense than Co-60: 15,000 times more intense at 1 hour; 35 times more intense at 1 week; 5 times more intense at 1 month; and about equal at 6 months. Thereafter fission drops off rapidly so that Co-60 fallout is 8 times more intense than fission at 1 year and 150 times more intense at 5 years. The very long-lived isotopes produced by fission would overtake the ^{60}Co again after about 75 years.

Fission-fusion-fission bombs

In 1954, to explain the surprising amount of fission-product fallout produced by hydrogen bombs, Ralph Lapp coined the term fission-fusion-fission to describe a process inside what he called a three-stage thermonuclear weapon. His process explanation was correct, but his choice of terms caused confusion in the open literature. The stages of a nuclear weapon are not fission, fusion, and fission. They are the primary, the secondary, and, in one exceptionally powerful weapon, the tertiary. Each of these stages employs fission, fusion, and fission.

Neutron bombs

A neutron bomb, technically referred to as an enhanced radiation weapon (ERW), is a type of tactical nuclear weapon designed specifically to release a large portion of its energy as energetic neutron radiation.

This contrasts with standard thermonuclear weapons, which are designed to capture this intense neutron radiation to increase its overall explosive yield. In terms of yield, ERWs typically produce about one-tenth that of a fission-type atomic weapon. Even with their significantly lower explosive power, ERWs are still capable of much greater destruction than any conventional bomb. Meanwhile, relative to other nuclear weapons, damage is more focused on biological material than on material infrastructure (though extreme blast and heat effects are not eliminated).

Officially known as enhanced radiation weapons, ERWs, they are more accurately described as suppressed yield weapons. When the yield of a nuclear weapon is less than one kiloton, its lethal radius from blast, 700 m (2300 ft), is less than that from its neutron radiation. However, the blast is more than potent enough to destroy most structures, which are less resistant to blast effects than even unprotected human beings. Blast pressures of upwards of 20 PSI are survivable, whereas most buildings will collapse with a pressure of only 5 PSI.

ERWs were two-stage thermonuclears with all non-essential uranium removed to minimize fission yield. Fusion provided the neutrons. Developed in the 1950s, they were first deployed in the 1970s, by U.S. forces in Europe. The last ones were retired in the 1990s.

A neutron bomb is only feasible if the yield is sufficiently high that efficient fusion stage ignition is possible, and if the yield is low enough that the case thickness will not absorb too many neutrons. This means that neutron bombs have a yield range of 1–10 kilotons, with fission proportion varying from 50% at 1-kiloton to 25% at 10-kilotons (all of which comes from the primary stage). The neutron output per kiloton is then 10–15 times greater than for a pure fission implosion weapon or for a strategic warhead like a W87 or W88.

Oralloy thermonuclear warheads

In 1999, nuclear weapon design was in the news again, for the first time in decades. In January, the U.S. House of Representatives released the Cox Report (Christopher Cox R-CA) which alleged that China had somehow acquired classified information about the U.S. W88 warhead. Nine months later, Wen Ho Lee, a Taiwanese immigrant working at Los Alamos, was publicly accused of spying, arrested, and served nine months in pre-trial detention, before the case against him was dismissed. It is not clear that there was, in fact, any espionage.

In the course of eighteen months of news coverage, the W88 warhead was described in unusual detail. *The New York Times* printed a schematic diagram on its front page. The most detailed drawing appeared in *A Convenient Spy*, the 2001 book on the Wen Ho Lee case by Dan Stober and Ian Hoffman, adapted and shown here with permission.

Designed for use on Trident II (D-5) submarine-launched ballistic missiles, the W88 entered service in 1990 and was the last warhead designed for the U.S. arsenal. It has been described as the most advanced, although open literature accounts do not indicate any major design features that were not available to U.S. designers in 1958.

The above diagram shows all the standard features of ballistic missile warheads since the 1960s, with two exceptions that give it a higher yield for its size.

- The outer layer of the secondary, called the "pusher", which serves three functions: heat shield, tamper, and fission fuel, is made of U-235 instead of U-238, hence the name Oralloy (U-235) Thermonuclear. Being fissile, rather than merely fissionable, allows the pusher to fission faster and more completely, increasing yield. This feature is available only to nations with a great wealth of fissile uranium. The United States is estimated to have 500 tons.
- The secondary is located in the wide end of the re-entry cone, where it can be larger, and thus more powerful. The usual arrangement is to put the heavier, denser secondary in the narrow end for greater aerodynamic stability during re-entry from outer space, and to allow

more room for a bulky primary in the wider part of the cone. (The W87 warhead drawing in the previous section shows the usual arrangement.) Because of this new geometry, the W88 primary uses compact conventional high explosives (CHE) to save space, rather than the more usual, and bulky but safer, insensitive high explosives (IHE). The re-entry cone probably has ballast in the nose for aerodynamic stability.

The alternating layers of fission and fusion material in the secondary are an application of the Alarm Clock/Sloika principle.

Reliable replacement warhead

The United States has not produced any nuclear warheads since 1989, when the Rocky Flats pit production plant, near Boulder, Colorado, was shut down for environmental reasons. With the end of the Cold War two years later, the production line was idled except for inspection and maintenance functions. The National Nuclear Security Administration, the latest successor for nuclear weapons to the Atomic Energy Commission and the Department of Energy, has proposed building a new pit facility and starting the production line for a new warhead called the Reliable Replacement Warhead (RRW). Two advertised safety improvements of the RRW would be a return to the use of "insensitive high explosives which are far less susceptible to accidental detonation", and the elimination of "certain hazardous materials, such as beryllium, that are harmful to people and the environment." Since the new warhead would not require any nuclear testing, it could not use a new design with untested concepts.

Weapon design laboratories

All the nuclear weapon design innovations discussed in this article originated from the following three labs in the manner described. Other nuclear weapon design labs in other countries duplicated those design innovations independently, reverse-engineered them from fallout analysis, or acquired them by espionage.

Berkeley

The first systematic exploration of nuclear weapon design concepts took place in mid-1942 at the University of California,

Berkeley. Important early discoveries had been made at the adjacent Lawrence Berkeley Laboratory, such as the 1940 cyclotron-made production and isolation of plutonium. A Berkeley professor, J. Robert Oppenheimer, had just been hired to run the nation's secret bomb design effort. His first act was to convene the 1942 summer conference.

By the time he moved his operation to the new secret town of Los Alamos, New Mexico, in the spring of 1943, the accumulated wisdom on nuclear weapon design consisted of five lectures by Berkeley professor Robert Serber, transcribed and distributed as the Los Alamos Primer. The Primer addressed fission energy, neutron production and capture, nuclear chain reactions, critical mass, tampers, predetonation, and three methods of assembling a bomb: gun assembly, implosion, and "autocatalytic methods," the one approach that turned out to be a dead end.

Los Alamos

At Los Alamos, it was found in April 1944 by Emilio G. Segrè that the proposed Thin Man Gun assembly type bomb would not work for plutonium because of predetonation problems caused by Pu-240 impurities. So Fat Man, the implosion-type bomb, was given high priority as the only option for plutonium. The Berkeley discussions had generated theoretical estimates of critical mass, but nothing precise. The main wartime job at Los Alamos was the experimental determination of critical mass, which had to wait until sufficient amounts of fissile material arrived from the production plants: uranium from Oak Ridge, Tennessee, and plutonium from the Hanford site in Washington.

In 1945, using the results of critical mass experiments, Los Alamos technicians fabricated and assembled components for four bombs: the Trinity Gadget, Little Boy, Fat Man, and an unused spare Fat Man. After the war, those who could, including Oppenheimer, returned to university teaching positions. Those who remained worked on levitated and hollow pits and conducted weapon effects tests such as Crossroads Able and Baker at Bikini Atoll in 1946.

All of the essential ideas for incorporating fusion into nuclear weapons originated at Los Alamos between 1946 and 1952.

After the Teller-Ulam radiation implosion breakthrough of 1951, the technical implications and possibilities were fully explored, but ideas not directly relevant to making the largest possible bombs for long-range Air Force bombers were shelved.

Because of Oppenheimer's initial position in the H-bomb debate, in opposition to large thermonuclear weapons, and the assumption that he still had influence over Los Alamos despite his departure, political allies of Edward Teller decided he needed his own laboratory in order to pursue H-bombs. By the time it was opened in 1952, in Livermore, California, Los Alamos had finished the job Livermore was designed to do.

Livermore

With its original mission no longer available, the Livermore lab tried radical new designs, that failed. Its first three nuclear tests were fizzles: in 1953, two single-stage fission devices with uranium hydride pits, and in 1954, a two-stage thermonuclear device in which the secondary heated up prematurely, too fast for radiation implosion to work properly.

Shifting gears, Livermore settled for taking ideas Los Alamos had shelved and developing them for the Army and Navy. This led Livermore to specialize in small-diameter tactical weapons, particularly ones using two-point implosion systems, such as the Swan. Small-diameter tactical weapons became primaries for small-diameter secondaries. Around 1960, when the superpower arms race became a ballistic missile race, Livermore warheads were more useful than the large, heavy Los Alamos warheads. Los Alamos warheads were used on the first intermediate-range ballistic missiles, IRBMs, but smaller Livermore warheads were used on the first intercontinental ballistic missiles, ICBMs, and submarine-launched ballistic missiles, SLBMs, as well as on the first multiple warhead systems on such missiles.

In 1957 and 1958 both labs built and tested as many designs as possible, in anticipation that a planned 1958 test ban might become permanent. By the time testing resumed in 1961 the two labs had become duplicates of each other, and design jobs were assigned more on workload considerations than lab speciality. Some designs were horse-traded. For example, the W38 warhead for the Titan I missile started out as a Livermore project, was given to Los Alamos when it became the Atlas missile warhead, and in 1959 was given back to Livermore, in trade for the W54 Davy Crockett warhead, which went from Livermore to Los Alamos.

The period of real innovation was ending by then, anyway. Warhead designs after 1960 took on the character of model changes, with every new missile getting a new warhead for marketing reasons. The chief substantive change involved packing more fissile uranium into the secondary, as it became available with continued uranium enrichment and the dismantlement of the large high-yield bombs.

Explosive testing

Nuclear weapons are in large part designed by trial and error. The trial often involves test explosion of a prototype. In a nuclear explosion, a large number of discrete events, with various probabilities, aggregate into short-lived, chaotic energy flows inside the device casing. Complex mathematical models are required to approximate the processes, and in the 1950s there were no computers powerful enough to run them properly. Even today's computers and simulation software are not adequate. It was easy enough to design reliable weapons for the stockpile. If the prototype worked, it could be weaponized and mass produced. It was much more difficult to understand how it worked or why it failed. Designers gathered as much data as possible during the explosion, before the device destroyed itself, and used the data to calibrate their models, often by inserting fudge factors into equations to make the simulations match experimental results. They also analyzed the weapon debris in fallout to see how much of a potential nuclear reaction had taken place.

Light pipes

An important tool for test analysis was the diagnostic light pipe. A probe inside a test device could transmit information by heating a plate of metal to incandescence, an event that could be recorded at the far end of a long, very straight pipe. The picture below shows the Shrimp device, detonated on March 1, 1954 at Bikini, as the Castle Bravo test. Its 15-megaton explosion was the largest ever by the United States. The silhouette of a man is shown for scale. The device is supported from below, at the ends. The pipes going into the shot cab ceiling, which appear to be supports, are diagnostic light pipes. The eight pipes at the right end (1) sent information about the detonation of the primary. Two in the middle (2) marked the time when x-radiation from the primary reached the radiation channel around the secondary. The last two pipes (3) noted the time radiation reached the far end of the radiation channel, the difference between (2) and (3) being the radiation transit time for the channel.

While x-rays would normally travel at the speed of light through a low density material like the plastic foam channel filler between (2) and (3), the intensity of radiation from the exploding primary created a relatively opaque radiation front in the channel filler which acted like a slow-moving logjam to retard the passage of radiant energy. Behind this moving front was a fully-ionized, low-z (low atomic number) plasma heated to 20,000 °C, soaking up energy like a black body, and eventually driving the implosion of the secondary. The radiation transit time, on the order of half a microsecond, is the time it takes the entire radiation channel to reach thermal equilibrium as the radiation front moves down its length. The implosion of the secondary is based on the temperature difference and resulting pressure difference between the hot channel and the cool interior of the secondary. Its timing is important because the interior of the secondary is subject to neutron preheat.

While the radiation channel is heating and starting the implosion, neutrons from the primary catch up with the x-rays, penetrate into the secondary and start breeding tritium with the third reaction noted in the first section above. This Li-6 + n reaction is exothermic, producing 5 MeV per event. The spark plug is not yet compressed and thus is not critical, so there won't be significant fission or fusion. But if enough neutrons arrive before implosion of the secondary is complete, the crucial temperature difference will be degraded. This is the reported cause of failure for Livermore's first thermonuclear design, the Morgenstern device, tested as Castle Koon, April 7, 1954.

These timing issues are measured by light-pipe data. The mathematical simulations which they calibrate are called radiation flow hydrodynamics codes, or channel codes. They are used to predict the effect of future design modifications. It is not clear from the public record how successful the Shrimp light pipes were. The data bunker was far enough back to remain outside the mile-wide crater, but the 15-megaton blast, two and a half times greater than expected, breached the bunker by blowing its 20-ton door off the hinges and across the inside of the bunker. (The nearest people were twenty miles (32 km) farther away, in a bunker that survived intact.)

Fallout analysis

The most interesting data from Castle Bravo came from radio-chemical analysis of weapon debris in fallout. Because of a shortage of enriched lithium-6, 60% of the lithium in the Shrimp secondary was ordinary lithium-7, which doesn't breed tritium as easily as lithium-6 does. But it does breed lithium-6 as the product of an (n, 2n) reaction (one neutron in, two neutrons out), a known fact, but with unknown probability. The probability turned out to be high. Fallout analysis revealed to designers that, with the (n, 2n) reaction, the Shrimp secondary effectively had two and half times as much lithium-6 as expected. The tritium, the fusion yield, the neutrons, and the fission yield were all increased accordingly.

As noted above, Bravo's fallout analysis also told the outside world, for the first time, that thermonuclear bombs are more fission devices than fusion devices. A Japanese fishing boat, the *Lucky Dragon*, sailed home with enough fallout on its decks to allow scientists in Japan and elsewhere to determine, and announce, that most of the fallout had come from the fission of U-238 by fusion-produced 14 MeV neutrons.

Underground testing

The global alarm over radioactive fallout, which began with the Castle Bravo event, eventually drove nuclear testing underground. The last U.S. above-ground test took place at Johnston Island on November 4, 1962. During the next three decades, until September 23, 1992, the United States conducted an average of 2.4 underground nuclear explosions per month, all but a few at the Nevada Test Site (NTS) northwest of Las Vegas.

The Yucca Flat section of the NTS is covered with subsidence craters resulting from the collapse of terrain over radioactive underground caverns created by nuclear explosions. After the 1974 Threshold Test Ban Treaty (TTBT), which limited underground explosions to 150 kilotons or less, warheads like the half-megaton W88 had to be tested at less than full yield. Since the primary must be detonated at full yield in order to generate data about the implosion of the secondary, the reduction in yield had to come from the secondary.

Replacing much of the lithium-6 deuteride fusion fuel with lithium-7 hydride limited the deuterium available for fusion, and thus the overall yield, without changing the dynamics of the implosion. The functioning of the device could be evaluated using light pipes, other sensing devices, and analysis of trapped weapon debris. The full yield of the stockpiled weapon could be calculated by extrapolation.

Production facilities

When two-stage weapons became standard in the early 1950s, weapon design determined the layout of the new, widely dispersed U.S. production facilities, and vice versa. Because primaries tend to be bulky, especially in diameter, plutonium is the fissile material of choice for pits, with beryllium reflectors. It has a smaller critical mass than uranium. The Rocky Flats plant in Boulder, Colorado, was built in 1952 for pit production and consequently became the plutonium and beryllium fabrication facility.

The Y-12 plant in Oak Ridge, Tennessee, where mass spectrometers called Calutrons had enriched uranium for the Manhattan Project, was redesigned to make secondaries. Fissile U-235 makes the best spark plugs because its critical mass is larger, especially in the cylindrical shape of early thermonuclear secondaries. Early experiments used the two fissile materials in combination, as composite Pu-Oy pits and spark plugs, but for mass production, it was easier to let the factories specialize: plutonium pits in primaries, uranium spark plugs and pushers in secondaries.

Y-12 made lithium-6 deuteride fusion fuel and U-238 parts, the other two ingredients of secondaries.

The Savannah River plant in Aiken, South Carolina, also built in 1952, operated nuclear reactors which converted U-238 into Pu-239 for pits, and converted lithium-6 (produced at Y-12) into tritium for booster gas. Since its reactors were moderated with heavy water, deuterium oxide, it also made deuterium for booster gas and for Y-12 to use in making lithium-6 deuteride.

Warhead design safety

Because even low-yield nuclear warheads have astounding destructive power, weapon designers have always recognised the need to incorporate mechanisms and associated procedures intended to prevent accidental detonation.

- Gun-type weapons: It is inherently dangerous to have a weapon containing a quantity and shape of fissile material which can form a critical mass through a relatively simple accident. Because of this danger, the propellant in Little Boy (four bags of cordite) was inserted into the bomb in flight, shortly after takeoff on August 6, 1945. This was the first time a gun-type nuclear weapon had ever been fully assembled. If the weapon falls into water, the moderating effect of the water can also cause a criticality accident, even without the weapon being physically damaged. Similarly, a fire caused by an aircraft crashing could easily ignite the propellant, with catastrophic results. Gun-type weapons have always been inherently unsafe.
- In-flight pit insertion: Neither of these effects is likely with implosion weapons since there is normally insufficient fissile material to form a critical mass without the correct detonation of the lenses. However, the earliest implosion weapons had pits so close to criticality that accidental detonation with some nuclear yield was a concern. On August 9, 1945, Fat Man was loaded onto its airplane fully assembled, but later, when levitated pits made a space between the pit and the tamper, it was feasible to use in-flight pit insertion. The bomber would take off with no fissile material in the bomb. Some older implosion-type weapons, such as the US Mark 4 and Mark 5, used this system. In-flight pit insertion will not work with a hollow pit in contact with its tamper.

- Steel ball safety method: As shown in the diagram above, one method used to decrease the likeiihood of accidental detonation employed metal balls. The balls were emptied into the pit: this prevented detonation by increasing the density of the hollow pit, thereby preventing symmetrical implosion in the event of an accident. This design was used in the Green Grass weapon, also known as the Interim Megaton Weapon, which was used in the Violet Club and Yellow Sun Mk.1 bombs.
- Chain safety method: Alternatively, the pit can be "safed" by having its normally-hollow core filled with an inert material such as a fine metal chain, possibly made of cadmium to absorb neutrons. While the chain is in the centre of the pit, the pit can not be compressed into an appropriate shape to fission; when the weapon is to be armed, the chain is removed. Similarly, although a serious fire could detonate the explosives, destroying the pit and spreading plutonium to contaminate the surroundings as has happened in several weapons accidents, it could not cause a nuclear explosion.
- Wire safety method: The US *W47* warhead used in *Polaris A1* and *Polaris A2* had a safety device consisting of a boron-coated wire inserted into the hollow pit at manufacture. The warhead was armed by withdrawing the wire onto a spool driven by an electric motor. Once withdrawn the wire could not be re-inserted.
- One-point safety: While the firing of one detonator out of many will not cause a hollow pit to go critical, especially a low-mass hollow pit that requires boosting, the introduction of two-point implosion systems made that possibility a real concern.

In a two-point system, if one detonator fires, one entire hemisphere of the pit will implode as designed. The high-explosive charge surrounding the other hemisphere will explode progressively, from the equator toward the opposite pole. Ideally, this will pinch the equator and squeeze the second hemisphere away from the first, like toothpaste in a tube. By the time the explosion envelops it, its implosion will be separated both in time and space from the implosion of the first hemisphere. The resulting dumbbell shape, with each end reaching maximum density at a different time, may not become critical.

Unfortunately, it is not possible to tell on the drawing board how this will play out. Nor is it possible using a dummy pit of U-238 and high-speed x-ray cameras, although such tests are helpful. For final determination, a test needs to be made with real fissile material. Consequently, starting in 1957, a year after Swan, both labs began one-point safety tests. Out of 25 one-point safety tests conducted in 1957 and 1958, seven had zero or slight nuclear yield (success), three had high yields of 300 t to 500 t (severe failure), and the rest had unacceptable yields between those extremes.

Of particular concern was Livermore's W47 warhead for the Polaris submarine missile. The last test before the 1958 moratorium was a one-point test of the W47 primary, which had an unacceptably high nuclear yield of 400 lb (180 kg) of TNT equivalent (Hardtack II Titania). With the test moratorium in force, there was no way to refine the design and make it inherently one-point safe. Los Alamos had a suitable primary that was one-point safe, but rather than share with Los Alamos the credit for designing the first SLBM warhead, Livermore chose to use mechanical safing on its own inherently unsafe primary. The wire safety scheme described above was the result. It turns out that the W47 may have been safer than anticipated. The wire-safety system may have rendered most of the warheads "duds," unable to fire when detonated. When testing resumed in 1961, and continued for three decades, there was sufficient time to make all warhead designs inherently one-point safe, without need for mechanical safing.

- Strong link weak link: A strong link/weak link and exclusion zone nuclear detonation mechanism is a form of automatic safety interlock.
- Permissive Action Links: In addition to the above steps to reduce the probability of a nuclear detonation arising from a single fault, locking mechanisms referred to by NATO states as Permissive Action Links are sometimes attached to the control mechanisms for nuclear warheads. Permissive Action Links act solely to prevent the unauthorised use of a nuclear weapon.

TACTICAL NUCLEAR WEAPON

A tactical nuclear weapon (or TNW) refers to a nuclear weapon which is designed to be used on a battlefield in military situations. This is as opposed to strategic nuclear weapons which are designed to threaten large populations, to damage the enemy's ability to wage war, or for general deterrence. Tactical nuclear weapons were a large part of the peak nuclear weapons stockpile levels during the Cold War.

Types

Tactical weapons include not only gravity bombs and short-range missiles, but also artillery shells, land mines, depth charges, and torpedoes for anti-submarine warfare, with nuclear warheads. Also in this category were the former nuclear-warheaded surface-to-air missiles (SAMs), ground-based or shipborne, and air-to-air missiles.

Small, two-man portable, or truck-portable, tactical weapons (sometimes misleadingly referred to as suitcase nukes), such as the Special Atomic Demolition Munition, have been developed, although the difficulty of combining sufficient yield with portability could limit their military utility. In wartime, such explosives could be used for demolishing "choke-points" to enemy offensives, such as at tunnels, narrow mountain passes, and long viaducts. Other new tactical weapons undergoing research include earth penetrating weapons which are designed to target enemy-held caves or deep-underground bunkers.

The yield of tactical nuclear weapons is generally lower than that of strategic nuclear weapons, but they are still very powerful, and some variable-yield warheads serve in both roles. Modern tactical nuclear warheads have yields up to the tens of kilotons, or potentially hundreds, several times that of the weapons used in the atomic bombings of Hiroshima and Nagasaki. Some tactical nuclear weapons have specific features meant to enhance their battlefield characteristics, such as variable yield which allow their explosive power to be varied over a wide range for different situations, or enhanced radiation weapons (the so-called "neutron bombs") which are meant to maximize ionizing radiation exposure while minimizing blast effects.

Controversy and criticism

The development of tactical weapons has often been criticized along a number of grounds. Many have argued that the promise of being able to wage a "limited" nuclear war with tactical weapons is dangerously misleading, and that any confrontation between nuclear powers could lead to escalation and eventually the use of strategic weapons. Additionally, the small size of many tactical weapons make them potential targets for theft and nuclear terrorism, especially during times of political instability (such as the case of Russia immediately after the dissolution of the Soviet Union). Tactical nuclear weapons have in the past made up a large part of the nuclear arsenals of the United States, the Soviet Union, the United Kingdom, and France, and they were a major part in the peak stockpile levels in the 1960s. For example, the British Army of the Rhine in Germany formerly was nuclear-armed, but not anymore. Conversely, some theorists argued during the Cold War that without tactical nuclear weapons, the United States and the United Kingdom would not have had a credible threat against the large armies of the Soviet Union, since it was unlikely that they would want to be the first to use strategic nuclear weapons in warfare. Because many felt that the use of *any* nuclear weapons against the Soviet Union would have triggered an exchange of strategic missile launches, though, the practical distinctions between tactical and strategic weapons might not have existed, in a way.

Uses

The uses on the battlefield for TNWs would include:

- Against a large ground force
- Against a fortified underground bunker
- Against remote and/or heavily-defended target locations difficult or impossible to reach with conventional weapons
- Against a carrier battle group or any collection of surface vessels
- Against a large amphibious invasion force
- Against a 100+ vehicle supply convoy
- Against a squadron of strategic bombers

Appearances

- In the video game Call of Duty: Modern Warfare 2 the player can utilize a Tactical Nuke as a reward in the game's online or offline multiplayer mode. Once the player has achieved 25 kills without dying, they may call in a tactical nuke to be dropped near the battlefield, resulting in a premature ending of the game and an automatic victory for whichever team the device was detonated by.
- In Day 6 of 24 the terrorists have acquired Russian suitcase nukes, which may be considered tactical nuclear devices. In one of the first five episodes, the terrorists succeed in detonating the device in Valencia, California just as a CTU S.W.A.T. team closes in.
- In the video game Mercanaries 2: World in Flames, the player must use a tactical nuke or a "Nuclear Bunker Buster" to destroy the heavily fortified bunker in which the primary antagonist is hiding at the end of the final mission.
- At the end of the film Resident Evil: Apocalypse, a tactical nuke is dropped on Raccoon City to "sanitize" the city of T-virus infected zombies.
- In the end of the Virtuous Mission chapter of Metal Gear Solid 3: Snake Eater, the GRU Colonel Volgin utilizes a newly acquired Davy Crocket Recoilless rifle to nuke the former research facility of rocket scientist Sokolov, which he had abducted.
- In the video game World In Conflict, Tactical Nukes play an important role both in the game's multiplayer and singleplayer modes. In multiplayer, they can be called in in the form of a missile hitting a specific point on the map where the player called in the strike, often without any long term consequences (Save for residual radiation in the direct blastzone) However, in Singleplayer, the Nuke is used to halt a Soviet advance, sending a large EMP and fallout wave throughout the area, scattering and destroying the majority of military units in the area.

NUCLEAR WARFARE

Nuclear warfare, or atomic warfare, is a military conflict or political strategy in which nuclear weapons are used. Compared to conventional warfare, nuclear warfare is vastly more destructive in range and extent of damage. A major nuclear exchange could have severe long-term effects, primarily from radiation release but also from possible atmospheric pollution leading to nuclear winter, that could last for decades, centuries, or even millennia after the initial attack. Nuclear war is considered to bear existential risk for civilization on Earth.

The first, and to date only, nuclear war was World War II: near the end of the war, the United States dropped atomic bombs on Hiroshima and Nagasaki, Japan. At the time of those bombings, the United States was the only country to possess atomic weapons. After World War II, nuclear weapons were also developed by the United Kingdom, France, the Soviet Union, and the People's Republic of China, which contributed to the state of conflict and tension that became known as the Cold War. In the 1970s, India and 1990s, Pakistan, countries openly hostile to each other, developed nuclear weapons. Israel, North Korea, and South Africa are also believed to have developed nuclear weapons, although South Africa subsequently abandoned them.

After the collapse of the Soviet Union in 1991 and the resultant end of the Cold War, the threat of a major nuclear war between the superpowers was generally thought to have receded. Since then, concern over nuclear weapons has shifted to the prevention of localized nuclear conflicts resulting from nuclear proliferation, and the threat of nuclear terrorism.

TYPES OF NUCLEAR WARFARE

The possibility of using nuclear weapons in war is usually divided into two subgroups, each with different effects and potentially fought with different types of nuclear armaments. The first, a *limited nuclear war* (sometimes *attack* or *exchange*), refers to a small scale use of nuclear weapons by one or more parties. A "limited nuclear war" would consist of a limited exchange between two nuclear powers targeting each other's military facilities, either as an attempt to pre-emptively cripple the enemy's ability to attack as a defensive measure or as a prelude to an invasion by conventional forces as an offensive measure. This term would apply to any limited use of nuclear weapons, which may involve either military or civilian targets.

The second, a *full-scale nuclear war*, consists of large numbers of weapons used in an attack aimed at an entire country, including military, economic and civilian targets. Such an attack would almost certainly destroy the entire economic, social, and military infrastructure of the target nation, and would possibly (depending on the severity of the nuclear exchange) have a devastating effect on Earth's biosphere.

Some Cold War strategists argued that a limited nuclear war could be possible between two heavily armed superpowers (such as the United States and the Soviet Union) and if so several predicted that a limited war could "escalate" into an all-out war. Others have called limited nuclear war "global nuclear holocaust in slow motion" arguing that once such a war took place others would be sure to follow over a period of decades, effectively rendering the planet uninhabitable in the same way that a "full-scale nuclear war" between superpowers would, only taking a much longer and more agonizing path to achieve the same result.

Even the most optimistic predictions of the effects of a major nuclear exchange foresee the death of a hundred million people within a very short amount of time; more pessimistic predictions argue that a full-scale nuclear war could bring about the extinction of the human race or its near extinction with a handful of survivors (mainly in remote areas) reduced quality of life and life expectancy for centuries after and cause permanent damage to most complex life on the planet, Earth's ecosystems, and the global climate, particularly if predictions of nuclear winter are accurate. It is in this latter mode that nuclear warfare is usually alluded to as a doomsday scenario. Such hypothesized civilization-ending nuclear wars have been a staple of the science fiction literature and film genre for decades.

Either a limited or full-scale nuclear exchange could be an *accidental nuclear war*, in which a nuclear war is triggered unintentionally. Possible triggers for this scenario have included malfunctioning early warning devices and targeting computers, deliberate malfeasance by rogue military commanders, accidental straying of planes into enemy airspace, reactions to unannounced missile tests during tense diplomatic periods, reactions to military exercises, mistranslated or misscommunicated messages, and so forth. A number of these scenarios did actually occur during the Cold War, though none resulted in a nuclear exchange. Many such scenarios have been depicted in popular culture, such as in the 1962 novel *Fail-Safe* (released as a film in 1964) and the film *Dr. Strangelove or: How I Learned to Stop Worrying and Love the Bomb*, also released in 1964.

HISTORY

Hiroshima to Semipalatinsk

The United States is the only nation to have ever used nuclear weapons during war, using two atomic bombs on the Japanese cities of Hiroshima and Nagasaki in 1945. Immediately after the bombings of Japan, the status of atomic weapons in international and military relations was unclear. Presumably, the United States hoped atomic weapons could offset the Soviet Union's superior conventional ground forces in Eastern Europe, and possibly be used to pressure Soviet leader Joseph Stalin into concessions. Stalin pursued his own atomic capabilities through scientific research and espionage against the American program. The Soviets believed that the Americans were unlikely to begin another world war with their limited nuclear arsenal and the Americans were not confident they could prevent a Soviet takeover of Europe, despite their atomic advantage.

Within the United States the authority to produce and develop nuclear weapons was removed from military control and put instead under the civilian control of the United States Atomic Energy Commission. This decision reflected an understanding that nuclear weapons had unique risks and benefits separate from other military technology.

For several years after World War II, the US developed and maintained a strategic force based on the Convair B-36 bomber that would be able to attack any potential enemy from bomber bases in the US. It deployed atomic bombs around the world for potential use in conflicts. Over a period of a few years, many in the US defence community became increasingly convinced of the invincibility of the United States to a nuclear attack. Indeed, it became generally believed that the threat of nuclear war would deter any strike against the United States.

Many proposals were suggested to put all US nuclear weapons under international control—for example, by the newly formed United Nations — as an effort to deter both their usage and an arms race. However no terms could be arrived at that made either the United States or the USSR feel secure.

On August 29, 1949 the USSR tested its first nuclear weapon at Semipalatinsk in Kazakhstan. Scientists in the United States from the Manhattan Project had warned that, in time, the Soviet Union would certainly develop nuclear capabilities of its own. Nevertheless, the effect upon military thinking and planning in the US was dramatic, primarily because American military strategists had not anticipated the Soviets would "catch up" so soon. However, at this time, they had not discovered that the Russians had conducted significant espionage of the project from spies at Los Alamos, the most significant of which was done by the theoretical physicist Klaus Fuchs. The first Soviet bomb was more or less a deliberate copy of the Fat Man device.

With the monopoly over nuclear technology broken, worldwide nuclear proliferation accelerated. The United Kingdom tested its first independent atomic bomb in 1952, followed by France in 1960 and then the People's Republic of China in 1964. While much smaller than the arsenals of the USA and the USSR, Western Europe's nuclear reserves were nevertheless a significant factor in strategic planning during the Cold War. A top-secret white paper produced for the British Government in 1959, compiled by the Royal Air Force, estimated that British atomic bombers were capable of destroying key cities and military targets in the Soviet Union, with an estimated 16 million deaths in the USSR (half of whom were estimated to be killed on impact and the rest fatally injured) *before* bomber aircraft from the United States' Strategic Air Command reached their targets.

1950s

Though the USSR had nuclear weapon capabilities in the beginning of the Cold War, the US still had an advantage in terms of bombers and weapons. In any exchange of hostilities, the US would have been capable of bombing the USSR, while the USSR would have more difficulties arranging the reverse.

The widespread introduction of jet-powered interceptor aircraft upset this balance somewhat by reducing the effectiveness of the US bomber fleet. In 1949 Curtis LeMay was placed in command of the Strategic Air Command and instituted a program to update the bomber fleet to one that was all-jet. During the early 1950s the B-47 and B-52 were introduced, providing the ability to bomb the USSR more easily.

Before the development of a capable strategic missile force in the Soviet Union, much of the war-fighting doctrine held by western nations revolved around using a large number of smaller nuclear weapons used in a tactical role. It is debatable whether such use could be considered "limited" however, because it was believed that the US would use their own strategic weapons (mainly bombers at the time) should the USSR deploy any kind of nuclear weapon against civilian targets. Douglas MacArthur, an American general, was fired by President Harry Truman, partially because he persistently requested permission to use his own discretion in deciding whether to use atomic weapons on the People's Republic of China in 1951 (as the Korean War was raging).

Several scares about the increasing ability of the USSR's strategic bomber forces surfaced during the 1950s. The defensive response by the US was to deploy a fairly strong layered defence consisting of interceptor aircraft and anti-aircraft missiles, like the Nike, and guns, like the Skysweeper, near larger cities. However this was a small response compared to the construction of a huge fleet of nuclear bombers. The principal nuclear strategy was to massively penetrate the USSR. Because such a large area could not be defended against this overwhelming attack in any credible way, the USSR would lose any exchange. This logic became ingrained in US nuclear doctrine and persisted for the duration of the Cold War. As long as the strategic US nuclear forces could overwhelm their USSR counterparts, a Soviet preemptive strike could be averted. Moreover, the USSR could not afford to build any reasonable counterforce as the economic output of the United States was far larger than that of the Soviets, and they would be unable to achieve nuclear parity. Soviet nuclear doctrine, however, did not match US nuclear doctrine. Soviet planning expected a large-scale nuclear exchange followed by a conventional war which itself would involve heavy use of tactical nuclear weapons. Unfortunately, US doctrine rather assumed that Soviet doctrine was similar—the *mutual* in Mutually Assured Destruction necessarily requiring that the other side see things in much the same way, rather than believing, as the Soviets did, that they could fight a large-scale, combined nuclear and conventional war.

A revolution in nuclear strategic thought occurred with the introduction of the intercontinental ballistic missile (ICBM), which the USSR first successfully tested in August 1957. In order to deliver a warhead to a target, a missile was more cost-effective than a bomber, and enjoyed a higher survivability due to the enormous difficulty of interception of the ICBMs due to their high altitude and speed. The USSR could now afford to achieve nuclear parity with the US in terms of raw numbers, although for a time they appeared to have chosen not to.

Photos of Soviet missile sites set off a wave of panic in the US military, something the launch of Sputnik would do for the public a few months later. Politicians, notably then-US Senator John Kennedy suggested a "missile gap" between the Soviets and the US. The US military gave missile development programs the highest national priority, and several spy aircraft and reconnaissance satellites were designed and deployed to observe Soviet progress.

1960s

Issues came to a head during the Cuban Missile Crisis in 1962. The Soviet Union placed medium range missiles 90 miles (140 km) from the US-a move considered by many as a direct response to American Jupiter missiles placed in Turkey. After intense negotiation, the Soviets ended up removing the missiles from Cuba and decided to institute a massive building program of their own. In exchange, the US dismantled its launch sites in Turkey, although this was done secretly and was not publicly revealed for over two decades. Khrushchev did not even reveal this part of the agreement when he came under fire by political opponents for mishandling the crisis. By the late 1960s, the number of ICBMs and warheads was so high on both sides that either the USA or USSR was capable of completely destroying the other country's infrastructure. Thus a balance of power system known as mutually assured destruction (*MAD*) came into being. It was thought that any full-scale exchange between the powers could not produce a victorious side and thus neither would risk initiating one.

One drawback of this doctrine was the possibility of a nuclear war occurring without either side intentionally striking first. Early warning systems were notoriously error-prone. On 78 occasions in 1979, for example, a "missile display conference" was called to evaluate detections potentially threatening to the North American continent. Some of these were trivial errors, spotted quickly. But several went to more serious levels. On September 26, 1983, Stanislav Petrov received convincing indications of a US first strike launch against the USSR but positively identified the warning as a false alarm. Though it is unclear what role Petrov's actions played in preventing a nuclear war, he has been honored by the United Nations for his actions. Similar incidents happened many times in the US, due to failed computer chips, flights of geese, test programs, and bureaucratic failures to notify early warning military personnel of legitimate launches of test or weather missiles. For many years, US strategic bombers were kept airborne on a rotating basis round the clock, until the number and severity of accidents persuaded policymakers it was not worthwhile.

1970s

By the late 1970s, citizens in the US and USSR (and indeed the entire world) had been living with MAD for about a decade. It became deeply ingrained into the popular culture. Such an exchange would have killed many millions of individuals directly and possibly induced a nuclear winter which could have led to the death of a large portion of humanity and, potentially, the collapse of global civilization.

In May 18, 1974, India conducted its first nuclear test in the Pokhran test range. The name of the operation was Smiling Buddha and India termed the test as a "peaceful nuclear explosion".

According to the 1980 United Nations report *General and Complete Disarmament: Comprehensive Study on Nuclear*

Weapons: Report of the Secretary-General, it was estimated that in total there were approximately 40,000 nuclear warheads in existence at that time with a total yield of approximately 13,000 megatons of TNT. By comparison, when the volcano Mount Tambora erupted in 1815 (turning 1816 into the Year Without A Summer due to the levels of ash expelled), it exploded with a force of roughly 1,000 megatons of TNT. Many people believed that a full-scale nuclear war could result in the extinction of the human species, though not all analysts agreed on the assumptions required for these models.

The idea that any nuclear conflict would eventually escalate was a challenge for military strategists. This challenge was particularly severe for the United States and its NATO allies because it was believed until the 1970s that a Soviet tank invasion of Western Europe would quickly overwhelm NATO conventional forces, leading to the necessity of escalating to tactical nuclear weapons.

A number of interesting concepts were developed. Early ICBMs were inaccurate, which led to the concept of countervalue strikes — attacks directly on the enemy population leading to a collapse of the enemy's will to fight. During the Cold War the USSR invested in extensive protected civilian infrastructure such as large nuclear-proof bunkers and non-perishable food stores. In the US, by comparison, smaller scale civil defence programs were instituted starting in the 1950s where schools and other public buildings had basements stocked with non-perishable food supplies, canned water, first aid, dosimeter and Geiger counter radiation measuring devices. Many of the locations were given "Fallout Shelter" designation signs. Also, CONELRAD Radio information systems were adopted, whereby the commercial radio sector would broadcast on two AM frequencies in the event of a CD emergency. These two frequencies can be seen on 50's vintage radios on online auction sites and museums, with many of these radios still in use on tabletops across America. Also, the occasional backyard fallout shelter was built by private individuals.

This strategy had one major and possibly critical flaw, soon realised by military analysts but highly underplayed by the US military: Conventional NATO forces in the European theatre of war were outnumbered by similar Soviet and Warsaw Pact forces, and while the western countries invested heavily in high-tech conventional weapons to counter this imbalance, it was assumed that in case of a major Soviet attack (commonly perceived as the "red tanks rolling towards the North Sea" scenario) that NATO, in the face of conventional defeat, would soon have no other choice but to resort to tactical nuclear strikes. Most analysts agreed that once the first nuclear exchange had occurred, escalation to global nuclear war would become almost inevitable.

As missile technology improved, the emphasis moved to counter-force strikes: ones that directly attacked the enemy's means of waging war. This was the predominant doctrine from the late 1960s onwards. Additionally the development of warheads (at least in the US) moved towards delivering a small explosive force more accurately and with a "cleaner" blast (with fewer long-lasting radioactive isotopes). In any conflict therefore, damage would have been initially limited to military targets, there may well have been "withholds" for targets near civilian areas. The argument was that the destruction of a city would be a military advantage to the *attacked*. The enemy had used up weapons and a threat in the destruction while the attacked was relieved of the need to defend the city and still had their entire military potential untouched.

Only if a nuclear conflict were extended into a number of "spasm" strikes would direct strikes against civilians occur, as the more accurate weapons would be expended early; if one side were "losing", the potential for using less accurate submarine-launched missiles would occur.

The 1980s

In the late seventies and early eighties the balance, in terms of nuclear weapons, shifted towards the Soviets. However, with the ascension to the presidency by Ronald Reagan, the US renewed its commitment to a powerful military, which required large spending on military programs. These programs, originally part of President Jimmy Carter's defence budget, included spending on conventional and nuclear weapons systems, as well as defensive systems like Strategic Defence Initiative.

Another major shift in nuclear doctrine was the development of the submarine-launched ballistic (nuclear) missile, the SLBM.

It was hailed by some military theorists as a weapon that would make nuclear war less likely. SLBMs, which can move with stealth virtually anywhere in the world, give a nation a "second strike" capability. Before the advent of SLBMs, thinkers feared that a nation might be tempted to initiate a first strike if it felt confident that such a strike would incapacitate the nuclear arsenal of its enemy, making retaliation impossible. With the advent of SLBMs, no nation could be certain that a first strike would incapacitate its enemy's entire nuclear arsenal. To the contrary, it would have to fear a retaliatory second strike from SLBMs. Thus a first strike was much less of a feasible option, and nuclear war was held to be less likely.

However, it was soon realized that submarines could "sneak up" close to enemy coastlines and decrease the warning time—the time between detection of the launch and impact of the missile—from as much as half an hour to under three minutes. This effect was especially significant to the United States, Britain, and China, with their capitals all within 100 miles (160 km) of their coasts. Moscow was more secure from this type of threat. This greatly increased the credibility of a "surprise first strike" by one of the factions and theoretically made it possible to knock out or disrupt the chain of command before a counterstrike could be ordered. It strengthened the notion that a nuclear war could be "won", resulting not only in greatly increased tension, and increasing calls for fail-deadly control systems, but also in a dramatic increase in military spending. The submarines and their missile systems were very expensive (one fully equipped nuclear powered nuclear missile submarine could easily cost more than the entire GNP of a third world nation), but the greatest cost came in the development of both sea-and land-based anti-submarine defenses and in improving and strengthening the chain of command. As a result, military spending skyrocketed.

South Africa developed a nuclear weapon capability during the 1970s and early 1980s. It was operational for a brief period before being dismantled in the early 1990s.

On Sept. 1, 1983, Korean Air Lines Flight 007 was shot down by Soviet Jet Fighters. On the 26th, a Soviet early warning station under the command of Stanislav Petrov falsely detected 5 inbound intercontinental ballistic missiles from US. Petrov correctly assessed the situation as a false alarm, and hence did not report his finding to his superiors. It is quite possible that this prevented World War III, as the Soviet policy at that time was immediate nuclear response upon discovering inbound ballistic missiles.

The world came unusually close to nuclear war (although perhaps not as close as during the Cuban Missile Crisis) when the Soviet Union thought the NATO military exercise Able Archer 83 was a cover up to begin a nuclear strike. The Soviets responded by readying their nuclear arsenal. Soviet fears of an attack went away once the exercise concluded without incident.

Post–Cold War

Although the dissolution of the Soviet Union ended the Cold War and greatly reduced tensions between the United States and Russia (the Soviet Union's formal successor state), both nations remained in a "nuclear stand-off" due to the continuing presence of a significant number of warheads in both nations. Additionally, the end of the Cold War led the United States to become increasingly concerned with the development of nuclear technology by other nations outside of the former Soviet Union. In 1995, a branch of the US Strategic Command produced an outline of forward-thinking strategies in the document "Essentials of Post-Cold War Deterrence".

The former chair of the United Nations disarmament committee states there are more than 16,000 strategic and tactical nuclear weapons ready for deployment and another 14,000 in storage. The U.S. has nearly 7,000 ready for action and 3,000 in storage and Russia has about 8,500 on hand and 11,000 in storage, he said. China has 400 nuclear weapons, Britain 200, France 350, India 80, and Pakistan 90. North Korea is confirmed as having nuclear weapons, though it is not known how many (a common estimate is between 1 and 10). Israel is also widely believed to have nuclear weapons. NATO has stationed 480 US nuclear weapons in Belgium, the Netherlands, Italy, Germany, and Turkey, with several other countries in pursuit of an arsenal of their own.

A key development in nuclear warfare in the 2000s has been the proliferation of nuclear weapons to the developing world, with India and Pakistan both publicly testing nuclear devices and North Korea conducting an underground nuclear test on October 9, 2006. The US Geological Survey measured a 4.2 magnitude earthquake in the area where the test occurred. A further test was announced by the North Korean government on May 25, 2009. Iran, meanwhile, has embarked on a nuclear program which, while officially for civilian purposes, has come under scrutiny by the United Nations and individual states.

Recent studies undertaken by the CIA cite the enduring India-Pakistan conflict as the most likely to escalate into nuclear war. During the Kargil War in 1999, Pakistan came close to using their nuclear weapons in case of further deterioration. In fact, Pakistan's foreign minister had even warned that they would "use any weapon in our arsenal", hinting at a nuclear strike against India; the statement was condemned by the international community with Pakistan denying it later on. It remains the only war between two declared nuclear powers. The 2001-2002 India-Pakistan standoff again stoked fears of nuclear war between the two countries.

Despite these very serious threats, relations between India and Pakistan have been improving somewhat over the last few years. A bus line directly linking Indian and Pakistani-administered Kashmir has recently been established. However, with the November 26, 2008 Mumbai terror attacks, India does not rule out war with Pakistan.

Another flashpoint which has analysts worried is a possible conflict between the United States and the People's Republic of China over Taiwan. Although economic forces have decreased the possibility of military conflict, there remains the worry that increasing military buildup (China is rapidly increasing their naval capacity) and a move toward Taiwan independence could spin out of control.

Israel is another possibility as it is thought to possess between one hundred and four hundred nuclear warheads. It has been asserted that the submarines which Israel received from Germany have been adapted to carry missiles with nuclear warheads, so as to give Israel a second strike capacity. Israel has been involved in wars with its neighbours on numerous occasions, and its small geographic size would mean that in the event of future wars the Israeli military might have very little time to react to a future invasion or other major threat; the situation could escalate to nuclear warfare very quickly in some scenarios.

In the Persian Gulf, Iran appears to many observers to be in the process of developing a nuclear weapon, which has heightened fears of a nuclear conflict in the Middle East, either with Israel or with Iran's Sunni neighbours.

POTENTIAL CONSEQUENCES OF A REGIONAL NUCLEAR WAR

A study presented at the annual meeting of the American Geophysical Union in December 2006 asserted that even a small-scale, regional nuclear war could produce as many direct fatalities as all of World War I and disrupt the global climate for a decade or more. In a regional nuclear conflict scenario in which two opposing nations in the subtropics each used 50 Hiroshima-sized nuclear weapons (ca. 15 kiloton each) on major populated centres, the researchers estimated fatalities from 2.6 million to 16.7 million per country. Also, as much as five million tons of soot would be released, which would produce a cooling of several degrees over large areas of North America and Eurasia, including most of the grain-growing regions. The cooling would last for years and could be "catastrophic" according to the researchers.

Sub-strategic use

The above examples envisage nuclear warfare at a strategic level, i.e. total war. However, many nuclear powers are believed to have the ability to launch more limited engagements.

The United Kingdom has reserved the possibility of launching a sub-strategic nuclear strike against an enemy, described by its Parliamentary Defence Select Committee as "the launch of one or a limited number of missiles against an adversary as a means of conveying a political message, warning or demonstration of resolve". This would see the deployment of strategic nuclear weapons in a very limited role rather than the battlefield exchanges of tactical nuclear weapons. Such a strategy is based on the assumption that an enemy country such as the Russian Federation or the People's Republic of China with a larger stockpile of nuclear weapons would not retaliate with far greater force than had been used by Britain.

British Trident-armed *Vanguard* class nuclear submarines are believed to carry some missiles for this purpose, potentially allowing a strike as low as one kiloton against a single target. Former Defence Secretary Malcolm Rifkind argued that this capacity offset the reduced credibility of fullscale strategic nuclear attack following the end of the Cold War.

Commodore Tim Hare, former Director of Nuclear Policy at the British Ministry of Defence, has described it as offering the Government "an extra option in the escalatory process before it goes for an all-out strategic strike which would deliver unacceptable damage". However, this sub-strategic capacity has been criticized as potentially increasing the acceptability of using nuclear weapons. The related consideration of new generations of limited-yield nuclear weapons by the United States has also alarmed anti-nuclear groups, who believe it will make the use of nuclear weapons more acceptable.

Nuclear terrorism

Nuclear terrorism by non-state organizations is an unknown factor in nuclear deterrence thinking, as states possessing nuclear weapons are susceptible to retaliation in kind, but sub- or trans-state actors are not. The collapse of the Soviet Union led to the possibility that former Soviet nuclear weapons might become available on the black market (so-called 'loose nukes'), while no warheads are known to have been mislaid, it has been alleged that suitcase-size bombs might be unaccounted for.

Another possible nuclear terrorism threat are devices designed to disperse radioactive materials over a large area using conventional explosives, called dirty bombs. The detonation of a dirty bomb would not cause a nuclear explosion, nor would it release enough radiation to kill or injure a lot of people. However, it could cause severe disruption and require potentially costly decontamination.

13

Understanding Network Centric Warfare

Network Centric Warfare (NCW) is the buzzword of choice in current Defence Department rhetoric. There is little doubt that the introduction of NCW is the defining paradigm of this decade in military affairs, and inevitably, we should see this reflected in Australia. How well NCW is understood in Australia's DoD is, however, another matter entirely. From a broad perspective the introduction of networking techniques into warfighting systems is the military equivalent of the digitisation and networking drive we observed in Western economies between 1985 and 1995. Military networking, especially between platforms, is far more challenging than industry networking due to the heavy reliance on wireless communications, high demand for security, and the need for resistance to hostile jamming. The demanding environmental requirements for military networking hardware are an issue in their own right. It should come thus as no surprise that the introduction of networking into military environments has proven more painful and more protracted than the industry experience of over a decade ago.

Why Networking?

Much has been written and said over the last decade as to why networking is essential, and how it improves warfighting capability. Unhappily, not all of the publications present robust arguments, and much of what has been written has been accepted as fact, rather than critically analysed.

At the most fundamental level networking aims to accelerate engagement cycles and operational tempo at all levels of a warfighting system. This is acheived by providing a mechanism to rapidly gather and distribute targeting information, and rapidly issue directives. A high speed network permits error free transmission in a fraction of the time required for voice transmission, and permits transfer of a wide range of data formats.

In a more technical sense, networking improves operational tempo (optempo) by accelerating the Observation-Orientation phases of Boyd's Observation-Orientation-Decision-Action (OODA) loop. Identified during the 1970s by US Air Force strategist John Boyd, the OODA is an abstraction which describes the sequence of events whihc must take place in any military engagement. The opponnent must be observed to gather information, the attacker must orient himself to the situation or context, then decide and act accordingly. The OODA loop is thus fundamental to all military operations, from strategic down to individual combat. It loop is an inevitable part of reality and has been so since the first tribal wars of 25,000 years ago, as it is fundamental to any predator-prey interaction in the biological world. Sadly, its proper understanding had to wait until the 1970s.

At a philosophical and practical level what confers a key advantage in engagements is the ability to stay ahead of an opponent and dictate the tempo of the engagement-to maintain the initiative and keep an opponent off balance. In effect, the attacker forces his opponent into a reactive posture and denies the opponent any opportunity to drive the engagement to an advantage. The player with the faster OODA loop, all else being equal, will defeat the opponent with the slower OODA loop by blocking or pre-empting any move the opponent with the slower OODA loop attempts to make.

The four components of the OODA loop can be split into three which are associated with processing information, and one which is associated with movement and application of firepower. Observation-Orientation-Decision are information centric while Action is kinematic or centred in movement, position and firepower. If we aim to accelerate our OODA loops to achieve higher operational tempo than an enemy, we have to accelerate all four components of the loop. Much of twentieth century warfighting technique and technology dealt with accelerating the kinetic portion of the OODA loop. Mobility, precision and firepower increases were the result of this evolution.

There are practical limits as to how far we can push the kinetic aspect of the OODA loop-more destructive weapons produce collateral damage, faster platforms and weapons incur ever increasing costs. Accordingly we have seen evolution slow down in this domain since the 1960s. Many weapons and platforms widely used today were designed in the 1950s may remain in use for decades to come, the B-52 being a good case study.

Observation-Orientation-Decision are all about gathering information, distributing information, analysing information, understanding information and deciding how to act upon this information. The faster we can gather, distribute, analyse, understand information, the faster we can decide, and arguably the better we can decide how and when to act in combat. Networking is a mechanism via which the Observation-Orientation phases of the loop can be accelerated, and the Decision phase facilitated.

Well implemented networking can contribute to improved effectiveness in other ways. One such technique is 'self synchronisation' which permits 'directive control'. Rather than micromanage a warfighting asset with close control via a command link tether, warfighters are given significant autonomy, defined objectives, and allowed to take the initiative in how they meet these objectives. A fighter pilot who receives continuous updates from an AEW&C aircraft over a network can make his own tactical decisions, exploiting the situational picture broadcast from the AEW&C aircraft. This is of course not a new model, but networking facilitates it in ways difficult to match-compare this example with the AM radio broadcasts issued in 1943-1945 by Luftwaffe air defence nodes to permit night fighters to autonomously hunt for Allied bombers. Both amount to a 'self synchronisation' scheme, but the underlying technology is five decades apart.

Networking is not a panacea, nor can it be. The ultimate limits on the combat effect produced by a warfighting system, and thus is capability, are bounded by the Action or 'kinetic' phase of the loop. Bombs or missiles delivered is the bottom line, and networking is a tool to facilitate this effect, it is not a sustitute for bombs and missiles on target as some proponents of NCW publicly advocate.

Until recently the mathematics underpinning capability gains in large networked warfighting systems had not been studied closely. Many scholars of NCW simply borrowed the well established Metcalfe's Law from the commercial domain and simply declared it to be valid for military systems. Metcalfe's Law states that the 'utility' of a network increases with the square of the number of nodes in the network-ten nodes (platforms) permit a hundred possible connections, a hundred nodes ten thousand. Unfortunately the mathematics of web site driven sales statistics are not particularly revelant to the behaviour of networked military forces. What we now understand is that Metcalfe's Law presents a possible best case scenario for distribution of information collected by sensors on platforms in a military system. At best it is an indicator of gains in situational awareness, assuming the data being distributed is valid, timely and relevant. The real limits to capability gains in networked systems arise from the Decision-Action phases of the OODA loop.

The Decision phase sees a commander exploiting knowledge acquired in the Observation-Orientation phases, and conferring as required with his superiors and subordinates to determine what is the best choice of action. In the Action phase the commander must deploy his assets and effect the engagement. Both of these phases of the loop, in mathematical terms, are queuing systems. The commander must wait for others to respond, and must marshal and position assets to engage. All of these events involve one entity waiting for another, in effect queueing up.

The mathematical model which contrains such systems is Amdahl's Law, like Metcalfe's Law a defining equation in the computer industry. The reality Amdahl defines is simple-increasing the number of assets in the system increases the achieved work or effect at best only by the number of assets added. The actual improvement is limited by the queuing effects seen in marshalling and positioning assets to perform engagements.

The mathematical bottom line in NCW is a very simple one: networking can permit a significant improvement in operational tempo, where a shortage of targeting information is the bottleneck to achieving a high operational tempo, but networking itself has very little impact on the absolute ability of a force to deliver weapons against targets, that being constrained by the capabilities and number of combat platforms in use.

A good example is the classic Desert Storm scenario of an air force attacking strategic targets and in situ battlefield targets like deployed armoured divisions. With ample targeting information, especially for fixed targets, networking of the attacking force would not have dramatically increased combat effect.

Accordingly we have seen networking produce its greatest gains in combat effect during battlefied strike and close air support operations, especially against highly mobile and fleeting ground targets. In such an environment, where the opponent is continuously on the move, networking can produce spectacular gains since the bottlneck limiting force capability lies in the flow of targeting information to strike aircraft.

No less interesting are the effects observed in demand for specific types of assets to support networked interdiction and strike operations. Short targeting cycles in strike operations require that the bomber be orbiting in close proximity to the intended target-this is persistent strike formally now labelled a killbox interdiction. In practice this has driven up the demand for tanker sorties and the demand for B-52H, B-1B and F-15E-all at the expense of the smaller F-16C and F/A-18 variants. Bigger is better in the networked strike game, so much so that a recent discussion piece by US analyst Price Bingham in the ISR Journal predicted the demise of the classical battlefield interdiction tasked fighter-bomber, in favour of larger bombers and UCAVs. This is a direct challenge to the basic rationale for the Joint Strike Fighter family of battlefield interdiction and close air support fighters, and the longer term use of legacy designs like the F-16 and F/A-18 variants.

Networking has produced other useful benefits. One is combat identification and deconfliction, where the JTIDS/Link-16 system has been used very effectively as a more capable substitute for conventional IFF, capable of supporting air, land and sea assets.

A key issue for all networking is the Intelligence-Surveillance-Reconnaissance capability supporting it. Networks like all computing systems obey the Garbage-In Garbage-Out rule-without accurate high quality ISR systems feeding the network, it is little more than high speed digital plumbing between platforms, with nothing useful to carry. In the US force structure, the pressure to introduce network developed mostly due to bottlenecks in pushing ISR derived targeting information out of existing ISR systems like AWACS, JSTARS and Rivet Joint.

Networking capabilities are not confined to Western nations. The diffusion of commercial computing and networking systems globally has contributed to a growing in focus by non-Western militaries. Russia has capitalised on this by aggressively marketing ISR platforms like the A-50 AWACS, digital datalinking products-the Soviets were deeply enamoured of digital air defence networks-and counter ISR systems. The latter include long range AAMs like the R-172, R-37 and Kh-31 variants, as well as airborne and land mobile high power jamming equipment, and very long range SAMs like the S-400 and Imperator series.

In summary the introduction of networking offers many benefits for an air force and should be actively pursued. It is however not a substitute for combat or ISR capabilities in a force structure and cannot be used as an excuse to justify downsizing of combat fleets.

THE TECHNOLOGICAL PERSPECTIVE

The technology supporting NCW is inherently complex, but not significantly moreso than the technology used to digitise and network the civilian world. It must however be more resilient physically, thermally, electrically and be better resistent to hostile penetration, and in wireless systems, hostile jamming. The prerequisite for an NCW capability is the digitisation of combat platforms. A combat aircraft with a digital weapon system can be seamlessly integrated in an NCW environment by providing digital wireless connections to other platforms. Without the digital weapon system, and its internal computers, NCW is not implementable. The growing gap between the US military and the EU military largely reflects the Europeans' reluctance to heavily invest in digitising their combat platforms.

Provision of digital wireless connectivity between combat platforms is a major technical challenge which cannot be understated. While civilian networking of computers can largely rely on cabled links, be they copper or optical fibres, with wireless connectivity as an adjunct, in a military environment centred in moving platforms and field deployed basing, wireless connectivity is the central means of carrying information.

The problems faced in providing military networking are generally well understood, but often push the boundaries of available technology. Key issues can be summarised thus:

1. Security of transmission. Since everybody does their best to eavesdrop, digital links have to be difficult to eavesdrop, and robustly encrypted to defeat any eavesdropping which might succeed. Even if a signal cannot be successfully decrypted, its detection provides an opponent with valuable information on the presence, position and often activity of the platform or unit in question.
2. Robustness of transmission. In the face of transmission impairments such as solar flares, bad weather and hostile jamming, networks must continue to function. If a signal cannot penetrate a rainshower or is blotted out by an opponent's barrage jammer, the link is broken and the NCW model also breaks.
3. Transmission capacity. How fast data can be transmitted is vital, especially where digitised imagery must be sent. If a 10 Megabyte recce image must be sent, or a 2 Megabit/sec digitised video feed observed, a 9600 bit/sec channel will be nearly useless. A popular misconception is that digital data compression solves this problem-the reality of Shannon's communication theory is very much at odds with this popular (in some

Canberra circles) fantasy. Robustness against jamming and the overheads of encryption both function at the expense of transmission channel capacity for a given radio communications link-the robust the link, the more capacity is soaked up with overheads to protect it.

4. Message and signal routing. Platforms must be able to specifically address and access other platforms or systems in an NCW environment. Just as email on a civilian network must have an address, so must a military messaging scheme. Such addressing must be able to cope with a fluid network topology, as platforms entre and leave an area of operations.
5. Signal format and communications protocol compatibility. It is essential that dissimilar platforms and systems can communicate in an NCW environment. This problem extends not only to the use of disparate signal modulations and digital protocols, but to the use of partially incompatible implementations of what is ostensibly the same signal modulation or communications protocol. The mutual incompatibility headaches we see in commercial computing are often more traumatic in the challenging military environment.

At the time of writing nearly all military datalinks used in NCW operate at speeds which would be considered intolerable in the civilian/commercial world, reflecting the realities of wireless communications. Moreover, the military world lives with a veritable Tower of Babel in both signal modulations, operating frequencies and digital communications protocols, and variations of nominally standard protocols.

To contextualise this, Western armed forces currently deploy systems using a wide range of current and legacy signal formats and protocols, examples being:

1. Link 1 at 1200/2400 bits per second used for air defence systems, devised in the 1950s.
2. TADIL A/Link-11/11B at 1364 bits per second used for naval links and ground based SAM systems, using original CLEW DQPSK modulation, or newer FTBCB convolutional coding at 1800 bits per second. It is 1960s technology.

3. TADIL C/Link-4 at 5,000 bits per second in the UHF band, used for naval aviation, AEW&C to fighter links, and fighter to fighter links on the F-14 series. It is also 1960s technology.
4. Link-14 used for HF transmission between naval combatants at low data rates.
5. TADIL J/MIDS/JTIDS/Link-16 which is a jam resistant L-band time division Spread Spectrum Multiple Access (SSMA)system based on 1970s technology. While its time slot model permits some allocation of capacity, in practical terms it is limited to kilobits/sec data rates, over distances of about 250 nautical miles. JTIDS is multi-platform and multi-service and widely used for transmitting tactical position data, directives, advisories, and for defacto Identification Friend Foe. Its limitation is that it is ill suited to sending reconnaissance imagery and inherently tied to master stations which generate its timebase-reflecting its origins of three decades ago. Satellite link and higher data rate derivatives exist but retain the basic limitations of its time division technique.
6. CDL/TCDL/HIDL/ABIT which are US high speed datalinks design primarily for satellite and UAV transmission of imagery. CDL family links are typically assymetric, using a 200 kilobit/s uplink for control and management, and a 10.71, 45, 137 or 234 Megabit/s high speed uplink, and a specialised for the control of satellite/UAVs and receipt of gathered data. ABIT is a development of CDL operating at 548 Megabits/s with low probability of intercept capabilities.
7. Improved Data Modem (IDM) is used over Have Quick II spread spectrum radios to provide low data rate but secure transmission of targeting coordinates and imagery. It has been used widely for transmission of targeting data to F-15E/F-16C strike fighters and F-16CJ Wild Weasels. It is essentially an analogue to commercial voiceband modems.
8. Army Tactical Data Link 1-ATDL 1 used for US Army Hawk and Patriot SAM batteries.
9. PATRIOT Digital Information Link-PADIL used by Patriot SAM batteries.

10. Tactical Information Broadcast System-TIBS used for theatre missile defence systems.
11. PLRS/EPLRS/SADL are a family of US Army/Marine Corps datalinks used for tracking ground force units, and providing defacto Identification Friend Foe of ground units. EPRLs is also used for data transmission between ground units.
12. TCP/IP (Internet) protocol implementations running over other channels, to provide connectivity between platforms and remote ground facilities.
13. Joint Tactical Radio System (JTRS), intended to supplant most legacy protocols with networking equipment which can communicate both in legacy prototols and modulations, and its own JTRS protocols and modulations. The JTRS Wideband Netwroking Waveform (WNW) is to provide multi-Megabit/s throughput.

This veritable menagerie of datalink modulations/protocols is by no means exhaustive, but reflects the realities observed in the computer industry in the decades predating the Internet. New protocols like the Joint Tactical Radio System (JTRS) are in part intended to incorporate mechanisms for translating such legacy protocols into formats which can be sent over a common channel. Separate from these multi-platform protocols and modulations are the type specific datalinks, such as the intra-and interflight datalinks used on the F/A-22A and later the JSF. As yet there has been little effort to capitalise on the new technology of ad hoc network protocols, designed for self organising networks of mobile platforms, although the JTRS WNW effort looks promising. The DARPA GLOMO program in the late 1980s saw considerable seed money invested, but did not yield any publicised dramatic breakthroughs. Ad hoc networking remains a yet to be fully explored frontier in the networking domain, one which is apt to provide a decisive technology breakthrough for NCW.

The technological issues in NCW often dominate the debate at the expense of the deeper philosophical and functional issues which is unfortunate, since both domains matter and getting either wrong results in an equally disfunctional end result.

NCW AND AUSTRALIA

In Australia networking has been very much in the limelight of the defence debate. Sadly, it has also been used to justify a great many dubious decisions, all predicated on premises which do not hold. Like most intellectually demanding and complex systems problems, NCW must be properly understood before it can be used as a basis for strategic planning decisions. Clearly this has not been the case in many key areas of the DoD, resulting in public statements which would be comical were not the circumstances so dire.

Perhaps the best exposition of this problem lies in the package of submissions presented earlier this year to the JSCFADT committee of Federal Parliament, especially the Air Combat Capability paper.

In this document we learn that networking can substitute for combat fleet numbers, despite the contrary experience in Afghanistan and Iraq, where aircraft size became the pivotal issue. We also learn that the combat effect of the system should exceed the sum of its parts despite the contrary mathematics underpinning this problem. Limitations in the F/A-18A and JSF we learn do not matter, since Australia will evidently have an asymmetric advantage in networking and AEW&C, despite regional buys of Russian/Israeli A-50 AWACS, and Russian marketing of TKS-2 digital datalinks on Su-30 fighters. We also learn in this document that AEW&C aircraft and networks will not be challenged, as evidently Russian R-172, Kh-31 and R-37 missiles, or high power jammers, will never be used in the region-regional buys notwithstanding. No differently, Australia need not invest in high power jamming aircraft since other nations will never use their AEW&C and networking systems. We also learn that five A330-200 tankers will improve the RAAF's combat persistence, since evidently the fuel carried in F-111s need not be counted. No less surprisingly we also discover that the mere AU$20M to 30M required to put networking into the F-111s is unusually expensive and not worth doing-evidently it is better to kill off the aircraft than invest into networking it.

The ugly reality is that networking has become a cure all panacea in the DoD bureacratic machine, one which can magically offset all force structure limitations, and one which magically only Australia can possess and use properly in the Pacrim.

The analytical perspective is very different, however. Most regional nations are now operating, deploying or shopping for AEW&C aircraft. Russia is actively marketing digital datalinks, like the TKS-2 and older APD-518, and marketing counter-ISR weapons like the Novator R-172 (KS-172) or Kh-31 series missiles. Russia is also marketing high power jamming equipment, especially pods using Digital RF Memory (DRFM) technology, and there is a good prospect of a Growler-ski based on the Su-32 materialising before the end of the decade.

In practical terms, by 2010-2015 regional opponents without AEW&C, long range counter-ISR missiles and jamming pods are likely to be the obliging exception to the rule. US thinking is not surprisingly centred in using F/A-22As to sanitise airspace permitting unhindered use of ISR platforms and networks, and the program to replace the lost capabilities of the EF-111A Raven with the B-52J or EB-52, equipped with high power stand-off jamming equipment to disrupt opposing networks and ISR sensors.

The reality we observe regionally and globally is, like the physics and mathematics which apply to the network problem, very different to the interpretation of these issues which we observe in the confines of Russell Offices. The Departmental leadership have effectively committed Australia to major strategic decisions, like the JSF program and F-111 retirement, on the basis of beliefs which are simply not supportable by fact. That a major fraction of virtually every public document dealing with the JSF and F-111 issues is dedicated to extolling the virtues of NCW is evidence in its own right.

14

The New Face of Class Warfare

For decades Democrats seemed to have a monopoly on class war with demagogy of "the rich." Today it is the rich who are instigating class war with attacks on middle class jobs. The ladders of upward mobility are being dismantled. America, the land of opportunity, is giving way to polarization between rich and poor. The assault on jobs predates the Bush regime. However, the loss of middle class jobs has become particularly intense in the 21st century, and, like other pressing problems, has been ignored by President Bush, who is focused on instigating war in the Middle East and a police state at home. The lives and careers that are being lost to the carnage of a gratuitous war in Iraq are paralleled by the economic destruction of careers, families and communities in the U.S. Since the days of President Franklin D. Roosevelt in the 1930s, the U.S. government has sought to protect employment of its citizens. Bush has turned his back on this responsibility. He has given his support to the offshoring of American jobs that is eroding the living standards of Americans. Whether this is an impeachable offence, it is another example of his betrayal of the public trust.

"Free trade" and "globalization" are the guises behind which class war is being conducted against the middle class by both political parties. Patrick J. Buchanan, a three-time contender for the presidential nomination, put it well when he wrote (March 10, 2006, World Net Daily column:) that NAFTA and the various so-called trade agreements were never trade deals.

The agreements were enabling acts that enabled U.S. corporations to dump their American workers, avoid Social Security taxes, health care and pensions, and move their factories offshore to locations where labor is cheap. The offshore outsourcing of American jobs has nothing to do with free trade based on comparative advantage. Offshoring is labor arbitrage. First world capital and technology are not seeking comparative advantage at home in order to compete abroad. They are seeking absolute advantage abroad in cheap labor.

Two recent developments made possible the supremacy of absolute over comparative advantage: the high speed Internet and the collapse of world socialism, which opened China's and India's vast under-utilized labor resources to first world capital.

In times past first world workers had nothing to fear from cheap labor abroad. Americans worked with superior capital, technology and business organization. This made Americans far more productive than Indians and Chinese, and, as it was not possible for U.S. firms to substitute cheaper foreign labor for U.S. labor, American jobs and living standards were not threatened by low wages abroad or by the products that these low wages produced.

The advent of offshoring has made it possible for U.S. firms using first world capital and technology to produce goods and services for the U.S. market with foreign labor. The result is to separate Americans' incomes from the production of the goods and services that they consume. This new development, often called "globalization," allows cheap foreign labor to work with the same capital, technology and business know-how as U.S. workers. The foreign workers are now as productive as Americans, with the difference being that the large excess supply of labor that overhangs labor markets in China and India keeps wages low. Labor that is equally productive but paid a fraction of the wage is a magnet for Western capital and technology.

Although a new development, offshoring is destroying entire industries, occupations and communities in the United States. The devastation of U.S. manufacturing employment was waved away with promises that a "new economy" based on high tech knowledge jobs would take its place. Education and retraining were touted as the answer. Reality has contradicted the glib economists. The new high tech knowledge jobs are being outsourced abroad even faster than the old manufacturing jobs. Establishment economists are beginning to see the light. Writing *in Foreign Affairs* (March/April 2006) Princeton economist and former Federal Reserve vice-chairman Alan Blinder concludes that economists who insist that offshore outsourcing is merely a routine extension of international trade are overlooking a major transformation with significant consequences. Blinder estimates that 42-56 million American service sector jobs are susceptible to offshore outsourcing. Whether all these jobs leave, U.S. salaries will be forced down by the willingness of foreigners to do the work for less.

Software engineers and information technology workers have been especially hard hit. Jobs offshoring, which began with call centres and back-office operations, is rapidly moving up the value chain. *Business Week's* Michael Mandel (September 15, 2005:) compared starting salaries in 2005 with those in 2001. He found a 12.7% decline in computer science pay, a 12% decline in computer engineering pay, and a 10.2% decline in electrical engineering pay. Marketing salaries experienced a 6.5% decline and business administration salaries fell 5.7%. Despite Sarbanes-Oxley, a make-work law for accountants, even accounting majors were offered 2.3% less.

Using the same sources as the *Business Week* article (salary data from the National Association of Colleges and Employers and BLS data for inflation adjustment), Professor Norm Matloff at the University of California, Davis, made the same comparison for master degree graduates. He found that between 2001 and 2005 starting pay for master degrees in computer science, computer engineering and electrical engineering fell 6.6%, 13.7%, and 9.4% respectively.

On February 22, 2006, CNNMoney.com staff writer Shaheen Pasha reported that America's large financial institutions are moving "large portions of their investment banking operations abroad." Offshoring is now killing American jobs in research and analytic operations, foreign exchange trades and highly complicated credit derivatives contracts. Deal-making responsibility itself may eventually move abroad. Deloitte Touche says that the financial services industry will move 20 percent of its total costs base offshore by the end of 2010. As the costs are lower in India, the move will represent more than 20 percent of the business. A job on Wall St is a declining option for bright young persons with high stress tolerance as America's last remaining advantage is outsourced.

According to Norm Augustine, former CEO of Lockheed Martin, even McDonald jobs are on the way offshore. Augustine reports that McDonald is experimenting with replacing error-prone order takers with a system that transmits orders via satellite to a central location and from there to the person preparing the order. The technology lets the orders be taken in India or China at costs below the U.S. minimum wage and without the liabilities of U.S. employees.

American economists, some from incompetence and some from being bought and paid for, described globalization as a "win-win" development. It was supposed to work like this: The U.S. would lose market share in tradable manufactured goods and make up the job and economic loss with highly-educated knowledge workers. The win for America would be lower-priced manufactured goods and a white collar work force. The win for China would be manufacturing jobs that would bring economic development to that country.

It did not work out this way, as Morgan Stanley's Stephen Roach, formerly a cheerleader for globalization, recently admitted. It has become apparent that job creation and real wages in the developed economies are seriously lagging their historical norms as offshore outsourcing displaces the "new economy" jobs in "software programming, engineering, design, and the medical profession, as well as a broad array of professionals in the legal, accounting, actuarial, consulting, and financial services industries". The real state of the U.S. job market is revealed by a *Chicago Sun-Times* report on January 26, 2006, that 25,000 people applied for 325 jobs at a new Chicago Wal-Mart.

According to the Bureau of Labor Statistics (BLS) payroll jobs data, over the past half-decade (January 2001—January 2006, the data series available at time of writing) the US economy created 1,050,000 net new private sector jobs and 1,009,000 net new government jobs for a total five-year figure of 2,059,000. That is seven million jobs short of keeping up with population growth, definitely a serious job shortfall.

The BLS payroll jobs data contradict the hype from business organizations, such as the U.S. Chamber of Commerce, that offshore outsourcing is good for America. Large corporations, which have individually dismissed thousands of their U.S. employees and replaced them with foreigners, claim that jobs outsourcing allows them to save money that can be used to hire more Americans. The corporations and the business organizations are very successful in placing this disinformation in the media. The lie is repeated everywhere and has become a mantra among no-think economists and politicians. However, no sign of these jobs can be found in the payroll jobs data. But there is abundant evidence of the lost American jobs.

During the past five years (January 01—January 06), the information sector of the U.S. economy lost 644,000 jobs or 17.4% of its work force. Computer systems design and related lost 105,000 jobs or 8.5% of its work force. Clearly, jobs offshoring is not creating jobs in computers and information technology. Indeed, jobs offshoring is not even creating jobs in related fields. U.S. manufacturing lost 2.9 million jobs, almost 17% of the manufacturing work force. The wipeout is across the board. Not a single manufacturing payroll classification created a single new job.

The declines in some manufacturing sectors have more in common with a country undergoing saturation bombing during war than with a super-economy that is "the envy of the world." In five years, communications equipment lost 42% of its workforce. Semiconductors and electronic components lost 37% of its workforce. The workforce in computers and electronic products declined 30%. Electrical equipment and appliances lost 25% of its employees. The workforce in motor vehicles and parts declined 12%. Furniture and related products lost 17% of its jobs. Apparel manufacturers lost almost half of the work force. Employment in textile mills declined 43%. Paper and paper products lost one-fifth of its jobs. The work force in plastics and rubber products declined by 15%.

For the five year period, U.S. job growth was limited to four areas: education and health services, state and local government, leisure and hospitality, and financial services. There was no U.S. job growth outside these four areas of domestic nontradable services.

Oracle, for example, which has been handing out thousands of pink slips, has recently announced two thousand more jobs being moved to India. How is Oracle's move of U.S. jobs to India creating American jobs in nontradable services such as waitresses and bartenders, hospital orderlies, state and local government and credit agencies?

Engineering jobs in general are in decline, because the manufacturing sectors that employ engineers are in decline. During the last five years, the U.S. work force lost 1.2 million jobs in the manufacture of machinery, computers, electronics, semiconductors, communication equipment, electrical equipment, motor vehicles and transportation equipment. The BLS payroll job numbers show a total of 69,000 jobs created in all fields of architecture and engineering, including clerical personnel, over the past five years. That comes to a mere 14,000 jobs per year (including clerical workers). What is the annual graduating class in engineering and architecture? How is there a shortage of engineers when more graduate than can be employed?

Of course, many new graduates take jobs opened by retirements. We would have to know the retirement rates to get a solid handle on the fate of new graduates. But it cannot be very pleasant, with declining employment in the manufacturing sectors that employ engineers and a minimum of 65,000 H-1B work visas annually for foreigners plus an indeterminate number of L-1 work visas.

It is not only the Bush regime that bases its policies on lies. Not content with moving Americans' jobs abroad, corporations want to fill the jobs remaining in America with foreigners on work visas. Business organizations allege shortages of engineers, scientists and even nurses. Business organizations have successfully used public relations firms and bought-and-paid-for "economic studies" to convince policymakers that American business cannot function without H-1B visas that permit the importation of indentured employees from abroad who are paid less than the going US salaries. The so-called shortage is, in fact, a replacement of American employees with foreign employees, with the soon-to-be-discharged American employee first required to train his replacement.

It is amazing to see free-market economists rush to the defence of H-1B visas. The visas are nothing but a subsidy to U.S. companies at the expense of US citizens. Keep in mind this H-1B subsidy to U.S. corporations for employing foreign workers in place of Americans as we examine the Labor Department's job projections over the 2004-2014 decade.

All of the occupations with the largest projected employment growth (in terms of the number of jobs) over the next decade are in nontradable domestic services. The top ten sources of the most jobs in "superpower" America are: retail salespersons, registered nurses, postsecondary teachers, customer service representatives, janitors and cleaners, waiters and waitresses, food preparation (includes fast food), home health aides, nursing aides, orderlies and attendants, general and operations managers. Note than none of this projected employment growth will contribute one nickel toward producing goods and services that could be exported to help close the massive U.S. trade deficit. Note, also, that few of these job classifications require a college education.

Among the fastest growing occupations (in terms of rate of growth), seven of the ten are in health care and social assistance. The three remaining fields are: network systems and data analysis with 126,000 jobs projected or 12,600 per year; computer software engineering applications with 222,000 jobs projected or 22,200 per year, and computer software engineering systems software with 146,000 jobs projected or 14,600 per year.

Assuming these projections are realized, how many of the computer engineering and network systems jobs will go to Americans? Not many, considering the 65,000 H-1B visas each year (bills have been introduced in Congress to raise the number) and the loss during the past five years of 761,000 jobs in the information sector and computer systems design and related.

Judging from its ten-year jobs projections, the U.S. Department of Labor does not expect to see any significant high-tech job growth in the U.S. The knowledge jobs are being outsourced even more rapidly than the manufacturing jobs. The so-called "new economy" was just another hoax perpetrated on the American people. If outsourcing jobs offshore is good for U.S. employment, why won't the U.S. Department of Commerce release the 200-page, $335,000 study of the impact of the offshoring of U.S. high-tech jobs? Republican political appointees reduced the 200-page report to 12 pages of public relations hype and refuse to allow the Technology Administration experts who wrote the report to testify before Congress. Democrats on the House Science Committee are unable to pry the study out of the hands of Commerce Secretary Carlos Gutierrez. On March 29, 2006, Republicans on the House Science Committee voted down a resolution (H.Res. 717) designed to force the Commerce Department to release the study to Congress. Obviously, the facts don't fit the Bush regime's globalization hype.

The BLS payroll data that we have been examining tracks employment by industry classification. This is not the same thing as occupational classification. For example, companies in almost every industry and area of business employ people in computer-related occupations. A recent study from the Association for Computing Machinery claims: "Despite all the publicity in the United States about jobs being lost to India and China, the size of the IT employment market in the United States today is higher than it was at the height of the dot.com boom. Information technology appears as though it will be a growth area at least for the coming decade."

We can check this claim by turning to the BLS Occupational Employment Statistics. We will look at "computer and mathematical employment" and "architecture and engineering employment". Computer and mathematical employment includes such fields as "software engineers applications," "software engineers systems software," "computer programmers," "network systems and data communications," and "mathematicians." Has this occupation been a source of job growth?

In November of 2000 this occupation employed 2,932,810 people. In November of 2004 (the latest data available), this occupation employed 2,932,790, or 20 people fewer. Employment in this field has been stagnant for four years. During these four years, there have been employment shifts within the various fields of this occupation. For example, employment of computer programmers declined by 134,630, while employment of software engineers applications rose by 65,080, and employment of software engineers systems software rose by 59,600. (These shifts probably merely reflect change in job title from programmer to software engineer.)

These figures do not tell us whether any gain in software engineering jobs went to Americans. According to Professor Norm Matloff, in 2002 there were 463,000 computer-related H-1B visa holders in the US. Similarly, the 134,630 lost computer programming jobs (if not merely a job title change) may have been outsourced offshore to foreign affiliates.

Architecture and engineering employment includes all the architecture and engineering fields except software engineering. The total employment of architects and engineers in the U.S. declined by 120,700 between November 1999 and November 2004. Employment declined by 189,940 between November 2000 and November 2004, and by 103,390 between November 2001 and November 2004.

There are variations among fields. Between November 2000 and November 2004, for example, U.S. employment of electrical engineers fell by 15,280. Employment of computer hardware engineers rose by 15,990 (possibly these are job title reclassifications). Overall, however, over 100,000 engineering jobs were lost. We do not know how many of the lost jobs were outsourced offshore to foreign affiliates or how many American engineers were dismissed and replaced by foreign holders of H-1B or L-1 visas. Clearly, engineering and computer-related employment in the U.S. has not been growing, whether measured by industry or by occupation. Moreover, with a half million or more foreigners in the U.S. on work visas, the overall employment numbers do not represent employment of Americans.

American employees have been abandoned by American corporations and by their representatives in Congress. America remains a land of opportunity—but for foreigners—not for the native born. A country whose work force is concentrated in domestic nontradable services has no need for scientists and engineers and no need for universities. Even the projected jobs in nursing and school teachers can be filled by foreigners on H-1B visas.

In the U.S. the myth has been firmly established that the jobs that the U.S. is outsourcing offshore are being replaced with better jobs. There is no sign of these jobs in the payroll jobs data or in the occupational employment statistics. When a country loses entry level jobs, it has no one to promote to senior level jobs. When manufacturing leaves, so does engineering, design, research and development, and innovation itself.

On February 16, 2006, the *New York Times* reported on a new study presented to the National Academies that concludes that outsourcing is climbing the skills ladder. A survey of 200 multinational corporations representing 15 industries in the U.S. and Europe found that 38 percent planned to change substantially the worldwide distribution of their research and development work, sending it to India and China. According to the *New York Times*, "More companies in the survey said they planned to decrease research and development employment in the United States and Europe than planned to increase employment." The study and the discussion it provoked came to untenable remedies. Many believe that a primary reason for the shift of R&D to India and China is the erosion of scientific prowess in the U.S. due to lack of math and science proficiency of American students and their reluctance to pursue careers in science and engineering. This belief begs the question why students would chase after careers that are being outsourced abroad.

The main author of the study, Georgia Tech professor Marie Thursby, believes that American science and engineering depend on having "an environment that fosters the development of a high-quality work force and productive collaboration between corporations and universities." The Dean of Engineering at the University of California, Berkeley, thinks the answer is to recruit the top people in China and India and bring them to Berkeley. No one seems to understand that research, development, design, and innovation take place in countries where things are made. The loss of manufacturing means ultimately the loss of engineering and science. The newest plants embody the latest technology. If these plants are abroad, that is where the cutting edge resides. The denial of jobs reality has become an art form for economists, libertarians, the Bush regime, and journalists. Except for Lou Dobbs, no accurate reporting is available in the "mainstream media."

Economists have failed to examine the incompatibility of offshoring with free trade. Economists are so accustomed to shouting down protectionists that they dismiss any complaint about globalization's impact on domestic jobs as the ignorant voice of a protectionist seeking to preserve the buggy whip industry. Matthew J. Slaughter, a Dartmouth economics professor rewarded for his service to offshoring with appointment to President Bush's Council of Economic Advisers, suffered no harm to his reputation when he wrote: "For every one job that U.S. multinationals created abroad in their foreign affiliates, they created nearly two U.S. jobs in their parent operations." In other words, Slaughter claims that offshoring is creating more American jobs than foreign ones.

How did Slaughter arrive at this conclusion? Not by consulting the BLS payroll jobs data or the BLS Occupational Employment Statistics. Instead, Slaughter measured the growth of U.S. multinational employment and failed to take into account the two reasons for the increase in multinational employment: (1) Multinationals acquired many existing smaller firms, thus raising multinational employment but not overall employment, and (2) many U.S. firms established foreign operations for the first time and thereby became multinationals, thus adding their existing employment to Slaughter's number for multinational employment.

ABC News' John Stossel, a libertarian hero, recently made a similar error. In debunking Lou Dobbs' concern with U.S. jobs lost to offshore outsourcing, Stossel invoked the California-based company, Collabnet. He quotes the CEO's claim that outsourcing saves his company money and lets him hire more Americans. Turning to Collabnet's web page, it is very interesting to see the employment opportunities that the company posts for the United States and for India.

In India, Collabnet has openings (at time of writing) for eight engineers, a sales engineer, a technical writer and a telemarketing representative. In the U.S. Collabnet has openings for one engineer, a receptionist/office assistant, and positions in marketing, sales, services and operations. Collabnet is a perfect example of what Lou Dobbs and I report: the engineering and design jobs move abroad, and Americans are employed to sell and market the foreign-made products.

Other forms of deception are widely practiced. For example, Matthew Spiegleman, a Conference Board economist, claims that manufacturing jobs are only slightly higher paid than domestic service jobs, so there is no meaningful loss in income to Americans from offshoring. He reaches this conclusion by comparing only hourly pay and leaving out the longer manufacturing work week and the associated benefits, such as health care and pensions. Occasionally, however, real information escapes the spin machine. In February 2006 the National Association of Manufacturers, one of offshoring's greatest boosters, released a report, "*U.S. Manufacturing Innovation at Risk*," by economists Joel Popkin and Kathryn Kobe. The economists find that U.S. industry's investment in research and development is not languishing after all. It just appears to be languishing, because it is rapidly being shifted overseas: "Funds provided for foreign-performed R&D have grown by almost 73 percent between 1999 and 2003, with a 36 percent increase in the number of firms funding foreign R&D."

US industry is still investing in R&D after all; it is just not hiring Americans to do the research and development. U.S. manufacturers still make things, only less and less in America with American labor. U.S. manufacturers still hire engineers, only they are foreign ones, not American ones. In other words, everything is fine for U.S. manufacturers. It is just their former American work force that is in the doldrums. As these Americans happen to be customers for U.S. manufacturers, U.S. brand names will gradually lose their U.S. market. U.S. household median income has fallen for the past five years. Consumer demand has been kept alive by consumers' spending their savings and home equity and going deeper into debt. It is not possible for debt to forever rise faster than income. The United States is the first country in history to destroy the prospects and living standards of its labor force. It is amazing to watch freedom-loving libertarians and free-market economists serve as apologists for the dismantling of the ladders of upward mobility that made the America of old an opportunity society.

Bibliography

Ackland, Len. *Making a Real Killing: Rocky Flats and the Nuclear West*. Albuquerque: The University of New Mexico Press, 1999.

Alperovitz, Gar. *The Decision to Use the Atomic Bomb*. New York: Vintage Books, 1996.

Arend, A.: *International Law and the Use of Force*, London, Routledge, 1993.

Bradley, John. *Learning to Glow: A Nuclear Reader. Tucson*: University of Arizona Press, 2000.

Bunn, Matthew, *Securing Nuclear Weapons and Materials: Seven Steps for Immediate Action*. Cambridge, MA: Harvard University, 2002.

Cochran, Thomas B. *Nuclear Weapons Databook*. Cambridge, MA: Ballinger Publishing Company, 1987.

Duncan, Francis. *Rickover and the Nuclear Navy: The Discipline of Technology*. Annapolis: Naval Institute Press, 1990.

Friedman, G.: *The Future of War: Power, Technology and American World Dominance in the 21st Century*, N.Y., Random House, 1996.

Garrelick, Renee. *M.I.T. Beginnings: The Legacy of Nuclear Metals*. Concord, MA: Nuclear Metals, Inc., 1995.

Gibson, James N.: *Nuclear Weapons of the United States: An Illustrated History*. Atglen, PA: Schiffer Publishing Ltd., 1996.

Gusterson, Hugh. *Nuclear Rites: A Weapons Laboratory at the End of the Cold War*. Berkeley: University of California Press, 1996.

Harris, Stephen L. : *Fire and Ice: The Cascade Volcanoes*, Seattle, The Mountaineers, 1980.

Huntington, S.P.: *The Soldier and the State*, N.Y., Vintage Books, 1964.

Kaufmann, Albert R. *Nuclear Reactor Fuel Elements: Metallurgy and Fabrication*. New York: Interscience Publishers, Inc., 1962.

Laskin, David : *Braving the Elements: The Stormy History of American Weather*, New York, Doubleday, 1996.

Mary, W.: *Asian Power and Politics: the Cultural Dimensions of Authority*, Cambridge, Belknap Press, 1985.

Nininger, Robert D. *Minerals for Atomic Energy*. New York: D. Van Nostrand Company, Inc., 1954.

Posen, B.R.: *The Sources of Military Doctrine, Ithaca*, 1984, Cornell Univ. Press.

Walker, Martin. *The Cold War: A History*. New York: Henry Holt and Company, 1993.

Worster, Donald : *Dust Bowl: The Southern Plains in the 1930s*, New York, Oxford University Press, 1979.

Index

❑❑❑